LIONS
IN THE
STREET

LIONS
IN THE
STREET

The Inside Story of the Great
Wall Street Law Firms

PAUL HOFFMAN

Saturday Review Press/E. P. Dutton & Co., Inc.

Published simultaneously in Canada by Doubleday Canada Ltd., Toronto

Library of Congress Catalog Number: 72-88654

ISBN 0-8415-0235-8

PRINTED IN THE UNITED STATES OF AMERICA

Design by Tere LoPrete

To my parents

Contents

LIONS
IN THE
STREET

1

The Congress of Vienna Sits on the Fifty-seventh Floor

Not so long ago there was an up-and-coming young lawyer at the prestigious firm of Cravath, Swaine & Moore. He had all the prerequisites for success: He was bright and personable; he was go-getting without being aggressive; he had a pretty and charming wife.

A junior partner took this young associate under his wing and gave him increasingly important assignments. The young man seemed to be going places—mostly out of town to handle aspects of a major case. One day he returned home unexpectedly and found the junior partner making love to his pretty, charming wife.

There was a brouhaha at Cravath the likes of which had not been seen since a "name" partner was indicted two decades before for bribing a federal judge. The upshot of it was that the cuckolded counsel was asked to leave—the firm found other employment for him—while the philandering partner went on to greater glory.

That's how the system works. "The fraternity takes care of its own," says a Cravath alumnus. "Nobody starves" is the unofficial motto. But nobody rocks the boat—or upsets the gravy train. It's a cozy, comfortable world where partners' salaries start at about $40,000 and can soar to ten times as much. It has a place for everybody—and everybody in his place.

The "system" is the Legal Establishment, the blue-chip bar, the Wall Street "law factories"—call it what you will—a collection of about three dozen high-powered law firms clustered around the canyons of Manhattan's financial district or stretched out along the flower beds of Park Avenue. The firms, as G. Edward White noted in the American Bar Association's *Journal*, "have been denounced as capitalist predators, hailed as responsible intermediaries between corporations and the public, seen as bureaucratic structures in an increasingly specialized and hierarchical world and viewed as the last bastions of nineteenth-century individualism."

They employ perhaps three thousand lawyers and twice that number of nonlegal personnel. But only a relative handful who have wormed and wiggled and waited until they reached the top—usually symbolized by a corner office with a panoramic view of New York harbor—can call the signals. They are the Brahmins of the Bar, the real movers and shakers of the Legal Establishment.

Except for a rare public personage like Richard Nixon or Arthur Goldberg, they are anonymous men, unknown to the general public and strangers to the street-corner practitioner. Consider this recent obituary:

> Henry E. Kelley, a senior partner in the New York law firm of Kelley, Drye, Warren, Clark, Carr & Ellis, died yesterday in St. Agnes Hospital, North White Plains. He was 77 years old and lived at 57 Edgemont Road [Scarsdale].
>
> Mr. Kelley, who was born in New Canaan, Conn., had

received his law degree in 1916 from New York Law School and was admitted to the bar a year later.

He received a field commission as second lieutenant while on National Guard duty on the Mexican border. In 1917 he fought with the 165th Infantry Regiment of the 42d Division in World War I.

After serving as an assistant United States Attorney for the Southern District of New York, he joined his present law firm, then Locke, Rathbone & Perry, in 1929.

Mr. Kelley was a former vice chairman of the grievance committee of the Association of the Bar of the City of New York and had served on its committee on the judiciary. He had also been chairman of the New York County Lawyers Association's committee on the Federal courts, the judiciary and nominations. He was also a member of the Catholic Lawyers Guild and the American Judicature Society.

Surviving are his widow . . .

But nothing to indicate what Kelley had done for thirty-three years! No mention of the fact that he was one of the leading corporate lawyers in New York. No word that he headed the firm that represents, among others, the Chrysler Corporation for 1971 fees of $570,233.

The blue-chip bar breeds no Perry Masons, no Percy Foremans, no Melvin Bellis or F. Lee Baileys. It indulges in no jury-swinging, headline-hunting histrionics. Its tools are the telephone and the memo-pad, its products the prospectus and the indenture. The Brahmins of the Bar rarely see the inside of a courtroom, and their knowledge of criminal cases is confined to movies and mystery novels.

Nor would the average man have occasion to consult these legal eagles, except in the rare event that he's being sued for violation of the antitrust laws or is about to float a loan for $50 million. The Brahmins of the Bar don't deal with the average legal problem. Their clients are the *"Fortune 500"* corporations, the commercial banks and investment houses, foreign governments and an occasional multimillionaire who needs a will drafted or a wife divorced—those willing to pay $250 an hour and up for expert advice, those able to shell out hundreds of thousands of dollars in annual retainers.

There is no other bar like it in the world. The fabled Inns of Court in London may rank it in tradition and prestige, but they cannot match its money or power. A Belli or a Bailey may gain greater glory than the Brahmins, but he'll never equal their entree into Whitehall or the White House. Firms in Boston, Chicago or San Francisco may rival the New York giants in size, but they are small by comparison when it comes to exerting influence in corporate executive suites, government offices or the world's money markets.

Here the law differs from the other learned professions. The Park Avenue physician may adopt a different bedside manner from the surgeon in the slums, but they both perform an appendectomy the same way. Similarly, a priest offers the same prayers for the man who bequeaths a new church as for the man who receives the bounty of the poor box. But the Brahmins of the Bar offer vastly different legal services for billion-dollar corporations from those the street-corner practitioners provide for America's Archie Bunkers.

A word from Sullivan & Cromwell, and a giant corporation is plunged into bankruptcy. A memo from Mudge Rose, and a state government gets the go-ahead to float a multi-million-dollar bond issue. A letter from Davis Polk, and the government backs down on a major antitrust case. A brief from Cravath, and a cherished government program is cut down by the courts.

The power comes not only from the wealth and influence of the clients on whose behalf the firms act and the importance of the matters with which they deal. The system itself nurtures power—from its recruitment, through its training, to its promotion and sponsorship of men able to cut through the thorny issues of business, finance and government. It is like an octopus with its head in Manhattan and its tentacles stretching into the power centers of American life. The brahmins sit on the boards of banks and businesses, foundations and universities. Its alumni go on to head these institutions. They graduate to posts in the Cabinet or seats on the Supreme Court. One supervises the national pastime, another the national government.

More than a century ago, de Tocqueville proclaimed lawyers the American aristocracy. As late as a half-century ago, the Wall Street lawyer was an individual, able to stretch and strut and shout. Some grew into giants—Elihu Root, John W. Davis, Henry L. Stimson, Charles Evans Hughes—and strode the national stage. Now it is not men, but institutions that hold the reins of power.

This is the age of the organization and of the "organization man." The processes of institutionalization and bureaucratization have tended to blur distinctions, making the lawyer "a member of the team," a cog in a giant machine, and the firms themselves as alike as restaurants along a thruway.

But the blue-chip bar is not yet a monolith. Law firms, like men, have distinct personalities—sometimes those of the present power brokers, sometimes those of partners long dead, sometimes those of powerful clients.

There are big firms and small firms; downtown firms and midtown firms; Republican firms and Democratic firms; Jewish firms and gentile firms; "white-shoe" firms and "law factories"; "green grocers," litigators and specialists in everything from taxes to trademarks—each one a subject worthy of scrutiny.

Let's start with Cravath. It's not the biggest. With two hundred lawyers Shearman & Sterling is New York's largest law firm.* It's not the oldest. Lord, Day & Lord was formed in 1845 and has retained the same name since, while other firms can trace their antecedents back to the 1790s. Nor is it necessarily the best. It's a subjective judgment, to be sure, but most New York lawyers rate Sullivan & Cromwell as No. 1. But Cravath

---

* Baker & McKenzie, an international firm with headquarters in Chicago and offices scattered around the globe, is even larger, with 240 lawyers.

is a model of how a blue-chip firm is organized and how it operates. It also provides an excellent example of how a law firm copes with changing conditions.

Seventy years ago, when law firms were casual collections of individual practitioners who combined for their mutual benefit and just as casually fell out again, Cravath deliberately set out to institutionalize itself, to create an entity that would transcend and outlive the influence of any one or two partners. The origins of the present Cravath, Swaine & Moore can be traced back to 1819, but the processes of institutionalization did not begin until 1906, when Paul D. Cravath took command of what was then Cravath, Henderson & deGersdorff.

A crusty, terrible-tempered tyrant, Cravath, according to the firm history written by his successor, Robert T. Swaine, "had a definite philosophy about the organization of his law firm."

First, like a symphony orchestra, it should be tyrannical; one man would call the tune and set the tempo.

Second, the firm would prosper not on *who* it knew, but on *what* it knew; it would live by merit, not by political pull. Within the firm merit would be the only qualification; lawyers would be hired and promoted on the basis of their legal acumen, not on their ability to bring in business. To ensure enforcement of this standard, there would be no nepotism, no hiring of partners' sons, nephews and in-laws.

Third, "The practice of law must be the primary interest and that practice shall be solely as a member of the Cravath team." It meant no sideline practice, no dabbling in business, and it pretty well precluded politics or public service. Cravath lawyers were also kept from possible conflicts of interest by being barred from owning stock in client corporations or serving on their boards of directors.

Fourth, members of the firm would be promoted through the ranks. Partners would not be brought in from the outside; instead, the cream of Ivy League law school graduates would be hired for what were then called "law clerks," paid a salary—a startling innovation at the turn of the century—

indoctrinated in Cravath's methods and groomed for leadership. "At the outset of their practice," said Swaine, "Cravath men are not thrown into the deep water and told to swim; rather they are taken into shallow water and taught strokes."

It was "up-or-out." If a clerk—later called an associate—couldn't navigate the deeper channels, he was sent elsewhere. "The frustrated man will not be happy and the unhappy man will not do a good job," Swaine explained. But "nobody starves." It was the responsibility of the firm to find other jobs for those who wouldn't become partners, either in the house-counsel offices of client corporations or in other law firms, often "satellite" firms living off the leftovers of Cravath's practice—most notably Olwine, Connolly, Chase, O'Donnell & Weyher, a midtown firm that had the ill fortune to get censured by the Appellate Division for letting *Life* magazine explore its inner workings.

It proved to be a system that pays dividends. "The alumni association at Cravath is very strong and active and loyal," says one of its members. "Very few leave with a bad taste in their mouth."

As other firms grew in size and found themselves—almost without asking for it—becoming institutions, they copied the Cravath system, especially its method of recruitment and promotion, now universal throughout the blue-chip bar.

At Cravath itself, some of the rules were more honored in the breach than in the observance. In its modern history the firm has recruited three partners from the outside, each to fill a gap in its ranks of specialists. For a few juniors, it wasn't "up-or-out," it was down-and-in: They became permanent associates, destined to serve out their careers at Cravath, confined to routine chores and never promoted to partner. At the insistence of some clients, Cravath lawyers wound up on boards of directors; Cravath himself served as chairman of Westinghouse. And some partners dabbled in business, primarily as tax-shelters; for a time, railroad freight cars were a favorite investment. The antinepotism rule was rigidly adhered to, but as other firms adopted it, they tended to take in each other's washing—or offspring: Cravath's current roster includes the sons of three senior partners of other blue-chip firms. Finally, there's no record that a man's ability to bring in business ever told against his advancement. Quite the contrary, Cravath developed a reputation as an able and aggressive business-hustler.

The one-man tradition held firm. "Cravath was an absolute czar," says Francis T. P. Plimpton, who has been a part of New York's legal scene for more than forty years. "The tradition was very strong. Swaine kept it up. Swaine couldn't have been nicer if you got him away from Wall Street, but in the office he was the apotheosis of the tough corporate lawyer."

Like his predecessors, Hoyt Moore was known as a "slave-driver" and under him Cravath maintained its well-deserved reputation as a "sweatshop." One recent associate recalls getting only three hours sleep a night for eighteen consecutive days while he worked on a major matter. Moore drove himself as hard as any of his underlings. "He was a prodigious worker," says Bruce Bromley, Cravath's top litigator, who has been with the firm for more than fifty years. "I never saw such a worker in my life."

The story in Swaine's history of the firm is admittedly apocryphal, but apt: Moore supposedly was approached by a partner who complained that the associates were being pushed too hard. "That's silly," he replied. "No one is under pressure. There wasn't a light on when I left at two this morning."

"He was a schoolteacher, a great grammarian," Bromley says of Moore. "He'd read an indenture and pick out a line, 'None of the leading bankers *were* insolvent.' He'd take that 'were' and cross it out so you couldn't see it and write in 'was.' "

Moore's special client responsibility was Bethlehem Steel. At Bethlehem's behest, Cravath entered the famous "sick-chicken" case, *Schechter* v. *U.S.*, in which a small kosher poultry concern in Brooklyn challenged the constitutionality of the New Deal's National Recovery Act. Hardly the typical Cravath client! But Bethlehem, perhaps the most reactionary of the "Little Steel" producers, found the case the ideal issue in its crusade against the NRA's production codes. With only two weeks' preparation, Cravath's lawyers argued the appeal and won a unanimous Supreme Court decision. A sick chicken felled the mighty Blue Eagle.

"No lawyer ever unreservedly gave more of himself to a client than Hoyt Moore gave to Bethlehem," Swaine wrote. But in his most celebrated case Moore gave *for* Bethlehem $500,000 in bribes to a federal judge so Bethlehem could acquire a bankrupt wire-rope company at bargain-basement prices. He showed more regard for the niceties of grammar than the letter of the law. There's no mention of it in Swaine's history, but Moore was indicted and successfully pleaded the statute of limitations. Although he had admitted his crime before a congressional committee, the Bar Association never took action against him, and his name remains today an honored part of the firm's shingle.

As senior partners came and left, the Cravath firm went through several name changes until the shingle was fixed at Cravath, Swaine & Moore in 1944. Cravath died in 1940 at age seventy-nine. Swaine headed the firm until his death in 1949. Moore ran it through the 1950s. When he died in 1959 at the age of eighty-eight, the firm had twenty-eight partners and eighty-eight associates.

The Cravath system tended to produce an able and hardworking, if narrow and unimaginative, lawyer—what law students call a "grind." Cravath himself wanted it that way. "Brilliant intellectual powers are not essential," he told a Harvard Law class in 1920. "Too much imagination, too much wit, too great cleverness, too facile fluency, if not leavened by a sound sense of proportion are quite as likely to impede success as to promote it. The best clients are apt to be afraid of those qualities. They want as their counsel a man who is primarily honest, safe, sound and steady."

Cravath has always been wary of the man who came on too fast, who posed a threat to the established order. It is significant that—until recent years—no one who remained with the firm distinguished himself outside it. The classic case is John J. McCloy.

As a young attorney in the years between world wars, McCloy attracted the attention of Henry L. Stimson for his handling of the "Black Tom" case, a $23 million claim arising from the explosion of a Bethlehem munitions plant during World War I. McCloy worked on the case for nearly two decades, doggedly tracking down the documentation that the German government had sabotaged the plant. The experience made him an expert on the German military. When Stimson became Secretary of War in 1940, he recruited McCloy as his assistant. "Probably no civilian other than the President himself had so direct a part in World War II military affairs and military decisions as did McCloy," Swaine boasted.

But when McCloy sought to return to Cravath after the war, Swaine's private position was much less effusive. "He thought it would dilute his position in the firm," McCloy recalls. "He made it clear that those who left the firm [during World War I] never amounted to much when they came back. He considered it sacrilege to leave the firm, abandonment of the cloth. If you ever left the Cravath firm, that was the end. It was put in such a way that it made my coming back less than enthusiastic. They were telling me not that I shouldn't come back, but that I shouldn't have any grand ideas."

Swaine himself glossed over the incident in his history: "All the partners hoped he would return, but . . ."

McCloy rebelled. He took his experience and expertise elsewhere, to become a name partner at what is now Milbank, Tweed, Hadley & McCloy and to go on to an even more distinguished career in law, banking and public service. He became, in Richard Rovere's satiric phrase, "Chairman of the Board of the American Establishment"—though McCloy himself scoffs at the idea that he's "Establishment," insisting that he's just a poor boy from the wrong side of the Philadelphia tracks.

The irony is that eleven years later, in 1960, when McCloy retired as chairman of the Chase Manhattan Bank, Cravath invited him to return. Instead, McCloy returned to *his* firm. Yet he, like most Cravath alumni, insists, "I have never had any rancor about it."

"The Cravath system is what everyone would tell you is old school," said one lawyer. "They are pure traditionalists. They do things the way they did them in the 1920s. They are very inbred. They would not consider taking in a partner who had not come up through the ranks. Bringing a guy up through the ranks produces a very narrow viewpoint, like raising a child in a convent school. They don't understand the government point of view. They don't understand consumer reaction. What amazes me is the narrowness of some of these Wall Street lawyers that I run into."

Another lawyer describes Cravath this way: "Their product is superb. The copy is clean. It comes out on time. The citations are all correct. It's as near perfection as an assembly-line product can be. But it lacks imagination."

Still the Cravath system produces esprit de corps, vital to keeping any law factory running smoothly. "When they're big, they have to be run like boarding schools," says author-attorney Louis Auchincloss, "or they fall apart."

They like to think of themselves as the pacesetter," says a fourth observer. And a fifth: "They practice law like the Congress of Vienna—'We have spoken.' "

The "Congress of Vienna" sits on the fifty-seventh floor of the Chase Manhattan Bank Building in the heart of the financial district. At last count it had forty-six partners and one hundred twenty-two associates, to rank as New York's third largest firm. A somber portrait of Paul D. Cravath graces the wall opposite the reception desk. The receptionist may be miniskirted and pants-suited secretaries may flit through the corridors, but Cravath's three floors have a definite masculine aura. Almost alone among Wall Street firms it still employs male stenographers and clerks, men with close-cropped hair and the dutiful manner of seminarians. Although it had female help as far back as 1897, women didn't make major inroads at Cravath until the manpower shortage of World War II.

By contrast, Cravath was one of the first firms to hire women lawyers. Helen L. Buttenwieser, a scion of the Lehman family who is now a senior partner in the medium-sized midtown firm of London, Buttenwieser & Chalif, served as an associate there in the 1930s. At the time, only one other Wall Street firm had a woman lawyer—Cadwalader, Wickersham & Taft. "They got a woman . . . and a Jew . . . and got to get rid of her in one year," Mrs. Buttenwieser recalls, also without rancor.

Cravath now has one woman partner and eight women associates—not enough though to keep it from being slapped with a sex-discrimination suit brought by a group of militant women law students.

Feminine intrusion was only one of the changes Cravath had to accept to keep pace with the times. The "gentiles-only" barrier fell in the 1950s when Cravath created its first Jewish partner—Edward Benjamin. Previously, it had had Jewish associates, but for all of them it had been "out," not "up." Benjamin's case touched off a furious fight in the Cravath councils. At one point in the discussions, Hoyt Moore, well in his eighties and set in the ways of an earlier era, reportedly called a colleague into the corridor and whispered, "All right, who's the first guy who's going to go in and yell, 'Jew! Jew!'?" When no one else would, Moore did, only to be outvoted—a rare rebellion against authority at Cravath. Benjamin's career was cut short in 1959 when he died in the crash of an American Airlines Electra in the East River. The firm has since promoted several Jews to partnerships.

With Moore's example in mind, the firm also took steps to provide for aging partners. But nothing was done until after his death.* Until 1967, Cravath had no retirement plan; partners stayed on into their dotage, exercising control, collecting their share of fees, preventing the rise of younger men. Under its present plan, partners are phased out starting at age sixty-five. For seven years their earnings are decreased each year according to individual formulas. Retirement is compulsory at seventy-two.

The provision did not apply to the three partners who had

---

* Until the passage of H.R. 10 (the Keogh Act) in 1962, it was impossible for law firms to set up tax-free pension plans. Aging partners could be retired, but any payments to them came out of the common kitty.

already reached retirement age—Bromley, Maurice "Tex" Moore (as his brother-in-law Henry Luce would say, no kin to Hoyt) and Edward Pinney.

A word about Bruce Bromley: For more than fifty years, he has been one of the nation's outstanding corporate litigators. According to courtroom rivals, he is a master at procrastination, an expert in devising ways to prevent any case likely to go against him from coming to trial. In the flesh, he's short and slight, a bantam of a man usually seen peering out at the world through dark glasses. He is also one of the last remaining "characters" in the corporate bar. "Obscene," "colorful," "ballsy" are the words other lawyers use to describe him.

"One of the outstanding leaders of the bar," said Governor Thomas E. Dewey when he gave Bromley an interim appointment to New York State's highest court, the Court of Appeals, in 1949. Bromley was defeated the following year when he ran for a full fourteen-year term.

An even more practical honor came when he was picked to represent the House of Representatives when Congressman Adam Clayton Powell appealed his ouster to the Supreme Court. Bromley's fee was $213,000.

As a litigator, "Judge" Bromley is not above a few clever courtroom ploys. He trained himself to read upside-down so he could decipher opposing attorneys' notes across the counsel table. Once, while arguing a case on behalf of General Motors, he noticed the opposing attorney scribbling his notes on a single sheet of yellow legal paper with a fountain pen. Bromley took a sip of water, spilled a thin film across the lectern, concluded his argument and sat down. The rival lawyer rose to reply, laid down his notes—and watched his carefully prepared argument dissolve.

On another occasion, Bromley tried to telephone Louis Nizer, but an officious secretary refused to put the call through. Would he care to leave a message?

The judge complied: "Bromley, Bruce. HA 2-3000. Fuck you, Louis!"

Within minutes, Nizer returned the call.

As aging partners were phased out, there was also a relative democratization at Cravath. Policy is thrashed out at Monday lunches in the Wall Street Club on the fifty-ninth floor; each of the forty-six partners has an equal vote. But day-to-day decisions remain in the hands of the presiding partner, always chosen from the corporate side of the firm, and the tradition of strong central leadership remains.

The current presiding partner is Roswell Gilpatric. His ascension to power symbolizes the most significant change at Cravath—the end of its policy of isolation. He has left the firm twice for government service—as Undersecretary of the Air Force in the Truman Administration, where he proved "a wizard at forestalling bottlenecks in aircraft production"; and as Deputy Defense Secretary under John F. Kennedy. Unlike McCloy, Gilpatric returned to the firm each time with enhanced stature and, according to critics, each time with a major defense contractor in tow as a Cravath client.

His tenure at Defense sparked another of those controversies to which Cravath, supposedly so staid, seems peculiarly prone. As Deputy Secretary, Gilpatric played a key role in pushing through the $6.5 billion contract to General Dynamics for construction of the ill-fated TFX jet fighter. General Dynamics was a Cravath client, having paid the firm more than $300,000 in fees between 1958 and 1963. Gilpatric himself had an office in General Dynamics' headquarters in Rockefeller Center and had advised the company on its acquisition of Material Services Corporation. After the TFX award, Cravath switched from being *a* counsel of General Dynamics to being *the* counsel, and "Tex" Moore went on its board of directors.

After a lengthy inquiry, the Senate Permanent Investigations Subcommittee—over the protests of its chairman, Arkansas Democrat John McClellan, and Washington's Henry "Scoop" Jackson, "the Senator from Boeing"—gave Gilpatric a 5-to-4 vote of confidence. And the Justice Department absolved him of any "legal or ethical conflict of interest." But seven years later, another Senate committee that looked into the contract concluded:

Deputy Secretary Roswell Gilpatric was guilty of a flagrant conflict of interest in the TFX award. . . . The record makes clear the fact that he was a top level policy counselor to General Dynamics for the two and one-half years immediately before his appointment and that he was a de facto member of the company's Board of Directors. The record shows that he participated in the TFX award proceedings and that he advised Secretary McNamara to give the contract to General Dynamics. . . . He obviously should have disqualified himself from taking any part in the decision.

Gilpatric is a handsome man in his mid-sixties, something of a dandy who keeps a handkerchief tucked up his sleeve. One lawyer's wife calls him "the suavest man I've met since Jimmy Walker."

He once described himself as "a colorless individual with a weakness for sailing and tennis." He forgot to mention women. Four times married, Gilpatric was a frequent escort of Mrs. Jacqueline Kennedy before she married Aristotle Onassis.

In February, 1970—just as he had pulled off one of his biggest coups, corralling CBS as a Cravath client—Gilpatric hit the headlines again when four handwritten letters from "Jackie" to "Ros" were put up for sale by autograph dealer Charles Hamilton. One had been sent from her honeymoon yacht:

> Dear Ros—I would have told you about the wedding before I left—but then everything happened so much more quickly than I'd planned. . . . I hope you know all you were and are and ever will be to me—with my love, Jackie

"A romantic," Gilpatric's third ex-wife, Madelin, called him. A Kennedy family friend described him as "a real lady-killer with those dancing blue eyes and blond hair. If I were a woman in New York looking for an attractive male to escort me, I'd look no further than Ros Gilpatric. But I doubt Jackie was ever very serious about Ros—he's notoriously impecunious thanks to his ex-wives."

Publication of the letters caused another scandal at Cravath. Gilpatric claimed they had been pilfered from his locked files by one of the rare disgruntled Cravath alumni—an ex-associate named Thomas Donson. Donson said the letters had been found in a wastebasket by one of the night stewards and passed on to him. The issue was never resolved. In May, Donson pleaded guilty to unauthorized possession of personal property and paid a $100 fine.* Three days later Gilpatric married for the fourth time. As for the purloined letters, Gilpatric got them back and gave them to the JFK Library.

Cravath's emergence from isolation also saw its partners taking a more active role in its clients' business affairs. Gilpatric sits on the boards of CBS, Corning Glass, Fairchild Camera and Eastern Airlines (not a Cravath client—yet), as well as the Federal Reserve Bank; Tex Moore on Time-Life, Chemical Bank and General Dynamics; Bromley on IBM.

Gilpatric insists it wasn't a change in policy, only "an expansion of exceptions" to the old rule. Yet he harbors Paul Cravath's old misgivings about the practice: "I think there's a conflict of interest when you're acting both as counsel and as a member of the board." It's a conflict Cravath has yet to resolve.

---

* Two years later Donson was arrested again, on charges of stealing prints from the Metropolitan Museum of Art—of which Gilpatric is a trustee.

2

Downtown, Midtown, All Around the World

Cravath also provides a convenient departure point for our tour of New York's Legal Establishment. It won't be an exhaustive survey. We'll hit the highlights, point out a few landmarks, perhaps linger longer at something that strikes our fancy. Later we'll return to look more closely at some of the more important structures.

The first leg of the tour will be by elevator, for the Chase Manhattan Bank Building is a mecca for the blue-chip bar.

Directly below Cravath—on the fifty-fifth floor—is Breed, Abbott & Morgan, an old firm headed for most of the past four decades by the late Charles Tuttle. A "pugnacious redhead," Tuttle was U.S. Attorney during Prohibition; a dry and a Republican, he had the ill fortune to run for governor in 1930 against Franklin D. Roosevelt; he lost by 725,000 votes. In size, the firm ranks just below the giants like Cravath; its clients include Eastman Dillon, Armco Steel and Union Chemicals.

On the fifty-fourth floor, a portrait of Wendell Willkie indicates the offices of Willkie, Farr & Gallagher. The firm is still headed by Harold Gallagher, the man who brought in Willkie after "the barefoot boy in Wall Street" lost the 1940 presidential election, also to FDR. Willkie's arrival inspired what may be the only poem ever written about a Wall Street law office—Melville Cane's verse that begins:

> *Let the so-called welkin tingle,*
> *Ring the bells both near and far,*
> *Wendell Willkie's hung his shingle*
> *Wendell Willkie's back at the bar . . .*

Actually, in the four years left of his life, Willkie gave the firm little more than the use of his name; he was too busy with politics and the war effort.

In size, Willkie, Farr & Gallagher also ranks just below the giants, representing a number of brokerage houses, Continental Can and organized baseball. As a Willkie Farr partner, Bowie Kuhn represented the major leagues and went on to become baseball commissioner.

On the forty-sixth floor is Milbank, Tweed, Hadley & McCloy—"Milbank Tweed" to everyone in the bar and, less reverently, "Milkweed" to its personnel. It is the legal arm of the Rockefeller family and the Chase Manhattan Bank, and one of the giants—150 lawyers spread over several floors.

Firms that represent banks are generally staid and gray. So it's strange that the firm produced so colorful a character as the late Harrison Tweed. Tweed, who died in 1969, was an earthy, ribald man, much in favor as an after-dinner speaker. A polo player in his youth, he was thrice married, once to the poetess Michael Strange. Once, when asked if he might marry again, he replied, "Why not? It isn't forever."

Tweed owned a summer house at Montauk, Long Island, a building designed by Stanford White and now owned by TV host Dick Cavett. In those pre-*Oh! Calcutta!* days, the Wall Street lawyer developed a unique method for chasing interlopers from his private stretch of sand: He'd simply stroll naked up and down the beach—and intruders fled in shock or shame.

For a decade, Tweed ran the Legal Aid Society, the blue-chip bar's favorite charity, then shifted over to rejuvenate the Bar Association after World War II. He wrote what has come to be the association's unofficial motto:

> I have a high opinion of lawyers. With all their faults they stack up very well against those in every other occupation or profession. They are better to work with or play with or drink with than most other varieties of mankind.

When it came time to inscribe the words in bronze in the association's Tweed Room, the sentence about "all their faults" was omitted.

The three floors below Milbank Tweed are occupied by Davis, Polk & Wardwell, known as "the Tiffany of law firms." Its clients include the J. P. Morgan interests, AT&T and ITT. The firm's modern era dates from 1921 when John W. Davis joined it. Perhaps the greatest appellate advocate of his day, Davis was the now-forgotten Democratic presidential candidate in 1924. He remained active in the firm until his death in 1955, but he was clearly a man whose time had passed. By the mid-1930s he was denouncing a New Deal law regulating holding companies as "the gravest threat to the liberties of American citizens that has emanated from the halls of Congress in my lifetime." Among his last acts was arguing the case *for* school segregation before the Supreme Court in 1953.

The two other names in the shingle belonged to Frank Polk, counselor to the State Department during World War I, who came to what was then Stetson, Jennings & Russell a few months before Davis and brought the future presidential candidate into the firm; and Allan Wardwell, Francis Stetson's son-in-law who served on Red Cross missions to Russia during the revolution and World War II and, as a result, got labeled "the Bolshevik of Wall Street."

Until he became "of counsel" in 1972, the firm in recent years was headed by Frederick A. O. Schwarz, of the toy store family. The present top man is D. Nelson Adams. Its leading litigator is Lawrence E. Walsh, the former federal judge who served as President Nixon's envoy at the Paris peace talks. Another partner is David Lindsay, the mayor's twin brother.

Davis Polk is the epitome of the "white-shoe" firm—so called because of the footwear once sported by Ivy League socialites. Its 122 lawyers probably include the highest proportion of Social Register names on Wall Street.

The story is told that when both Davis Polk and Cravath were at 15 Broad Street one could tell in the elevator which were Cravath associates and which Davis Polk's. The Cravath men would talk about the work they've done the night before, Davis Polk's about what they'd have for lunch.

"The Davis Polk lawyer may have worked just as late the night before as the Cravath fellow," one lawyer explained. "He just doesn't brag about it. Davis Polk's people pride themselves on being gentlemen, and a gentleman doesn't brag about being a greasy grind."

Now that both firms are once again housed in the same skyscraper, we can see if it still holds true as we descend to the lobby to continue our tour on foot.

We cut across the plaza toward the East River, past the Down Town Association where the Brahmins gather for lunch. At 80 Pine Street is Cahill, Gordon, Sonnett, Reindl & Ohl, an outgrowth of a firm founded in 1918 by William Gibbs McAdoo, Woodrow Wilson's Treasury Secretary and son-in-law. Over the years it went through a number of changes in personnel, personality and name—from McAdoo, Cotton & Franklin; to Cotton, Franklin, Wright & Gordon; to Wright, Gordon, Zachry, Parlin & Cahill; to the present combination. There are still some old-timers around town who call it "Cotton Franklin," a name it hasn't used since the 1920s.

The present firm dates from the end of World War II with

the group assembled by the late John T. Cahill, the New Deal era U.S. Attorney best remembered for his 1939 prosecution of Court of Appeals Judge Martin T. Manton, the highest-ranking federal jurist ever convicted of corruption in office.

Unlike most blue-chip firms, Cahill Gordon thrives on litigation and has grown into one of the giants, with 125 lawyers. It has the reputation for being a bunch of tough Irish gut-fighters. "They never ask you for anything and they never give you anything," one lawyer says. "You really bust your chops when you go up against Cahill Gordon." Among those whose chops got busted were the Hughes Tool Company in TWA's $145 million antitrust suit and the U.S. government in its attempt to suppress the Pentagon Papers.*

We go a short block south to Wall Street. With the rash of new building on the fringes of the financial district only a handful of "Wall Street" firms can still be found physically on the artery that symbolizes American capitalism.

At No. 67 is Hawkins, Delafield & Wood. A medium-sized firm founded in 1892, it specializes in municipal-bond certification. Among its corporate clients is ABC. Its trusts and estates division is headed by Louis Auchincloss, many of whose novels and stories are set in Wall Street law offices.

At the corner of Wall and William Streets—No. 53—is a squat, imitation Greek temple that houses the First National City Bank. On one side is Shearman & Sterling, New York's largest law firm. Both literally and figuratively, it rests on the foundation of Citibank, its biggest client. "They're very gray, very stodgy, very traditional—like a bank," says one lawyer. Shearman & Sterling also handled the incorporation of Merrill Lynch, Pierce, Fenner & Smith and various transactions for Aristotle Onassis.

The firm was founded in 1873 by Thomas G. Shearman and John W. Sterling and got its start by representing Jay Gould in the battles of the robber barons. Sterling made a fortune in-

---

* Busted chop and all, Hughes had the last laugh. After eleven years of litigation, on January 10, 1973, the Supreme Court threw out the award to TWA—and Cahill Gordon's $7.5 million fee.

vesting in suburban real estate and left $35 million to Yale when he died in 1918. At the time, the firm had two partners and eleven associates.

Its greatest growth came after World War II when General Boykin C. Wright and several colleagues split off from what became Cahill Gordon to give Shearman & Sterling a needed injection of new blood and a new name—Shearman, Sterling & Wright. Wright, a nonpareil business-getter, died in 1956 and five years later the firm reverted to its time-honored name. But the Wright influence still prevails over the fading legacy of Shearman & Sterling: Wright's successors, Charles Parlin and Frederick Eaton, were both part of the group that followed him into the firm.

Across the street, on the eighteenth floor of the Bank of New York Building at 48 Wall is Sullivan & Cromwell, probably dollar-for-manhour the world's most lucrative law firm. Its basic business is "green goods"—securities and indentures. Among its clients are the First Boston Corporation, Goldman Sachs, International Nickel, the Marine Midland Bank and the Bank of New York.

Among laymen, Sullivan & Cromwell is best known as the firm of the late Dulles brothers—John Foster, the Secretary of State; and Allen, the CIA spymaster. Foster Dulles was "chairman" of the firm for twenty-five years, until he received an interim appointment to the Senate in 1949. He was succeeded by Arthur H. Dean, who later served as the chief American negotiator at the Panmunjom peace talks and the Geneva disarmament discussions.

Dean stepped down in 1972 and was succeeded by Wm. Ward Foshay, whose career has been shrouded in the anonymity appropriate to a corporate lawyer. His only venture into the public eye came through an eleven-year term as president of the U.S. Golf Association. ("I hope I can still get in the high 70s.") Sullivan & Cromwell's 155 lawyers also include Norris Darrell, a tax specialist who heads the American Law Institute, and David Peck, the former Presiding Justice of the Appellate Division who is chief of litigation.

The firm was founded in 1879 by Algernon Sullivan and William Nelson Cromwell. Sullivan died within the decade, but Cromwell lived on until 1948, a bachelor recluse who will go down in history as the mastermind behind the international intrigue that led to the Panamanian revolution of 1903 and the construction of the Panama Canal.

Through most of his life Cromwell was an absentee lawlord. "[He] conducted his practice principally from his residence," Foster Dulles observed. "An imposing suite was kept [at the office] for his use. But his appearances there were rare and far between. He was usually to be found at 12 West 49th Street in a mansion of mid-Victorian character, crowded with tapestries, paintings and statuettes."

Cromwell is generally credited with being the first man to urge corporations to make public disclosure in their reports, and, under his auspices, Sullivan & Cromwell lawyers played a major role in drafting much of the New Deal's securities legislation. "A pioneer," Arthur Dean called him.

Despite his legal pioneering, Cromwell resisted such progress as the typewriter, telephone and telegraph. As Foster Dulles noted: "Some of the older partners felt that the only dignified way of communication between members of the legal profession was for them to write each other in Spencerian script and to have the message thus expressed delivered by hand. They resented and rejected the innovations of dictation and the telephone which they deeded incompatible with their sense of privacy and decorum." At Cromwell's insistence that "accidents . . . are permitted to happen by fools who take no thought of misadventure," as late as the 1930s, "every air mail letter had to be followed by one sent regular mail and every telegram confirmed by mail."

Cromwell left an estate of $19 million, mostly to charity. As a Sullivan & Cromwell associate, Louis Auchincloss represented the estate at a routine transfer of property to Columbia University. The school's lawyer asked the whereabouts of the executors—Foster Dulles and Eustace Seligman, another Sullivan & Cromwell partner.

"I represent them," said Auchincloss.

The Columbia counsel refused to sign the necessary papers unless Dulles and Seligman were also present to sign.

"I'll tell you what," Auchincloss said. "You produce Eisenhower [then Columbia's president] and I'll produce Dulles and Seligman." The closing was completed.

No. 48 Wall also houses Emmet, Marvin & Martin, a small firm dealing mostly in trusts and estates. "I remember," says a Wall Street old-timer, "the old dowagers pulling up in their carriages every time they wanted their wills changed." The firm was founded in 1921 as Emmet, Marvin & Roosevelt. The Roosevelt was FDR, who described his duties as "mostly estates, wills, etc., all of which bore me to death." Within three years he left to join Basil O'Connor in a more congenial practice and to return to the political wars.

Next door at 40 Wall Street are the elegant, old-fashioned offices of Winthrop, Stimson, Putnam & Roberts, perhaps the last remaining firm in New York with wood-burning fireplaces. It, of course, was the firm of Henry L. Stimson and, before him, of Elihu Root. Its leading light today is Merrell "Ted" Clark, Jr., who scarcely fits the image of a Wall Street lawyer with his Texas tooled belts and bow ties. Winthrop Stimson's clients include Bristol Myers, the Singer Company and Irving Trust.

At 14 Wall Street, in the Bankers Trust Annex, is White & Case. "The distinctive thing about White & Case," says one lawyer, "is they're gentlemen. You never have to put anything in writing with White & Case."

The firm was founded in 1901 by J. DuPratt White and George B. Case. Two years later the fledgling firm helped organize Bankers Trust, which it has represented ever since. Its other major client is U.S. Steel. White, who died on the eve of World War II, was a Nyack native long active in the fight to preserve the Palisades. Case, who died in 1955, is remembered by sports historians as the man who invented the "squeeze play" while a member of Yale's baseball team in the 1890s.

For years the firm was headed by Colonel Joseph M. Hartfield, who died in 1964 at the age of eighty-two. Hartfield was a dwarf—the "Colonel" was a Kentucky appellation—a bachelor who could be seen galavanting around town in the company of chorus girls a foot taller and forty years younger. But, according to one legal veteran, "he was the best damned business-getter I ever saw."

With 156 lawyers, White & Case is New York's fourth largest firm. Its current partners include Orison S. Marden, who has served as president of the city, state and American bar associations, and Roger Blough, the former chairman of U.S. Steel.

Cutting south again, we pass the New York Stock Exchange—a Milbank Tweed client—till we come to 20 Broad Street, whose top five floors are occupied by Mudge, Rose, Guthrie & Alexander, the firm that gave the nation President Nixon and Attorney General Mitchell. We'll return for a closer look later.

At the tip of Manhattan are two ultramodern towers overlooking Battery Park. One State Street Plaza houses Cleary, Gottlieb, Steen & Hamilton, the newest addition to the blue-chip bar, a 1946 split-off from what was then Root Clark Ballantine. Former U.N. Ambassador George Ball was one of the founders and is currently "of counsel" in its Washington office.

At 1 Battery Park Plaza is Simpson Thacher & Bartlett, one of the giants—144 lawyers—whose clients include Manufacturers Hanover bank, Lehman Brothers and Gulf + Western. It was the firm of the late Edwin F. Weisl, an ace business-getter and business-advisor best known as Lyndon Johnson's "man in New York."

The firm's senior partner is Whitney North Seymour. A tall man with a majestic manner—he likes to sport Chesterfield coats and bowler hats—he's a collector of medallions and ornate piggy banks. He won't fly—which caused no end of trouble when he had to hop-scotch the country as president of the American Bar Association. He's also a confirmed Anglophile. When the A.B.A. held its 1971 convention in London, Seymour escorted Princess Margaret at a garden reception. One observer noted that "the only lady who curtseyed to her was Lola [Mrs. Seymour] because Lola thinks she's English."

Seymour also has a bawdy strain. Among other things, he's a

burlesque buff. "It's the funniest thing in the world," says a colleague, "when he's out of town on a case, at the end of the day, after dinner, to see him stride down the aisle of a burlesque house, bowler hat and Chesterfield and all, followed by Lola—who's very striking herself—followed by a retinue of a half-dozen associates toting briefcases."

In the complex antitrust case *Ferguson* v. *Ford Motor Co.*, Seymour represented Henry Ford II at a six-week deposition of the auto magnate. During the preparation, he noticed that Ford had bladder problems and advised him to wear a "motorman's helper"—a rubber receptacle strapped beneath the trousers—so he wouldn't have to keep dashing from the deposition to the men's room. After the case was settled, Ford sent Seymour the apparatus as a souvenir, which he often trots out to show off to visitors.

Until his election to the Senate, New Jersey Republican Clifford Case was a partner. The firm's rising star today is Cyrus Vance, the former Deputy Defense Secretary and international troubleshooter for LBJ. Among Wall Street firms, Simpson Thacher & Bartlett is the most conspicuous violator of the antinepotism rule. Three generations of Thachers have served there. Edwin L. Weisl, Jr., is a partner and, until his appointment as U.S. Attorney, so was Whitney North Seymour, Jr.

We head up Broadway to the Cunard Building, No. 25. On the eighth floor is Lord, Day & Lord, founded in 1845 by Daniel Lord, his son Daniel, Jr., and his son-in-law Henry Day, and headed today by Herbert Brownell, Eisenhower's Attorney General.

Eight floors above is Chadbourne, Parke, Whiteside & Wolff, another old firm whose chief client is American Brands (formerly American Tobacco Company). The firm got mixed up in the Manton scandal, and a name partner, Louis Levy, was disbarred as a result. Levy had acted as middleman in securing a $250,000 loan—never repaid—for Manton while American Tobacco had a $6 million stockholders' suit pending before the judge.

At 61 Broadway, a private elevator leads to the office of Stroock & Stroock & Lavan, one of New York's oldest "Jewish" firms. Founded in the nineteenth century by Saul and William Stroock, it has long represented many "Our Crowd" families. Peter I. B. Lavan (originally Levine), who joined it more than fifty years ago, brought in the Julius Rosenwald interests as clients. Among gentile lawyers, it's spoken of slightly condescendingly as "a fine, high-class firm."

In recent years, Stroock & Stroock & Lavan has blossomed with a colorful nosegay of political talent—Maxwell Rabb, Secretary to the Cabinet in the Eisenhower Administration; Congressman Herman Badillo; William vanden Heuvel, a Kennedy aide at Justice who now heads the city's Board of Corrections; and several refugees from the Lindsay Administration. Robert B. Anderson, Treasury Secretary in the last years of the Eisenhower Administration, is "of counsel."

Across Broadway, in the Irving Trust Company Building at 1 Wall Street, are three firms of distinguished lineage. On the forty-first floor is Patterson, Belknap & Webb, a 1938 offshoot of Milbank Tweed. Until his death in a 1952 plane crash, it was headed by Robert Patterson, Stimson's successor as War Secretary. The firm represents the Rockefeller philanthropies.

On the twenty-sixth floor, a bronze bust of Charles Evans Hughes indicates the offices of Hughes, Hubbard & Reed. Although he once headed the firm, it is doubly ironic that the bust is there. First, the "Hughes" of the shingle is properly Charles, Jr., who took command of the firm when his father was named Chief Justice in 1930. Second, Hughes, Sr., never believed in trading on the names of dead partners.

In 1904 Hughes was the No. 2 man at Carter, Hughes, Rounds & Schurman, as it was then called. Otto Koegel noted in his history: "[A visitor] called at the Carter office . . . soon after the death of Walter Carter. He found they were removing the name from the door and inserting the name of the new firm. Mr. Hughes explained that he believed in standing on his own name. The view has been held by some that law firms should not carry on the names of deceased partners. Hughes was one of them."

On the twenty-fourth floor is Cadwalader, Wickersham & Taft. The firm traces its origins to 1818. John Cadwalader came along in 1878; the present name dates from 1914 with the ascension of George W. Wickersham, President Taft's Attorney General, and Henry W. Taft, the President's brother. It has long been one of Wall Street's leading specialists in railroad reorganization.

Across the street, at 2 Wall, is Donovan, Leisure, Newton & Irvine, the firm founded in 1929 by the late General William J. Donovan, commander of the "Fighting 69th" in World War I and of the O.S.S. in World War II. Like Charles Tuttle, "Wild Bill" also had the misfortune to run for governor as a Republican in a depression year; he lost to Herbert Lehman in 1932 by more than 800,000 votes. George Leisure, nearing eighty but still active in the firm, assisted Clarence Darrow at his last trial—the Massie murder case in Hawaii in 1932. Like Cahill Gordon, Donovan Leisure thrives on litigation, especially antitrust cases such as the complex welter of suits involving American Cyanamid in the 1960s.

However, Donovan Leisure will not be here by the time we take our tour. In April, 1973, the firm is scheduled to move into larger quarters in the RCA Building in Rockefeller Center. It will be the largest exodus of a Wall Street firm to midtown since the shifts started a generation ago.

A block uptown is the Equitable Building at 120 Broadway, an antique skyscraper with a vaulted lobby and brass fittings. In the days before central air-conditioning, it housed a large proportion of the blue-chip bar. But few firms remain today.

One that does is Fried, Frank, Harris, Shriver & Jacobson, a recent outgrowth from an earlier merger of two Jewish firms— Riegelman, Strasser, Schwartz & Spiegelberg and Fried & Frank. It is as much a Washington as a Wall Street firm. The Washington partners include R. Sargent Shriver, the Kennedy in-law who headed the Peace Corps and the War on Poverty, then went on to become George McGovern's running mate; and Max Kampelman, a member of Hubert Humphrey's inner circle. The Washington office's area of esoteric expertise is Indian law; it's the registered lobbyist for many tribes.

In the next block, at 140 Broadway, is the modern tower of the Marine Midland Building. On the forty-sixth floor is

Dewey, Ballantine, Bushby, Palmer & Wood, the firm headed for eighteen years by the late former Governor Thomas E. Dewey. In size, it's New York's second largest—174 lawyers. We'll star it for a later look.

Twenty-five years ago our tour would have ended here. Until the end of World War II the blue-chip bar was confined to the canyons of the financial district. The midtown firms were considered upstarts, beyond the pale. They were small; few had as many as twenty lawyers or clients that needed the services of more. They were largely Jewish, further fueling Wall Street's sense of superiority.

Several things happened. The midtown firms developed expertise in areas of the law that the old guard overlooked— labor relations, for example. They cultivated clients in new and expanding segments of the economy; some soared with the airlines while Wall Street rivals chugged into oblivion on the railroads. They grew by quantum leaps, avoiding the slow inbreeding of Wall Street by recruiting specialists from government. By the mid-1950s several midtown firms had grown enough in size and strength to match the across-the-board services that Wall Street offered.

The postwar building boom struck midtown about fifteen years before it hit the financial district. Lured by the city's access to the media, finance and foreign markets, corporations from all over the country relocated their executive offices in the heart of Manhattan. New York City's biggest business became the "executive industry." Many of these executives found it easier to deal with lawyers located around the corner than with those a taxi ride across town.

As the Wall Street firms grew, they needed more space. It was available midtown in modern, air-conditioned buildings. In the 1950s and 1960s, several Wall Street firms moved to Park Avenue, while others opened midtown branches. The exodus probably would have been even greater had not downtown redevelopment, spurred by David Rockefeller and the Chase Manhattan Bank, started in the mid-1960s.

Until the building boom hit the financial district, there was a distinct difference in physical setting between downtown and midtown firms. Downtown was dark-paneled suites, period furniture, ship models and Currier & Ives prints; only senior partners rated a window air conditioner in the sweltering summer months. By contrast, midtown was glass and sunlight, abstract art on the walls and functional furniture in centrally air-conditioned offices.

The style differences were reflected in the personnel. Midtown lawyers tended to dress more flamboyantly, perhaps in reflection of those around them—ad men and theater folk, as opposed to bankers and brokers. But Wall Street caught up: Downtown lawyers—at least in the younger echelons—now sport as many wide ties and hirsute chins as their midtown counterparts.

Similarly, as hemlines soared in the late 1960s, downtown secretaries lagged several inches behind those midtown. In part, it was employer conservatism; in part, employee. Midtown secretaries are largely career girls, caught up in the "swinging singles" scene of the Upper East Side; downtown's tend to be commuters living at home in the Catholic communities of Brooklyn and New Jersey. But here, too, downtown caught up. At staid Sullivan & Cromwell—where a lawyer once described the wall color as "shit brown"—miniskirted receptionists now adorn a setting more suited to shirtwaists and bustles.

As with dress and decor, so with counsel and clients. Gradually many of the distinctions between "midtown" and "downtown" disappeared, though Wall Street firms still have a monopoly on the banks and underwriters and trade more heavily in "green-goods," while, with a few exceptions, midtown firms tend to be newer, smaller, more Jewish and more litigious. But every passing year blurs the distinctions further.

The midtown leg of our tour starts in the Pan Am Building, 200 Park Avenue. On the fifty-second floor is Royall, Koegel & Wells, which started as a mid-1930s split-off of the Hughes firm and which mushroomed in the 1950s under the leadership of Kenneth Royall, Truman's Secretary of the Army. During his eight-year hiatus between serving as Eisenhower's Attorney General and Nixon's Secretary of State, William P. Rogers was a name partner.

After his defeat by Robert F. Kennedy in 1964, Senator Kenneth Keating joined the firm, but left the following year when he was elected to the state Court of Appeals. (He later became ambassador to India.) In his short stint with the firm the white-thatched politico brought in one major client, the way many "public partners" do—from appointment by a friendly office-holder. He was named trustee in bankruptcy for Yale Express Systems, collecting $40,000 for his six-month service, while the firm, which acted as the trustee's attorney, got $68,000.

Since Rogers' departure to Foggy Bottom, Royall's death in 1971 and the virtual retirement of founder Otto Koegel, the firm of ninety-three lawyers has been headed by John A. Wells, a member of Governor Rockefeller's inner circle.

Royall Koegel is highly political, operating out of both Washington and New York. Almost alone among the blue-chip bar it is a registered lobbyist in Albany, representing R. L. Polk & Company, the Detroit mailing-list concern; Proctor & Gamble; Schaefer breweries; Pinkerton's; North American Mortgage Investors; and the Lefrak Organization, one of New York's largest real-estate developers. Wells served as counsel to Yes for Transportation, Inc., the highway lobby that pushed for passage of Rockefeller's unsuccessful $2.5 billion bond issue in 1971.

Despite its close ties to the Nixon Administration, the firm represented the *Washington Post* in the Pentagon Papers case. Among its nonpolitical clients is Dreyfus & Company.

On the thirteenth floor is Coudert Brothers, an old family firm specializing in international law, though its founder, Frederic Rene Coudert, used to bristle at the appellation, saying that if a fellow practitioner introduced him as an "international" lawyer, he suspected the man of trying to steal his domestic clients. His son, Frederic, Jr., who died in 1972, served as the "Silk Stocking" district's ultraconservative congressman during the decade after World War II. Among its present partners is Sol M. Linowitz, the former chairman of Xerox and LBJ's ambassador to the Organization of American States.

Back at ground level, we head north through the arcade of the New York General Building into the glass-walled gulch of Park Avenue.

At No. 300—the Colgate-Palmolive Building—is Proskauer, Rose, Goetz & Mendelsohn, one of the first large Jewish firms, headed for forty years by the late Joseph M. Proskauer, a former Appellate Division justice who was one of Al Smith's closest advisors. Among its clients is Warner Brothers.

In the ITT Building—No. 320—is Debevoise, Plimpton, Lyons & Gates, a firm founded in 1931 by two Davis Polk associates—Eli Whitney Debevoise, son of the counsel to the Rockefeller family, and William Stevenson, later president of Oberlin College. They were joined in 1933 by Francis Plimpton, Debevoise's law school classmate. Martin Lyons, a tax specialist, and Samuel Gates, an aviation law expert, joined after World War II. Among its 109 lawyers is George Lindsay, another mayoral sibling. Its clients include Phelps Dodge, American Airlines and the Ford Foundation.

Across the street, at 345 Park Avenue, is Paul, Weiss, Rifkind, Wharton & Garrison, a political powerhouse whose partners have included Adlai Stevenson, Arthur Goldberg and enough lesser talent to fill an entire Democratic slate. We'll star it for a later look.

Filling four floors of 425 Park Avenue is Kaye, Scholer, Fierman, Hays & Handler, which swelled from 16 lawyers in 1947, to 43 in 1958, to 116 in 1972. Part of its growth came when it absorbed a small firm headed by Stanley Waxberg and acquired the burgeoning Franklin National Bank as a client. Part came when Milton Handler, Columbia Law's antitrust expert joined. But a large part remains inexplicable.

"We really don't believe it," says one partner. "We feel—we hope—it's professional. We're not interested in getting our names in the paper."

That Kaye Scholer has managed to avoid. It has risen to the ranks of New York's dozen largest firms with a minimum of publicity. It has handled no headline cases. And although a few lower-level partners have been active in politics—Paul Curran, for example, is chairman of the State Commission of Investigation—none of the name partners is a name familiar to the general public.

Although generally regarded as a "Jewish" firm, Kaye Scholer is now about one-fourth gentile. Still, one partner— Julius Berman—is an ordained rabbi, and several others are so orthodox that kosher meals have to be catered for the partners' lunches.

Across the street, at 430 Park Avenue, is another mushrooming firm, Marshall, Bratter, Green, Allison & Tucker, which went from twelve to ninety-five lawyers in a dozen years, primarily by riding the real-estate boom. When former I.R.S. Commissioner Mortimer M. Caplin was chosen as trustee of Webb & Knapp, William Zeckendorf's bankrupt real-estate empire, he picked Marshall Bratter as his attorneys; in five years, the fees ran to more than $460,000.

At 57th Street we cut west to Madison Avenue. At No. 575 is Rosenman, Colin, Kaye, Petschek, Freund & Emil, another of the Jewish giants. It is headed by Samuel I. Rosenman, one of the grand old men of the New York bar, a former state Supreme Court justice who is always identified in news accounts as "former FDR speechwriter." He coined the terms "New Deal," and "Nine Old Men" as well as Roosevelt's best remembered phrase, "The only thing we have to fear is fear itself," and the rhythmic cadence, "Martin, Barton and Fish."

Now nearing eighty, Rosenman is stone deaf, but still spry. During the 1970 election, he broke with his party to head Democrats for Rockefeller. One of the governor's aides went to Rosenman's office to pick up the judge's endorsement statement. He was dismayed at its seventeen-page length—the Bar Association once satirized Rosenman's long-windedness with a song, "Sam, You Made the Speech Too Long"—but he was delighted with the ringing rhetoric of Rosenman's peroration.

"It sounds just like Franklin Roosevelt," he said.

Without blinking, Rosenman replied, "It is."

At 477 Madison Avenue, we come to Phillips, Nizer, Benjamin, Krim & Ballon—less a law firm than an amalgam of two law firms and a movie company. One lawyer there describes it as "a good-sized business that's administered as if it were still a candy store. It's a system of happy anarchy." The firm has no managing partner to coordinate the flow of work. And, until recently, its lawyers did not fill out time-sheets; partners plucked figures from the air for billing clients.

Phillips Nizer is a tough litigator, with a reputation for serving papers at 5 P.M. Friday, returnable Monday, thus forcing opposing counsel to work through the weekend.

Louis Nizer, of course, is a legendary figure in the law. He has set out his own accounts of his more famous courtroom triumphs—Quentin Reynolds' libel suit against Westbrook Pegler, John Henry Faulk's battle against the blacklisters, Eleanor Holm's divorce from Billy Rose.

"The eleventh floor [the firm's litigation department] survives because people come to Nizer with difficult cases," says one of its members. "The thing that makes it so unusual is that they are all one-shots." The transient nature of this business worries many younger lawyers there. "When he goes, the firm goes."

The other two-thirds of the firm seem more stable. Charles Ballon heads the corporate side, which handles much of New York's "rag trade"—the garment industry. The firm has long been active in movie work. Arthur Krim—one of the Democratic party's top fund-raisers—and Robert Benjamin run United Artists from the law office. Nizer is currently counsel to the Motion Picture Producers Association.

A recent addition to Phillips Nizer is Arnold M. Grant, long a lone wolf of the legal world and best known to the public as the ex-husband of former Miss America (and present Ms. Consumer) Bess Myerson. Grant has acquired a reputation for legal ingenuity. He is credited with inventing the "collapsable corporation" for movie stars' tax savings and the "sale-and-lease-back" method now universal in real-estate development. "Packaging property," Grant calls it.

At 437 Madison Avenue is Greenbaum, Wolff & Ernst, a small firm of literary lawyers. Its chief client is Harper & Row, which it defended against the Kennedy family's effort to suppress William Manchester's *Death of A President*. The late Edward S. Greenbaum headed the firm for fifty-five years. Brigadier general in World War II, he was active in civic affairs. Among his last acts was arranging Svetlana Stalin's flight to the United States. Morris Ernst, still active in his eighties, is a noted author, legal scholar and civil liberties lawyer. He argued the landmark censorship case that let James Joyce's *Ulysses* clear customs. But he won fewer plaudits in the 1950s for his defense of the late dictator Rafael Trujillo in the Galindez affair—the case of Jesus de Galindez, a Dominican exile on the Columbia University faculty. He stepped onto a subway platform one night and was never seen again. Most observers believed that he was kidnaped and murdered by Trujillo's agents. Even within the firm there was opposition to Ernst's defending the dictator, and he had to handle the case as a personal—not a firm—matter.

We cut west to Rockefeller Center. In the General Dynamics Building is Webster, Sheffield, Fleischmann, Hitchcock & Brookfield. Its chief client is Liggett & Myers, its chief glory Bethuel Webster. A courtly gentleman of the old school, "Beth" Webster is the epitome of an Establishment Republican, a former member of The Hague's Permanent Court of Arbitration and, as much as any man can claim the mantle, John Lindsay's mentor. Until his election as mayor, Lindsay was a member of the firm and for several years afterward Webster kept Lindsay's old office vacant in case he chose to return.

Finally, we turn south to 44th Street. Midway between Fifth and Sixth Avenues, at No. 42 West, is the headquarters of the Association of the Bar of the City of New York (hereinafter called the Bar Association). Here the Legal Establishment convenes to proclaim its policies. Here, too, its members meet to socialize and relax over cocktails.

It seems a good place for us to pause.

We could continue—but the trip would be by Metroliner or jet plane.

Given the importance of government in today's economy, most of the major firms maintain branch offices in Washington. In the case of Fried Frank and Cleary Gottlieb, the Washington offices are co-equals and powers in their own right. But for most firms, the Washington offices are small—holding operations usually manned by a partner and an associate who do little more than keep tabs on government and file papers with the appropriate agencies.

Some firms have expert "knife-throwers," men who know the government's decision-making process inside-out and who can direct the New York partners who hop the 8 A.M. Metroliner or the 9 A.M. shuttle to "the man who . . ." A prime example is Breed, Abbott & Morgan's Joseph P. Tumulty, Jr., the former New Jersey congressman.

Similarly, many of the larger firms maintain offices in Europe to handle their clients' overseas affairs—in Paris, London, or more popularly in the past decade, Brussels. The offices are small—staffed by one or two junior lawyers, often resident nationals who serve as functionaries, not decision-makers. Given the state of the world's economy, in the next decade we can expect to see the New York firms opening branch offices in Tokyo.

Closer to home, Cravath has quietly opened not so much an office as an outpost in suburban White Plains to service one of its biggest clients, IBM, headquartered in nearby Armonk. Given the spurt of recent shifts of corporate offices to suburbia, Cravath once again could be setting the trend. And a decade from now we may find Wall Street law firms with branches not only on Park and Pennsylvania avenues, the Ginza and the Rue de la Paix, but in Greenwich and Great Neck, Pleasantville and Paramus.

3

The $100-an-hour
Toll Collectors

Lawyers pride themselves on their ability to write, though only a few have the felicity with words to turn out the best-selling memoirs of a Louis Nizer or the highly acclaimed fiction of a Louis Auchincloss. But a closely reasoned brief that will sway the Supreme Court, an iron-clad contract that leaves no loophole, a will that will withstand the challenge of cut-off-without-a-cent relatives—these are the products of legal authorship.

Yet the most important writing done by members of the Legal Establishment comes when they fill out their time-sheets, divvying their days and hours into six- or ten-minute blocks to determine how much the client will be billed. The Canons of Ethics may be filled with pious pronouncements about an attorney's duty to his clients, to the courts, to the law of the land and the concept of justice; but Cravath, Sullivan & Cromwell,

White & Case and all the rest exist not to chase the elusive butterflies of abstract ideals, but to make money.

The business of the blue-chip bar is business. It's apparent from the priorities a law firm sets for itself. Law schools and legal publishers have made great strides in computerizing the statute books—press a button and a precedent pops up on the print-out—though the process is far from perfected. But when the blue-chip firms installed computers, they were placed not in the law libraries, but in the accounting offices. The electronic brains are used not for legal research, but for billing.

A firm of one hundred lawyers can expect billings of more than $10 million a year. The following financial statement is based on actual 1971 figures for a firm of seventy-five lawyers —thirty partners, forty-five associates—and twice that number of nonlegal personnel:

Gross Receipts—fees		$6,000,000
Operating Expenses		
Payroll		
Legal	$1,100,000	
Nonlegal	1,100,000	
Employee taxes and benefits	220,000	
Pension and death benefits—		
Employees	50,000	
Partners	150,000	
	2,620,000	
Office costs, rent and depreciation	830,000	
		3,450,000
Net to thirty partners		$2,550,000

The partners average $85,000 before taxes.

Such big businesses require businesslike organization—structures that are a far cry from the casual informality of the law offices we see in the novels of Dickens or the teleplays about Perry Mason. The structure varies from firm to firm, but essentially the framework is the same.

First, the vertical pyramid:

We'll draw a heavy horizontal line two-thirds of the way up, a barrier beyond which none may rise. Above the line are the lawyers; below it, the nonlegal personnel—secretaries, stenographers, receptionists, librarians, messengers, clerks, accountants, telephone operators, etc. None will ever have a say in the management of the firm, though an office manager may have authority to hire, fire and assign the lay staff.

In the smaller pyramid on top we'll draw another line two-thirds of the way up, a dotted line dividing the partners from the associates. Associates are also salaried employees, but in time some will filter up through the dotted line to the coveted ranks of partnership at the peak of the pyramid.

Just outside the peak, we may place a period or two—to indicate the lawyers who are "of counsel" to the firm. They are outside the hierarchy—either semiretired seniors like Theodore Kiendl and George Brownell at Davis Polk or part-time practitioners like Robert Anderson at Stroock, George Ball at Cleary Gottlieb or Roy Cohn at Saxe, Bacon & Bolan. They are provided with the courtesy of an office and use of the facilities, but no share of the profits or say in the management; their clients are their own.

On this vertical structure we'll superimpose a horizontal segmentation.

We'll divide the pyramid into a series of wedges to indicate the different departments, each headed by a senior partner. The names may differ from firm to firm, but every Wall Street and Park Avenue law office starts with the same basic four—corporate, tax, trusts and estates, and litigation. In some firms, banking is split off from corporate and antitrust from litigation. Firms with esoteric specialities have separate departments for them—municipal bonds at Mudge Rose, theater at Paul Weiss, labor relations at Kaye Scholer.

Such elaborate organizations need direction. In theory, a firm is run by the partners; in practice, the management of a three hundred-, four hundred- or five hundred-man organization is no job for a committee of fifty men, each with his own work to do, so the task is delegated. Here again, there are wide variations from firm to firm. Policy may be decided by all the partners, usually at weekly or bi-weekly luncheon meetings; or by an executive committee of four to six partners; or by both. Day-to-day decisions will be made by the managing partner—sometimes the strongman of the firm, like the "presiding partner" at Cravath or the "chairman" at Sullivan & Cromwell. More often, the routine chores of administrations are handled by a middle-level partner.

Sometimes power may devolve—not to the best lawyer, or the top business-getter, but to the man who takes command of the internal administrative apparatus, often a man wholly unknown to the outside world. As one lawyer put it, "The man who really runs the firm is the guy who tells the secretaries whether or not they have to work on Washington's Birthday." Orison Marden of White & Case notes: "Where the outside world would think of Mr. Jones as the strongman, those in a position to know say it's Mr. Smith."

Beyond these top-level management chores, special tasks are delegated to other partners—hiring, assignment of associates, supervision of the library, etc.

The blue-chip bar provides far more than first-class legal service—it offers across-the-board expertise in the ins and outs of government, the ups and downs of business, the whys and wherefores of foreign governments.

"Because of their widely held reputation for knowhow," a Merrill Lynch report notes, "lawyers are consulted more frequently for advice on nonlegal matters."

The senior partners rarely crack a law book. They are negotiators, lobbyists and management consultants, with wide knowledge and contacts. From their skycraper offices on Wall Street and Park Avenue they have a better perspective of the political picture or economic outlook than the businessman in Detroit, Dayton or Des Moines.

This is especially true of the lawyers who serve as corporate directors, making basic business decisions for their clients. John J. McCloy, of Milbank Tweed, is on the boards of AT&T,

Metropolitan Life, Allied Chemical, United Fruit and Westinghouse. Frederick M. Eaton, of Shearman & Sterling, is on Monsanto, New York Life, Con Edison and the First National City Bank. Ward Foshay, of Sullivan & Cromwell, is on International Nickel, Pitney-Bowes and the Marine Midland Bank. The list could be extended for pages.

Such men are consulted as lawyers and retained as directors not so much for their legal ability as for their knowledge, contacts and judgment. When he returned as a name partner to Milbank Tweed in 1960, McCloy had practiced law only one year in the previous twenty. Would Mount Sinai or Columbia-Presbyterian hire a chief surgeon who hadn't touched a scalpel for two decades? This suggests that the law—at least as practiced at the upper levels of the blue-chip bar—is not so much a profession as a discipline, a pattern of thinking, an ability to assimilate information, a capacity for switching from one subject to another, all the while combining the patience of a psychiatrist and the passion of a preacher.

"I had a real question in my mind if I could come back to the law," McCloy recalls. But, "You have a feeling of where the red flags are and where the thin ice is that sticks with you. After I got into it again, I had the feeling of coming home."

Many of a corporate lawyer's functions could be—and often are—performed by an astute businessman, banker or broker, if only he had the fiduciary relationship and a team of attorneys to back him up. It doesn't take a lawyer to negotiate a corporate merger or settle a labor dispute—only to seal the deal in the boilerplate, the agate clauses of the contract.

Even in a law firm's other departments, the lawyers often perform largely nonlegal functions. In tax, they advise corporations on how to escape with the lowest levies possible—or as one lawyer put it more bluntly, "how to fuck the government out of money." It's largely an accountant's job.

Tax is a burgeoning area of the bar, simply because taxes are becoming more pervasive and the I.R.S. code more complex. In Louis Auchincloss' *Powers of Attorney* one lawyer muses, "I sometimes wonder what the hell lawyers did before big taxes.

Fuss around with the commerce clause, I guess, and try to break wills."

Trusts and estates used to be the mainstay of many a blue-chip firm, but it has declined in importance as corporate wealth has superceded personal fortunes. The legal work is the simplest possible: The basic task is administering the estate, a nonlegal function that is often handled by bankers and businessmen—and even housewives! It's also one of the few areas of the law where blue-chip lawyers don't bill by the hour; they're paid a percentage of the estates they administer.

"One big estate can carry a firm for years, with a very small amount of work," says Auchincloss, who handles trusts and estates for Hawkins, Delafield & Wood. "There's not much difference between administering a $750 million estate and a $1 million estate."

Finally, there's litigation—which brings to mind the classic confrontations of counsel before judge and jury. In the blue-chip bar litigation is usually an extension of the negotiating process, and very few cases ever come to trial. One lawyer notes that "litigation is where one party sends the other party a piece of paper, and the other party sends the first party a piece of paper . . . and nothing ever happens."

"They like to call themselves litigators," another lawyer adds, "except they don't try cases. They come in at nine, press a button and the papers roll out. They throw up a great deal of paper. Now paper is very good for billing clients, because the clients sees it."

Few firms make money from litigation. They look upon the litigation department as a loss-leader, something to lure clients into the office. As David L. Bazelon, a lawyer turned social critic, observes:

> Trial lawyers, the really good ones, are a breed apart. They are like intellectual matadors or fifty-mission war aces. Whole firms are built around a single one, because the mystique of a trial-winner is a great lodestone for clients who are money-winners. The money in legal practice,

however, does not come directly from trying cases—and the best lawyers are always those who keep their clients out of court. But every once in a long while . . . the gauntlet is offered and cannot be refused. Then you run for Simon Rifkind or Bruce Bromley, Milton Pollack or Louis Nizer, or somebody who carried a briefcase for someone who was trained by Max Steuer. That is, if you really want to win, and can afford to pay the price.

The bills—not just for litigation—can be astronomical. Clients pay six-figure retainers for the services of Wall Street and Park Avenue firms.

A researcher named William J. Hudson, Jr., plowed through fifty-five files containing cases of reports submitted to the Securities and Exchange Commission to compile the most comprehensive study yet of corporate legal fees—payments made from 1,919 corporations to 1,182 firms. Yet he noted that these payments "represent only the tip of the iceberg," since the S.E.C. requires disclosure only when the fee is paid to the firm of an officer or director of the corporation.

Among the top fees for 1971 which Hudson discovered were:

Corporation	Firm	Fee
First National City Corp.	Shearman & Sterling	$2,210,000
Leasco Corp.	Willkie, Farr & Gallagher	1,854,683*
Alleghany Corp. (and subsidiaries)	Donovan, Leisure Newton & Irvine	1,097,724
CBS	Cravath, Swaine & Moore	949,350
Singer Co.	Winthrop, Stimson, Putnam & Roberts	933,800
Howmet Corp.	Seward & Kissel	933,140
Gulf + Western	Simpson Thacher & Bartlett	926,548
Tesoro Petroleum	Dewey, Ballantine, Bushby, Palmer & Wood	811,039
American Electric Power	Simpson Thacher & Bartlett	778,500

*Sum of fees 1968-71

Corporation	*Firm*	*Fee*
Kinney Services	Paul, Weiss, Rifkind, Wharton & Garrison	748,500
Supermarkets General Corp.	Nickerson, Kramer, Lowenstein, Nessen & Kamin	623,000
Wheelabrator-Frye	Palmer & Series	610,575
American Metal Climax	Sullivan & Cromwell	580,000
Chrysler Corp.	Kelley, Drye, Warren, Clark, Carr & Ellis	570,233
Continental Can	Willkie, Farr & Gallagher	557,073
Becton, Dickinson & Co.	Kane, Dalsimer, Kane, Sullivan & Kurucz	556,955
Continental Corp.	Kelley, Drye, Warren, Clark, Carr & Ellis	540,880

Undoubtedly, there are other fees as large, or larger.* But the exact amounts are known only to those who paid and received them.

Curiously, in the S.E.C. reports, only one company disclosed the hourly breakdown of the legal services it paid for—Merrill Lynch, which shelled out $704,000 for fifteen thousand hours put in by lawyers at Brown, Wood, Caldwell & Ivey, an average of about $47 an hour.

Clients willingly pay such fees—though some may be hard-pressed to say what they actually get for the money. Lawyers sow not, neither do they reap; they do not produce, nor do they market. Their role is adjunctive. At best, it can be said that they facilitate; at worst, that their services are a necessary evil—like license fees, a cost of doing business. One client likens them to toll collectors: "You can't get on the road unless you pay the toll." But no attendant with his hand out along the Pennsylvania Turnpike ever charged $100 an hour.

---

* What is believed to be the largest legal fee ever—$7.5 million—was awarded to Cahill Gordon in the case of *TWA* v. *Howard Hughes*. But the fee—still in dispute—was to be paid not by Cahill Gordon's client, TWA, but by the Hughes Tool Company, which lost the antitrust action. The judge's breakdown showed that Cahill Gordon attorneys put in 58,600 hours on the eleven-year-long case, about 20,000 by partners, 38,000 by associates—for an average of $125 an hour.

The blue-chip bar is also a booming business. The following table shows how the major firms have grown in the past fourteen years:

	1958	1968	1972
Shearman & Sterling*	35-90/125	49-120/169	56-144/200**
Dewey, Ballantine, Bushby, Palmer & Wood	23-82/105	36-111/147	47-127/174
Cravath, Swaine & Moore	28-88/116	39-108/147	46-122/168
White & Case	34-75/109	45-90/135	56-100/156
Sullivan & Cromwell	32-53/85	48-65/113	50-105/155
Milbank, Tweed, Hadley & McCloy	28-66/94	45-83/128	50-100/150
Simpson Thacher & Bartlett	23-74/97	41-83/124	49-95/144
Paul, Weiss, Rifkind, Wharton & Garrison	19-31/50	—	45-93/138
Cahill, Gordon, Sonnett, Reindl & Ohl	28-56/84	46-60/106	45-80/125
Davis, Polk & Wardwell	30-67/97	42-82/124	42-80/122
Mudge, Rose, Guthrie & Alexander	20-35/55	—/105	39-79/118
Kaye, Scholer, Fierman, Hays & Handler	—/43	38-68/106	51-65/116
Donovan, Leisure, Newton & Irvine	21-37/58	—	37-78/115

---

* Present names are used.
** Partners-associates/total. In some years figures were not available for all firms.

The firms, as we have noted, also employ scores of nonlegal personnel. The ratio of laymen to lawyers is generally about 2 to 1, and would be even greater were it not for three wonders of modern technology—the automatic typewriter, the Xerox copier and the computer.

The growth is evident. The reasons for it are more difficult to discern. At some firms—Paul Weiss, Mudge Rose and Kaye Scholer—it was dramatic, and idiosyncratic. At the others, it was steady, and across-the-board.

Undoubtedly the chief reasons for the growth arise from the increasing complexity of the law itself and the increasing intrusion of government into business. No corporation can make a move today without encountering a government regulation, and that entails a legal opinion, often the judgment of a specialist. The growth of government influence in the 1960s has been nowhere near as dramatic as that of the New Deal or World War II. "But the trends," says Sullivan & Cromwell's Foshay, "started then."

The growth has also been spurred by business conditions. A large part stems from the trend toward merger and conglomeration. Then there has been a flood of antitrust cases, both government and private, which eat up legal manpower like an invasion of cannibal tribes. Some growth stems from the stockmarket booms of 1961–62 and 1965–68 and the spate of new-issues work for lawyers. And the Nixon recession and the increase in bankruptcies, borrowings and corporate reorganizations have also added to this trend. Good times or bad, the blue-chip bar prospers.

But contra-growth trends are equally evident. The 1960s also saw a dramatic growth in the number and size of house-counsel staffs—from 21,054 lawyers in 1957, to 32,222 in 1966, to an estimated 45,000 in 1972. Much of the routine legal work once done on Wall Street or Park Avenue is now handled in corporate executive suites. "The kind of work which I did when I first came here the young fellows don't do today," says Foshay.

And much of the work once done on Wall Street is now done

on Chicago's LaSalle or San Francisco's Market Street, or in Milwaukee and Minneapolis, Denver and Dallas. Just as the Park Avenue firms grew to rival those downtown, so have many outside New York.

To keep pace, the blue-chip bar has had to diversify, to branch out and take in clients it would have shunned a decade ago, in numbers it never thought possible. A partner at Willkie, Farr & Gallagher estimates that in 1950 one client constituted 20 per cent of the firm's business; today none can claim as much as 5 per cent.

"We used to be specialized practitioners for America," he explains. "We're still that. But we're also becoming general practitioners for the metropolitan area. We're more like drug stores—all of us."

Still he sees one big benefit from this client mix—less dependence on the business of one or two major clients and less need to kowtow to the whims of one or two eccentric executives. "Lawyers have become as independent as they say they are."

Whatever the reasons, the blue-chip bar keeps growing—most of it. "We would prefer not to," says Orison Marden, of White & Case. "It just seems to be forced by a need to serve clients. It's more fun when you're a small family. You see more of each other."

A few firms deliberately resisted growth, feeling that gigantism would impair their ability to function and destroy their sense of individual identity. "When I started out," says Louis Auchincloss, "there was a distinct difference between Sullivan & Cromwell and Davis Polk. Now you can't tell them apart." The upper limits vary from firm to firm—75, 100, 125 lawyers. New business that forces a firm to expand beyond that point is turned away.

There are several dangers in this: First, the client that's turned away could be the big income-producer of the future, while those that remain could decline in importance—and so will the firm. Second, limiting size may limit the service a firm can provide its clients, especially those that are mushrooming themselves. Then the client may leave, and the firm declines even further. Finally—and most important—limiting size limits the openings for new partners. Able associates will be forced to seek places elsewhere, and such a firm quickly acquires a reputation as a "dead-end," holding little appeal for top law-school graduates. In a short span of time, such a firm can become second-rate.

When their firms were both at 575 Madison Avenue, Lloyd K. Garrison, of Paul Weiss, would occasionally encounter Samuel Rosenman in the elevator. At such times he'd tease the judge by reciting a bit of doggerel:

> More euphonious name ne'er was coined,
> Than Rosenman, Colin, Kaye, Petschek & Freund.

Alas for euphony, the name of the firm is now Rosenman, Colin, Kaye, Petschek, Freund & Emil.

It illustrates one of two contradictory trends in firm names. At newer—or recently rejuvenated firms—the names get longer. Each new arrival to a position of power presses for a place on the shingle. As the firms age, the new arrivals must compete not only with present powers, but with dead or retired partners.

For years there was an unwritten rule that shingles would include no more than five names. But under the pressures of the 1960s the rule gave way and several firms went to six. Rosenman's firm is one example. Two more prominent ones are Paul Weiss after Arthur Goldberg joined and what was then Nixon Mudge when it took in John Mitchell.

Among older, more stable firms the contrary trend can be seen. They revert back to a shingle of founders when present powers retire or die—Shearman, Sterling & Wright to Shearman & Sterling; Davis, Polk, Wardwell, Sunderland & Kiendl to Davis, Polk & Wardwell; Willkie, Farr, Gallagher, Walton & Fitzgibbon to Willkie, Farr & Gallagher.

Reversion solves several problems: It saves money and effort sending out notices and reprinting stationery with every name change; it squelches a major source of possible conflict among partners; and, as one attorney put it, "It gives the firm more of an institutional sense." It's a sign that the firm has become established, institutionalized, no longer subject to the vicissitudes of partners' departures or deaths.*

A short, snappy name also has commercial value. It's far easier to remember and to repeat. Better a client should say, "My lawyers are Sullivan & Cromwell," or "White & Case," than "My lawyers are Smith, Jones, Johnson, Jenkins and whatshisname . . . or is it Jones, Jenkins, Johnson and whatshisname?"

Some have suggested a subtler motive for the trend. As racial barriers have fallen in the blue-chip bar, Jews have risen to positions of power in many old-line firms. Reversion prevents the possibility, say, of Cravath, Swaine & Moscowitz; Lord, Day & Lipschitz; or Davis, Polk & Warshavsky.

Shingle stabilization is only a surface manifestation of institutionalization, itself a relatively recent development in the blue-chip bar. Only two of New York's thirteen largest firms have shingles composed wholly of names of men who did not live into the postwar period—Shearman & Sterling and Simpson Thacher & Bartlett. Only four more have shingles composed wholly of names of dead partners—Cravath; Sullivan & Cromwell; White & Case and Davis Polk.

True, a number of firms in the second rank have shingles of long-gone partners—Hawkins, Delafield & Wood; Lord, Day & Lord; Carter, Ledyard & Milburn, to name but three. But these firms have not grown like the giants. There may be a

---

* One place old names persist is cable addresses. Debevoise Plimpton's is "DEBSTEVE" from its 1931 founding as Debevoise & Stevenson. Emmet, Marvin & Martin's is "EMMARO" from its 1921 founding as Emmet, Marvin & Roosevelt; two letters are all that remain to mark FDR's days as a Wall Street lawyer. The Botein, Hays, Sklar & Herzberg cable address is "HAYGREEN" from its turn-of-the-century partnership of Daniel Hays and Samuel Greenbaum (Edward Greenbaum's father). Some cable addresses are appropriate: Battle Fowler's is "COUNSELLOR"; the internationally oriented Baker & McKenzie's, "ABOGADO."

lesson here. Perhaps institutionalization is the first step on the road to stagnation and ossification.

Lawyers are conservative creatures, resistant to change and innovation, witness Cromwell's attitude toward the telegraph and Cravath's toward women. So it is with the bar's latest augury for change—incorporation.

New York was one of the last states to allow lawyers and other professionals to incorporate. In 1970, Mayor Lindsay, hard-pressed as always for funds, came hat-in-hand to Albany. One of the bones the legislature tossed him was the right to impose a 4 per cent tax on unincorporated businesses. But it coupled its gift with an escape clause allowing professionals to incorporate.

Far from accepting the innovation, the blue-chip bar fought it vigorously. Bernard Botein, the Bar Association's president, called it "a direct attack on the traditional organization of the practice of law in this country."

Consequently, there was no rush on Wall Street or Park Avenue to form Perfect Patent Lawyers, Inc., or Admiralty Attorneys Corporation. And no investors rang their brokers to buy shares in Sullivan & Cromwell. Actually, neither the law nor the canons allow such titles, only the words "Professional Corporation" or the initials "P.C." at the end of the shingle. And the only shareholders allowed are participating lawyers.

Few lawyers or law firms took advantage of the opportunity to incorporate,* although R. Palmer Baker, Jr., of Lord, Day & Lord, recently presented a paper at the Tax Forum—a monthly meeting of the blue-chip bar's tax specialists—urging the major firms to incorporate. He noted that the major opposition to such a move was psychological. But, he said, "it is hard to believe that an established New York City firm would tar-

---

* No figures are available. The New York Secretary of State's office, which registers corporations, does not keep occupational breakdowns, though it reported that most of the filings for professional corporations were by physicians. A cursory check of the 1972 *Manhattan Yellow Pages* shows nine firms and eight individuals listing themselves as "professional corporations."

nish its image and name by adding the abbreviation 'P.C.' "

Baker sees the chief advantage in incorporating as economic —especially in escaping taxes and funding pension and profit-sharing plans. He notes that tax-free pension plans, currently limited to $2,500 a year at law firms, could be boosted to 20 per cent of annual earnings at professional corporations—quite a tax saving for those in the $100,000-plus income bracket.

He also foresees the prospect of the state's tacking on its own unincorporated business tax, for a total bite of 7 per cent. "The amount would be substantial, the effect would be staggering," he says. In such a case, incorporation would offer a tax saving enough to cover funding of a firm's pension plan.

But having proposed incorporation in the abstract, Baker did not urge it in the particular. He did not suggest that Lord, Day & Lord become Lord, Day & Lord, P.C. "Being cautious lawyers, I don't think any of the Wall Street firms are going to incorporate until we've looked at it a little more," he explains. "We're all looking at it very carefully."

Even that is progress. "Ten years ago," Baker continues, "I couldn't conceive of this firm incorporation." But then, as Sullivan & Cromwell's Foshay notes, "If anyone had said thirty-five years ago that all the brokers on the New York Stock Exchange would be incorporated, I would have said they were crazy."

Crazy or not, unwanted or not, incorporation, in the view of many lawyers, is inevitable. A corporation, according to Blackstone, is designed to perpetuate a business beyond the lives of those who began it. It would be the final act of institutionalization of the blue-chip bar.

Institutionalization breeds bureaucratization. The blue-chip bar now offers its partners security equivalent to IBM's—and the equivalent regimentation. The climb up the ladder is no longer by leaps and bounds, but by measured steps. One sign of this is the increasing age of those who attain the seats of power. Fifty years ago, John Foster Dulles became "chairman" of Sullivan & Cromwell at age thirty-seven; two decades ago, his successor, Arthur Dean, took command at fifty-one; in 1972, when Dean stepped down, his successor, Ward Foshay, was sixty-one. This trend may be reversed as more and more firms adopt pension plans and compulsory retirement. More likely, it will probably mean merely that those at the top enjoy a shorter period of power.

Institutionalization also breeds anonymity. With increasing specialization and division of labor in the blue-chip bar, the individual lawyer—especially a younger one—has no opportunity to stand out.* The firms become the powers, not the men in them. People stop thinking in terms of "John W. Davis' firm," but of "Davis Polk," and no one ever thinks of it as "Fritz Schwarz' firm." Or as one lawyer puts it: "Who *are* the partners at Shearman and Sterling? No one knows."

"The old Romans seem to be gone," says Orison Marden, himself one of the last of the breed.

The handful of brahmins known to the general public generally earned their reputations not at the bar, but in politics or public service.

In short, the blue-chip bar has become a place for a man to make money, not to make his mark.

---

* Two illustrations of this:

The Bar Association has to pick targets to "roast" at its annual Twelfth Night shows. The target must be of both sufficient stature to attract an audience and sufficient color to provide material for a forty-five minute revue. The field is expanded because retiring judges are included in the lists, contracted because potential political candidates are not. Since 1959, when its present format was launched, Twelfth Night targets have been (in chronological order): Judge Harold Medina; Morris Ernst; Whitney North Seymour; Judge Charles Clark; Bruce Bromley; the late James B. Donovan (of the Powers–Abel spy swap); Thomas E. Dewey; Samuel Rosenman; Simon Rifkind; Judge Bernard Botein; Theodore W. Kheel and Francis Plimpton (George Plimpton portrayed his father). In 1972 there was a joint entry—Judges Edward Lumbard and Leonard Moore—further illustration of the dwindling pool of legal giants. According to one member of the association's entertainment committee, Louis Nizer's name has been suggested from time to time, but always rejected because "He's his own publicity man; why should we do anything to advertise him?"

In 1958 *Fortune* picked portraits of ten men to illustrate its article on Wall Street lawyers: Harrison Tweed; Arthur Dean; Theodore Kiendl, of Davis Polk; Eli Whitney Debevoise; Seymour; Bromley; Dewey; Norris Darrell; Frederick Eaton and Alan Klots, of Winthrop Stimson. When I asked various lawyers to name ten men to illustrate such an article today, there was a general paucity of names. Many could not complete the list. Those named were mostly old men, many holdovers from the *Fortune* list fourteen years before. If I imposed the judicial cut-off of age seventy, scarcely a name remained.

Even the money is not what it once was, relatively. *Forbes* may hail the law as "the gilt-edged profession" and the top men in the Wall Street and Park Avenue firms may have annual earnings in six figures. But their income is paltry in comparison with that of corporate executives—and it's taxable at much higher rates. No lawyer today can amass a fortune like William Nelson Cromwell's—at least not solely from the practice of law.

"Lawyers as lawyers," says one Wall Street lawyer, "no longer have impact. There's got to be another handle of some kind."

Though the old established firms forbid the practice, the "handle" for many lawyers in the smaller, newer midtown firms is to cut themselves in for a share of the client's business. It's not a course that can be charted with U.S. Steel or Standard Oil, but for a lawyer whose client is a newly formed company, it can be a path to instant fortune—especially during stock-market booms for new issues like those of the early- and mid-1960s.

"The easiest game in town—to make money," said one lawyer. "Most people go into the law to make money, but they find they can't make much money just practicing law, even if they bill at a hundred dollars an hour. They make much more money putting deals together. They're really businessmen with law degrees, and they need a firm to service their clients."

Consider the career of Ted Kheel: Appropriately for a man who would make his mark as a labor mediator, his very name is a compromise—Theodore Woodrow Kheel, first name for a Republican President, middle one for a Democrat. A native New Yorker, Kheel graduated Cornell Law in 1937 and went to work in the legal office of the new National Labor Relations Board; a few years later he switched over to the War Labor Board.

"When the war ended, I thought very hard about what I wanted to do," he says. "I almost went with a firm of labor relations consultants. But a friend said to me, 'You're silly not to be a lawyer. When you're a lawyer you can do anything else. But you can't practice law if you're not a lawyer.' "

Kheel decided to practice law—and work part-time for the labor relations outfit. "I even got a ruling from the Bar Association. A lawyer can participate in somebody else's fee, but nobody else can participate in his, which I thought was a very fine ruling."

However, the labor relations consulting fell through and Kheel went back to government service—this time with the city's division of labor relations. In 1949, he joined a small midtown firm which became Battle, Fowler, Stokes & Kheel and he soon established a reputation as the city's top labor mediator, handling touchy maritime, newspaper and transit disputes. He became a familiar figure on the TV tube—a handsome, husky, crew-cut man announcing an eleventh-hour settlement or pausing for an interview as he shuttled along a hotel corridor in the midst of a marathon negotiation.

He also built up a thriving legal practice. His clients include the National Football League owners and the movie composers who have filed a $300 million antitrust action against the motion picture producers.

In 1965, Kheel was widely touted for the Democratic mayoral nomination, but he turned down the bid. "It's money," explained a political insider who had pushed him. "He must make about $150,000 a year—and he spends every cent of it. He likes to live well—and he's got six kids to see through college. He can't afford the pay cut of being mayor."

Yet he kept active in politics and public affairs. In recent years he's become the city's resident gadfly on mass transit. In 1971, he single-handedly took on the whole of the Establishment by opposing passage of Governor Rockefeller's $2.5 billion transporation bond issue. The measure was backed by a gamut ranging from Mayor Lindsay to Senator James Buckley, from *The New York Times* to the highway lobby—"the triple-A bunch," as Kheel calls them—who mounted a high-pressure ad campaign whose chief effect was to provide Kheel with free TV time for rebuttal. Only Kheel—and the voters—opposed the bond issue.

Rockefeller was plainly piqued at the rejection of his pet

project. "He wants to be mayor," he sneered when Kheel's name was mentioned. But the day after the bond issue went down, Kheel went on TV to proclaim: "I covenant with the people of this city and state never to run for any public office of any description, in this state or any other state in the United States, so help me God!"

Kheel estimates that "fifty per cent of the work I do I don't get paid for." But it keeps him in the public eye. As *The New York Times'* labor expert A. H. Raskin noted, "Much of his private income stems from the prestige . . . his strike-settling activities have brought him."

Late in 1965, Kheel announced that he was bowing out of future newspaper disputes "to devote more time to my family and my business activities." The announcement came the day after Kheel was named board chairman of the new Republic National Bank of New York. Kheel had handled the firm's filing for a charter.

Through the following five years, he dabbled increasingly in business. Currently, he's listed as a director of Athlone Industries, Stirling Homex Corporation, Combustion Equipment Associates, Inc., and Western Union. He's also president of the Punta Cana Club, a luxury resort in the Dominican Republic. And he bought an interest in Le Pavillon—not so much as an investment as to ensure getting a good table at what was, until it folded, one of New York's finest French restaurants.

Kheel says he always buys an interest in the companies he serves as director. "You'd like to have some reason for being a director." For example, he purchased five hundred shares of Western Union—a non-client—through his broker. At Athlone—a holding company that's half steel, half soft goods ranging from shoes to lingerie—he was given an option to buy three thousand shares of convertible preferred at $4.25 a share. Hardly investments that would enable him to retire to the Punta Cana Club.

But to those who scan the fine print of corporate prospectuses, the eye-opener came with Stirling Homex, a manufacturer of modular housing that Kheel helped organize in 1968.

For his legal work, Battle Fowler received fees of $50,000 in 1970.

And Kheel's potential profit was far greater. In June, 1969, Stirling Homex gave Kheel an option to buy 200,000 shares of its stock at $1 a share. Kheel exercised the option. The following February, the company went public, offering its shares for $16.50 each.

On the first day of trading, the stock soared to 36½ and reached a high of 51½ later that year. On paper, Kheel's profits ranged from $3.1 million to $10.1 million.

It's not disclosed whether or at what profit he sold his shares. For his sake, one hopes he got out early. Within two years, Stirling Homex shares had fallen to $5 each and the company, unable to repay $38.8 million in bank loans, filed for bankruptcy.

At least one government agency looked into Kheel's holding in Stirling Homex, but found no basis for action. As one official explained, "As long as you make full disclosure, it's perfectly legal." And the single sentence of disclosure was there—buried in the middle of the prospectus.

4

Some Partners Are
More Equal than Others

There's a story told about a lawyer at Chadbourne who never spoke at partners' meetings. For years he sat silent while his colleagues debated and decided the future of the firm. Then, at one meeting, the promotion of associates to partnership was being considered. A name was put before the panel.

"I don't want him," one partner said. "I just don't like him."

The long-silent partner ahem-ed for attention, and the others bent forward, wondering what words of wisdom he had to utter at so long last.

"I don't see what that has to do with it," he said. "I don't like any of you."

There's nothing in the books—or partnership agreements— that says partners have to like each other. Some firms manage to exist, like the Gilbert and Sullivan collaboration, with the members barely even speaking to each other. But the partners

have to find some sort of accommodation if the firm is to remain viable.

Internal dissension can arise from any number of factors—
personality differences, policy disputes, one partner's politicking or another's handling of a controversial case, the order of
names on the shingle. But most involve that old devil, the
dollar.

It's not an easy subject for an outsider to probe. On no subject is the blue-chip bar so secretive than about what it earns
and how it's divided.

One smaller Wall Street firm reportedly has solved conflicts
over money matters by paying all partners an equal share. But
every other firm in town operates on the Orwellian principle
that some partners are more equal than others.

Once a year, usually around Christmastime, the partners sit
down to decide how the firm's income should be divvied—
"hacking the pie," as it's called. Partners are paid a percentage
of the firm's net income and the totals are expressed in "points":
one point, 1 per cent; ten points, 10 per cent. Occasionally,
newly promoted juniors or recent recruits from the outside will
be given a guaranteed minimum in dollar figures.

In many firms, a partner's points determine how many votes
he casts at partners' meetings. One ten-point partner thus out-
votes nine one-point members. Such a situation makes it
doubly difficult for the juniors to grab a bigger slice of the
pie.

During the year, a partner may "draw" against his antici-
pated earnings—either monthly or quarterly, depending on
firm policy. Coudert Brothers, though, holds to the gentlemanly tradition of paying out earnings only at the year's end.
One associate there, who had been receiving a monthly salary,
was recently promoted to partnership—and found himself
without an income. He had to borrow to meet his bills.

In past years, when the firms were smaller, and their seniors
nationally known figures, the top men took whopping percent-
ages of the firms' incomes. The original Sullivan & Cromwell
partnership agreement, a handwritten document framed on
the office wall, gave Algernon Sullivan two-thirds, William

Nelson Cromwell one-third—and exempted Sullivan's fees as Public Administrator from the common kitty. As late as the 1920s, when the firm had a dozen partners, Paul D. Cravath reportedly received a fifty-point slice of the pie.

But today, when firms have thirty to fifty partners and net incomes ranging up to $10 million, it's doubtful that any lawyer in the major firms pulls more than a seven- or eight-point share, while the juniors must settle for fractions.

The pie-hacking sessions generally devolve into one of two basic confrontations. The first pits the "rainmakers" against the workers, those who bring in the clients against those who service them. The rainmakers usually win, because they control the clients, and their money. But in recent years the differences have tended to level out. As the client becomes institutionalized, he's less subject to the control of one man, and as a firm grows, the rainmaker's value is reduced. When a firm has 150 to 200 lawyers, it's difficult for any one partner to bring in a new client so large as to add significantly to the pie. U.S. Steel, Standard Oil and Citibank aren't about to switch law firms at the behest of one man. Even a $100,000 retainer is only one-tenth of 1 per cent for a law firm grossing $10 million.

The second confrontation pits the middle-level partners against the seniors, sometimes men no longer able to pull their own weight, but who refuse to relinquish their prerogatives —or paychecks. As a firm grows and ages, the problem becomes especially acute, with a lot of deadwood floating at the top. What to do about such men, in the words of one managing partner, is "the most difficult problem any law firm has." In recent years, though, it's been diminished somewhat by the introduction of compulsory retirement and pension plans.

Usually, conflicts are compromised by slicing off a fraction of a point here, adding a fraction there. If a firm's business is booming, a senior partner can afford to suffer some point-shaving without an actual loss of income. But sometimes the squabbles erupt into the open. Before he was appointed to the federal bench by John F. Kennedy, Inzer Wyatt twice threatened to quit Sullivan & Cromwell unless he was given a bigger slice of the pie. Once he went so far as to submit his resignation from the firm, and Arthur Dean even circulated a memo through the office announcing his departure. But cooler heads managed to reconcile the pair.

Sometimes a lawyer discovers a more devious method of moving up the ladder. In *Powers of Attorney*, Louis Auchincloss' protagonist is the senior partner of a large Wall Street firm who discovers that his second-in-command is angling to have him named president of his college alma mater so the second-in-command can take over as head of the firm. There are real-life parallels. When Edward Costikyan, then a junior at Paul Weiss, was Tammany leader, he managed to have his firm's chief of litigation, Samuel Silverman, nominated and elected to the state Supreme Court. Silverman's ability was unquestioned, but the more cynical suggested that Costikyan was less interested in the caliber of the judiciary than in moving up a notch in the Paul Weiss hierarchy.

For a breed that specializes in churning out pages of boilerplate to cover every eventuality, dotting every *i* and crossing every *t*, lawyers are strangely cavalier in their dealings with each other. Many major firms do not have partnership agreements. "We operate entirely on the basis of trust in each other," says Cravath's Roswell Gilpatric. And sociologist Erwin Smigel quoted one Cravath alumnus as recalling, "Mr. deGersdorff, of Cravath, used to say, 'We don't want people for partners with whom we need written agreements.' "

It is surprising that there are not more open breaks. In recent years, the blue-chip bar has remained remarkably stable. There has not been a significant split in a major Wall Street or Park Avenue firm for more than twenty-five years. Except for departures to government service, none has lost more than one partner at a time. Also, when partners leave a firm, they generally go into government, business or academic life. Only a handful quit one firm to practice with another.

Unlike business executives or college professors, the Brahmins of the Bar don't shop around for better-paying positions. A partner at Sullivan & Cromwell won't drop a hint to the powers at White & Case that he's available for a little more money. And, as if by an unwritten agreement, there is almost

no "raiding" by one firm of another's talent. The most significant exception is the recent feud between the bond sections of
Mudge Rose and Hawkins, Delafield & Wood. After John Mitchell became Attorney General, Mudge Rose helped fill the
gap he left by luring a partner and his associate from Hawkins,
Delafield & Wood, which responded by snaring a partner from
Mudge Rose.

In other cities where the bar is more personal and less institutionalized, a lawyer may bounce from firm to firm like a
rubber ball. For example, in less than a decade, John Sharon,
of Cleary Gottlieb's Washington office, went first to Clark
Clifford's firm, then to a partnership with former Supreme
Court Justice Abe Fortas. But on the upper levels of the New
York bar, the shifts are so rare that lawyers can tick them off
on their fingers.

On closer inspection, though, the reasons for such stability
are not difficult to discern. A half century ago, if partners fell
out, one would simply pack his briefcase and set up shop in an
office across the street, taking his clients with him. But in this
era of the institutionalized law firm, it's not so simple. First,
one or two men can't do it: A corporate law firm today requires across-the-board expertise, something attainable only
with a team of a dozen or more first-rate lawyers. Second,
there's the expense: Setting up a properly equipped corporate
law office today requires an investment of several hundred
thousand dollars, and even the best of lawyers will balk before
giving up a sure thing to chance such an outlay on an uncer-
tain future. Third, as clients become "locked-in," there's less
likelihood that they'll follow a lawyer who leaves. And, finally,
there's the lawyer's equity in his pension.

As a result, we don't have a contemporary example. So we'll
have to turn back the clock to look at the last significant split in
a blue-chip firm, one that went through not one, but two internal upheavals in less than a decade.

At the end of World War II, there was no finer array of legal
talent in New York than the aggregation known as "the Root

Clark firm." It was founded in 1909 by Elihu Root, Jr., and Grenville Clark and quickly earned a reputation as one of the city's leading corporate law firms. In its early years it handled the estates of Andrew Carnegie and Marshall Field and represented the beer brewers in their legal fight to thwart the Volstead Act.

After he retired from the Senate in 1915, Elihu Root, Sr., became "of counsel" to the firm and remained with it until his death in 1937. For two decades thereafter, the firm's stationery listed his name with the dates "1915–1937" but nothing to indicate that he'd never actually been a member.

The younger Root was something of a dilettante, a yachtsman and an esthete who in later life took to painting finely detailed nudes. Clark, by contrast, was deeply involved in public affairs. "Publicly inconspicuous," said *The New York Times*, but "privately a man of enormous influence with uncommon powers of persuasion." Long an apostle of world government, though he held no official position, he played a major role in both World Wars. An advocate of preparedness, he organized the Plattsburgh Movement to train military men in the months before America's entry into World War I. In 1940, he helped draft the Selective Service Act and induced FDR—once his fellow associate at Carter, Ledyard & Milburn —to recruit Henry L. Stimson and Robert Patterson for the War Department. But his friendship with Roosevelt did not prevent him from organizing the bar's opposition to the President's "court-packing" plan.

Behind Root and Clark was an able trio of name partners who made the firm flower in the two decades between the wars—Emory Buckner, its leading litigator, who served a term as U.S. Attorney in the 1920s; Silas Howland, who left in 1930 to become counsel to the Guggenheim Brothers; and Arthur A. Ballantine, former counsel to the I.R.S., who became "the brain trust of the Republican right wing through the Roosevelt era." Behind them was a bench strength unmatched on Wall Street—more than a dozen first-rate junior and middle-level partners, mostly men sent down from Harvard Law by Felix

Frankfurter. An old friend of Buckner's, Frankfurter, until his appointment to the Supreme Court, served as "a one-man employment agency" for Root Clark.

The "bench" was strong enough so that the top men had plenty of free time for their private pursuits—be it the arts, public service or golf. It became a standing joke in the office that whenever a partner was away on the course, callers would be told, "Mr. —— is out in Westchester [or Long Island or New Jersey or wherever] going over a piece of property."

By the end of World War II, the real force in the firm had become Wilkie Bushby, a man not so fondly remembered by almost all who worked under him as "a mean son-of-a-bitch." Bushby, who died in 1970, also deserves a footnote in history for leading the successful fight to keep the infant United Nations from settling in his home town of Greenwich, Connecticut.

In 1945, Clark retired. That led to an internal reshuffling and eventually to an open break, as George Cleary and Leo Gottlieb led a parade of middle-level partners out of the firm. The exact causes of the breach remain shrouded in secrecy; none of the living participants was willing to discuss it, and the papers of those who have died since are not yet available to the public.

Some attribute the split to a simple money squabble, others to Gottlieb's insistence on and Bushby's refusal for a place on the shingle, still others to a simple desire of those who left to become their own bosses. Most likely, it was a combination of all three.

So the firm of Cleary, Gottlieb, Friendly & Hamilton (now Cleary, Gottlieb, Steen & Hamilton) was born. Though his name came second, Leo Gottlieb was clearly the dominant partner. "Impressive, gracious, urbane, obviously very smart, but a little distant," in the words of one lawyer, he also had a shrewdness that some of his more ivory-towered partners lacked. At one Root Clark billing conference—the story goes—the partners were discussing how much to ask for a court-appointed assignment. Root had calculated an amount based on the hourly rate, while Gottlieb pressed for an inflated figure, on grounds that the judge was bound to trim whatever sum was requested. Root carried the day—and the judge cut his request by about a third.

A protégé of Buckner's who had been with the firm since 1920, Gottlieb took with him some of its largest clients—Federated Department Stores, Salomon Brothers and the estates of several of the Guggenheims and Lehmans. It's easy to see how such a man might have harbored the ambition to become the first Jewish name partner in a major WASP Wall Street firm.

In benign, soft-spoken George Cleary, the new firm got one of Wall Street's leading tax lawyers. The third name partner, Henry Friendly (now chief judge of the U.S. Court of Appeals), was shy and withdrawn, almost a caricature of the Jewish intellectual; but he was general counsel of Pan American Airlines and brought the new firm another major client. The fourth name partner, Fowler Hamilton, came out of wartime service with the government, most notably as counsel to the Department of Justice where he earned a reputation as a "lawyer's lawyer." Glib and urbane, he has been described as a man who "makes a better first impression than a second." He later served a not-so-successful stint as Foreign Aid Administrator under JFK.

From the start, Cleary Gottlieb was as much a Washington firm as a New York one. Another recruit from government was picked to head the Washington office—George Ball, later Undersecretary of State and U.N. ambassador. For a time, the Washington firm was named Cleary, Gottlieb, Friendly & Ball. As clients, Ball brought in the French government (Vichy France, like the Third Republic, had been represented by Coudert Brothers) and, through his friendship with Jean Monnet, first the European Coal & Steel Community, then the Common Market, seeds of Cleary Gottlieb's thriving international business.

Cleary Gottlieb now claims 135 lawyers, which would put it among New York's ten largest firms, except it counts its Washington office separately. (The firm also has branches in Paris and Brussels.) The New York office has 70 lawyers.

The split was a bitter blow for Root, Ballantine, Harlan, Bushby & Palmer, as Root Clark was renamed. "Cleary Gottlieb took with them all the Jews and liberals," said one observer. "All they had left were these stodgy, senior people. They were losing clients hand over fist." Root Ballantine rebuilt slowly. Charles McLean went to night school to learn tax law and thus fill the gap Cleary had left. New associates were brought in, but there was a general feeling that those who joined in the postwar years were not up to the caliber of Frankfurter's recruits. "It wasn't like the period twenty years before when everyone wanted to join," says one lawyer. "It wasn't a very pleasant place to work."

Root retired in 1952, becoming "of counsel" to the firm. Then in 1954 came a double blow. First, it lost its brightest star—John Marshall Harlan, the firm's leading litigator, who had defended DuPont in the biggest antitrust action ever brought by the U.S. government. President Eisenhower named him to the Court of Appeals and, a few months later, to the U.S. Supreme Court. Second, it looked as if it would lose its biggest client—the Bank of Manhattan, about to be absorbed by the Chase. Something had to be done—*fast*—before the firm sank into oblivion.

In 1954, Thomas E. Dewey announced that he would not seek a fourth term as governor. Although derided as "the dummy on top of a wedding cake," Dewey had solid achievements in politics and a good grounding in law. His meteoric rise started in 1935 when Governor Lehman named him special prosecutor to clean up the rackets in New York. He came on like gangbusters, winning election to a full term as district attorney in 1937. By the time he retired in 1941, he had successfully prosecuted gangsters Lucky Luciano and Louis Lepke, Tammany leader Jimmy Hines, American Nazi leader Fritz Kuhn, New York Stock Exchange President Richard Whitney, as well as uncovered the evidence that sent Judge Manton to jail. In 1942 he was elected to the first of three terms as governor. Twice he ran for President, finally becoming a figure of fun—the man who "snatched defeat from the jaws of victory." But in Albany he had proved an able administrator, who whipped the bureaucracy into line and reshaped the reactionary Republican party upstate to a progressive image. He was the archetype of the Establishment Republican. Surely, such a man would be an asset for any law firm. Bushby set out to snare him.

R. Burdell Bixby, who served as Dewey's secretary in Albany, recalls: "Mr. Bushby met with him here in the Roosevelt Hotel in New York [Dewey's downstate headquarters] and in substance issued an invitation to him to join his firm. There was some discussion and it was decided on both sides of the table. And on January 1, 1955, we both arrived at the offices at 31 Nassau Street."

But before Dewey arrived, the firm went through another internal upheaval. Perhaps Dewey himself could have averted it, but Bushby did not have the politician's tact. The cause, though, was Dewey's ego. For a while, he had explored the possibility of joining the Eisenhower Administration. But he was not about to play second-fiddle to anyone—in Washington or in his new law firm. He insisted on being No. 1—not only the head of the firm, but the first name on the shingle. It was a galling blow to the semiretired Elihu Root, Jr. According to one account, the final blow came when Bushby informed Root that he'd have to vacate his office to make room for the firm's new senior partner.

Root resigned and his name came off the shingle of the firm he had founded forty-five years before. Teaming once again with Grenville Clark, the pair joined with the rebels of eight years before, becoming "of counsel" to Cleary Gottlieb where they remained until they died, a few months apart, in 1967.

From October, when Root resigned, until January, when Dewey joined, the firm was Ballantine, Bushby, Palmer & Wood. Then Dewey's name was added—first.

"One of the first personal decisions that he made was a matter of policy," says the adulatory Bixby, who serves as chairman of the authority that runs the Thomas E. Dewey Thruway. "He reviewed Wendell Willkie's experience of returning to a law firm and continuing in politics. He reviewed Adlai Stevenson's experience. He decided that he was going to return to law and that he was going to practice law full time and that he would refrain from any active, sustained participation in politics.

"He felt that people who sought his legal advice would want to see him personally. 'I will be in the office,' he announced. And from January 1, 1955, until the day he died [in 1971]—except for two absences—he was here every day.

"He felt that if all the firm had was his name at the top of the flagpole, and he was traveling the world and everything else, it was a clear indication that he wasn't practicing law and that clients wouldn't come to the firm."

Dewey himself relished the change. "This is the life," he said the first day he arrived at the office. "I feel about ten years younger. I'm looking forward to private life more than I ever looked forward to anything before."

Five months later *Newsweek* would comment:

> All too frequently, a politician will join a law firm simply to capitalize on his name and connections. This isn't true of Dewey. He isn't merely a figurehead in the firm, but a key member. His friends say that it's his ambition to become known as the leading attorney in the United States.

As head of a large corporate law firm, Dewey was a triple-threat quarterback. First, he was a courtroom advocate who argued many major cases. Among them were two tax suits on behalf of Schenley Industries; defending the Port Authority's Austin Tobin on a contempt of Congress citation and representing New York State on a reapportionment case before the Supreme Court, for a fee of $63,982.

Second, he was an able business-getter. "The demand for his services exceeded his ability to handle it," says Bixby, one of whose duties was to screen out "crackpot" clients. "He was sought after by businessmen. The fact is that as governor he was more immersed in business decisions than in politics— finance, borrowing, bonds. Because he was immersed in these business considerations, he was an excellent businessman as well as a lawyer. He wasn't consulted on decisions involving the state government or federal government. He was consulted on corporate business judgments and the legal implications of those judgments."

Despite Dewey's disclaimer that the firm was not going to engage in any lobbying, one of the first clients he attracted was the Turkish government, which was seeking additional American aid—for a $150,000 annual retainer—and Dewey himself had to register as a foreign agent.

Finally, Dewey took charge with the same firm hand he had shown as D.A. and governor. He was also something of a martinet and he had a strong sense of protocol. It was *de rigueur* that everyone in the office called him "Governor," not "Tom" or "Mr. Dewey."

He had no sense of humor about himself. At the firm's annual dinners, held then at the University Club, it is customary for the younger lawyers to present a show satirizing their seniors. At the first dinner Dewey attended, when the character portraying the twice-defeated presidential candidate made his entrance, the band struck up "Hail to the Chief." Dewey walked out, never to attend another firm dinner. Bixby tried to explain his absences by saying that Dewey disliked attending formal functions, especially on weekends, when the dinners were held.

Bixby's own relationship with Dewey did not escape the younger lawyers' ridicule. At one firm dinner, the character portraying Dewey turned to the one portraying Bixby and snorted:

"Bix, did you fart?"

"No, Governor. Do you want me to?"

Though he insisted that everything be just so, Dewey proved a gracious and considerate boss. Although he avoided the formal firm dinners, he was an eager participant at "Wranglers," the firm's monthly bull-sessions started by Buckner years before at which the lawyers discussed their cases.

His chief difficulty—surprisingly for a politician—was an astonishingly bad memory for names. During the summer, law students would "intern" at the firm under the supervision of an associate. Sometime during the season, each associate would take his intern to meet the boss, and each went through the same ritual: The associate would leave the intern in the reception room and enter Dewey's outer office, where he'd tell Dewey's secretary his first name and the intern's last name; then he'd rejoin the intern in the reception room. A few minutes later, they'd be ushered in to meet Dewey, who greeted them with an effusive: "How are you, Jim! Pleased to meet you, Mr. Smith!"

If Dewey was adamant about practicing law and not participating in politics, he was equally dedicated to making money. His "draw," well into six figures, was said to be the highest in any Wall Street firm. He was also an acknowledged expert at putting the "bite" on a client. One middle-class businessman reportedly brought a legal problem to Dewey. When he sat down, the governor flipped an hour-glass.

"When that sand runs out," he explained, "you'll owe me five hundred dollars."

The businessman rose. "That's a little too steep for me. I'll leave fifty dollars with your secretary." And he left.

Under Dewey, the firm, in decline for a decade, revived and prospered. As it grew, it moved first to 40 Wall Street, then to the forty-fourth floor of the modern Marine Midland Building, whose block-square plaza included the firm's old Nassau Street address. "Back on the same real estate," Bixby notes. Dewey Ballantine also opened offices in Paris and Brussels. By the time Dewey died of a heart attack at age sixty-eight, the firm had 174 lawyers—47 partners and 127 associates—to rank as New York's second largest.

Dewey had been brought in to rejuvenate a declining firm and he succeeded. He also institutionalized it, so that there was little of the panic that normally follows the death of so dominant a figure at the peak of his powers.

"Of course, no one can fill all of his shoes or do all of the things he did," said Bixby. "But we fully expect and hope that the reputation of the firm is resting on solid foundations."

Since Dewey's death, there's no indication that any major client is looking elsewhere. Dewey might have brought the clients in, but he could devote only a small percentage of his time to their problems; it took the team he assembled over eighteen years to service them. And the team is still going strong.

Clarence Darrow once observed that he'd never killed anyone, "but I have read some obituary notices with great satisfaction." Sad but true, lawyers on Wall Street or Park Avenue may read the death notices of their multi-point seniors and smile. After Dewey died, one observer summarized the situation at his firm: "The older partners were running around trying to reassure each other that everything was going to be okay. The younger partners were jubilant, because they'd get to divvy up his cut."

5

The Care and Feeding
of Corporate Clients—I

Buried back among the stock-market tables in *The New York Times* is a column headed "Advertising." It chronicles the comings and goings of Madison Avenue, reporting events like: Accidental Airlines is shifting its account from White, Lies & Exaggeration to Half, Truth & Platitude, which will launch a new $15 million multimedia ad campaign.

But if Accidental Airlines shifted its legal business from Boodle, Boodle, Graft & Corruption to Ambulance, Chaser & Shyster to draw up a $150 million indenture, chances are not a line about it would appear in the public press, nor even in the *New York Law Journal*, the daily devoted to legal doings.

First, the word would not go out. Blue-chip practitioners don't discuss their clients—or their fees. Ostensibly, this discretion stems from a strict adherence to the Canons of Ethics. Actually, it's more a part of proper protocol, less following the letter of the law than observing the social graces. Talking about clients and fees just isn't done, not even when lawyers gather among themselves over lunch at the Recess Club or over cocktails at the Bar Association.

Law firms outside New York usually list "Representative Clients" in the Martindale-Hubbell *Law Directory*, primarily to impress New York firms that they're equipped to handle whatever local business might be thrown their way. Virtually no New York firm does. When asked why not, they say it smacks of advertising. Some firms—like Winthrop Stimson and Simpson Thacher & Bartlett—even go so far as to avoid listing themselves under "Lawyers" in the *Yellow Pages*, while Cravath considers calling cards unethical.

Yet even if the blue-chip bar sent out press releases every time a new client walked through the front door, it's doubtful that the *Times* would have a column headed "Law" devoted to the comings and goings of Wall Street and Park Avenue, because there wouldn't be enough news to fill the space.

In the blue-chip bar client shifts are rare. A partner in one Wall Street firm estimates its turnover in dollar volume at 5 per cent a year, mostly in one-shot litigation. A corporation that thinks nothing of changing advertising agencies every six months may stick with the same law firm for sixty years.

That's why the CBS shift came as such a surprise, so much so that more than two years later the blue-chip bar is still talking about it.

In late April, 1969, Bates Lowry, director of the Museum of Modern Art, phoned Ralph Colin, a name partner of Rosenman, Colin, Kaye, Petschek, Freund & Emil. Colin was a MOMA trustee, a noted collector in his own right, administrative vice president and counsel of the Art Dealers Association.

But if art was his life, CBS was his livelihood. It was CBS money that enabled him to hobnob with the Rockefellers and Whitneys on the museum board, CBS' money that enabled him to line the walls of his Park Avenue apartment with Dubuffet paintings and prints, CBS' money that enabled his daughter,

Pamela, the London editor of *Vogue*, to swim in the social circles where she could meet and marry Britain's Lord Harlech.

For forty-three years, Colin had been counsel to William S. Paley's broadcasting empire. In fact, his association with CBS antedated Paley's by a year. He had been Paley's personal attorney since 1928, a member of the CBS board since 1937. In addition, he was president of the CBS Foundation and a director of the William S. Paley Foundation. The bonds linking CBS to Judge Rosenman's firm seemed as solid as those tying U.S. Steel to White & Case or the Morgan interests to Davis Polk—until Bates Lowry placed his call.

"I called Ralph, whom I consider to be a friend," Lowry recalls, "and said, 'In view of what has happened, I'm calling you and I'd like to approach'—and I named somebody in his firm—'to represent me. I thought I should ask you first.'

"And he said, 'What are you talking about,'"

The *what* was that Lowry had just been fired as director of the museum by William S. Paley, MOMA's president. Not only had Paley's fellow trustees not been consulted, they had not even been informed.

"So I was the unwitting bearer of the news," Lowry continues, "which perhaps, knowing Ralph, meant even more. There had been at least three or four days in which he could have been informed."

On May 2, the official announcement was made by Paley and David Rockefeller, MOMA's chairman, that Lowry—in office less than ten months—had resigned "for personal considerations." Few failed to see through the verbal subterfuge. "Has MOMA gone network?" one critic asked.

Lowry was liked by his staff and respected in the art world for his acquisition of Gertrude Stein's collection of early Braques and Picassos. But he had shown an independent streak and had failed to kowtow properly to the centimillionaires who considered the museum their personal plaything.

Ralph Colin also had an independent streak. "A man of unusual integrity, which is so rare in this age of universal toadyism," says Louis Auchincloss, who had served with Colin on the Bar Association's Ethics Committee. On May 15, an angry Colin brought up the matter of Lowry's ouster at a meeting of the MOMA trustees.

"The issue was very simple," he explained afterward. "The discharge was made without calling a meeting of the board of trustees. I felt that was an improper procedure and I said so." Colin did not question the reasons for Lowry's ouster, only the way it was done. "If the board of trustees was not consulted on this matter, I don't know what a board of trustees is for. [Choosing a director] is about as vital a decision as a board is called on to make."

Ironically, Colin had attempted to resign from the board the year before because he had not been consulted about Lowry's hiring, but David Rockefeller had dissuaded him.

"Ralph is very direct, to the point," says one who worked with him at the museum. "He doesn't mess around with a lot of verbiage."

His words obviously didn't sit well with the imperious Paley. The next day Colin found out that his services could be dispensed with as easily as Arthur Godfrey's or Ed Sullivan's —or Bates Lowry's. Paley summoned Colin to his office in Eero Saarinen's CBS building on Sixth Avenue and discharged him as his personal attorney.

Colin's long association with the Museum of Modern Art was also coming to an end. He felt the trustees should present a united front and did not precipitate an open break—a fruitless move, as it turned out, since fellow trustee John de Menil publicly protested Paley's action. But he refused to attend another board meeting and in December submitted his resignation to David Rockefeller. "In view of recent happenings," he said, he felt he could no longer be a "useful or effective member."

It was apparently the last blow for Paley. On January 26, while Paley was vacationing in the Bahamas, CBS President Frank Stanton called Colin to his office and told him that his law firm's long association with CBS was severed.

"It was a tremendous blow to Judge Rosenman," says one

observer. "He tried to get them back together again. Paley absolutely refused."

Colin's term on the CBS board wasn't up for another year. Some at CBS feared he might linger on as a disruptive force, a gadfly who knew where the bodies were buried. But within the week he dictated a letter of resignation as CBS director: "The only reason for this [the firm's discharge] was that the change would be 'desirable in the long run.' We have been told of no reason why this change suddenly became desirable." Before the month was out, Colin's connections with the CBS and Paley Foundations were also severed.

Some observers doubted that an argument on the museum board alone could have ended a client-counsel association of forty-two years. *The Wall Street Journal* suggested that CBS was irked because Colin advised the network to comply with government subpoenas for "outtakes"—broadcast film clips —of Black Panther interviews. Colin insisted that his ouster "had nothing to do with the subpoenas," and Stanton, breaking an otherwise rigid silence on the subject said, "Colin was not to my knowledge consulted at any time about the subpoenas."

Variety put the question directly to Colin: "Wasn't it strange that such a long and close relationship could be ended by an issue entirely unrelated to CBS?"

"You're telling *me!*" Colin replied.

It did not surprise Bates Lowry, who had been the cause of it all. "It was pique on Paley's part and a strong sense of position on Ralph's part," he says. "Paley seemed to me totally in character."

Both Paley and Stanton have declined to discuss the matter. Colin talked to *Variety*'s reporter, but has since kept silent. I made an appointment to see him, but a few days later he called me back to cancel it.

"After thinking it over, I decided that I don't want to talk to you," he said. "The article in *The New York Times* covered it all."

"The article was very sketchy," I replied. "As I gather, there was quite a clash of personalities involved."

"That's just what I don't want to talk to you about."

Like many corporations, CBS sometimes farmed out bits of its legal business to other firms—especially Cravath, which had a background in broadcasting, having served as counsel to RCA and NBC in the 1930s.

After Edward R. Murrow made his famous attack on Joseph R. McCarthy, Cravath's Bruce Bromley was called in by CBS to prepare for the senator's inevitable counterattack. When dealing with McCarthy, better to be represented by a Republican judge than the firm of a New Deal speechwriter.

Cravath also represented CBS on several stockholder suits and counseled the network when it was forced to sever its ties with Broadcast Music, Inc. On that matter, Judge Rosenman's firm had a conflict of interest, since its third-ranked partner, Sidney Kaye, was counsel and chairman of BMI.

Cravath has a reputation that once it gets a piece of a client it never lets go until it has swallowed it whole. Though Bromley insists, "All we did was come in on certain litigation," another Cravath lawyer says, "Make no mistake about it—we made a major pitch for that business every year."

In 1970 the long years of pitching paid off. On February 11, CBS announced the appointment of a new director—Roswell Gilpatric, presiding partner at Cravath. Gilpatric doesn't face the prospect of a fall-out with Paley over museum management; he's on the board of the Metropolitan Museum of Art.

A CBS may come and go—even after forty-two years. But a bank, like a diamond, is forever. A bank is the epitome of a locked-in client. Once it retains a firm, a bank is stuck with it. Law firms' banking departments are so large, their personnel so expert in the often arcane affairs of their one client that it's virtually impossible for a bank—even if it chose—to switch to another firm. No other could handle the load, at least not for several years. About the only way a law firm can lose a banking client is for the bank to fold or merge.

In turn, a bank impresses its indelible stamp on its law firm. Indeed, it's sometimes a question of which is the tail and which the dog. In Louis Auchincloss' *Powers of Attorney*, a law firm faces the loss of its biggest client, a bank, because of a pending merger. One character muses: "Tower, Tilney without Standard Trust! Why it was like Davis, Polk without Morgan's! Or Milbank, Tweed without the Chase!"

The Chase, of course, is the Rockefellers' bank. And Milbank Tweed has existed for its more than forty years under what Harrison Tweed termed "the Rockefeller surveillance." The firm's founding in 1931 was dictated by John D. Rockefeller, Jr. The firm of Murray, Aldrich & Webb represented the bank. But its strength had been sapped because "Mister Junior" had plucked its senior partner, his brother-in-law Winthrop Aldrich, to take over the chairmanship of the Chase. So he pressed for the firm's merger with Masten & Nichols, which represented the family.

"Frankly," said Tweed, "we did not like the idea of a merger with the whole Masten & Nichols outfit. The original idea had been that we could bring into our firm the lawyer who was at that time the head of Masten & Nichols, Albert Milbank. . . . Mr. Milbank had John D. Rockefeller's confidence, they having been college friends. However, Mr. Milbank wasn't willing to leave his firm in the lurch. So the problem was to merge the whole kit and kaboodle."

The negotiations were difficult. According to Tweed, several of his partners at Murray, Aldrich & Webb wanted to say, "To hell with the whole thing! Let's go ahead and see where we end up without any Milbank, or Masten & Nichols, or perhaps without any Rockefeller!" But few say "no" to a Rockefeller, especially when he signs the paycheck. So the negotiations continued.

The money division caused the toughest problem, because the two firms were structured differently. Eventually, Milbank proposed the solution—a fifty-fifty split, the old Masten & Nichols firm to divide its half among its partners and associates however it chose, Murray, Aldrich & Webb to do the same, "no questions asked."

So the firm of Milbank, Tweed, Hope & Webb was born.

How was the name chosen? "Almost trial by combat," Tweed said. There were to be two names from each of the old firms, alternating. As "boss," Milbank came first. The choice of the second name was complicated because Murray, Aldrich & Webb itself was the product of a merger two years before of Murray & Aldrich with Webb, Patterson & Hadley, and each claimed a place on the shingle. With Aldrich's departure, Vanderbilt Webb was the senior partner, but he came from the junior firm. So Tweed's name was placed second. Then Walter Hope, from Masten & Nichols. And finally Webb.

At its inception, Milbank Tweed had twenty partners and twenty-eight associates—and the Chase Bank. For any law firm a banking client is a business bonanza. A bank generates legal work, far more than any one firm can handle.

According to a preliminary report by "Nader's Raiders," the First National City Bank, now New York's largest, is also "New York City's number one plaintiff"—filing more than ten thousand law suits in 1969, more than fifteen thousand in 1970, "more than all the other banks and more than the ubiquitous Telephone Company or Consolidated Edison." Most of the cases were routine collections to recover unpaid personal loans or credit-card purchases. Sixty per cent were handled by Citibank's house counsel, the remainder distributed among three firms specializing in collections. But if a case went beyond the routine, it was turned over to the bank's big guns—Shearman & Sterling.

A bank is also a magnet for legal business. It naturally refers customers with legal problems to its law firm and the inter-city banking network serves as a funnel for out-of-town clients. But a bank may also dictate which clients its firm *can't* handle.

Tweed explained: "A firm which represents a big banking organization loses the opportunity to represent a number of corporations. . . . The corporations are borrowers or are otherwise financially dependent on the bank, and no firm in a situation like that can give its complete loyalty to both of them. On the other hand, the *quid pro quo* was well worth it. The amount of business they gave us on their own—from the

Chase—and the amount of work they would steer to us without getting into any questions of divided loyalty far more than made up for the disqualifications."

A bank has other assets to offer its law firm. Lawyers can call upon the bank's resources in nonrelated matters. An attorney in a firm that represents one of New York's largest banks explains:

"Let's say that you file a suit against one of our clients. All I have to do is call up——[the bank] and the next morning I'll have on my desk a complete credit report on you, where you've worked, what you're worth, how much you owe. I'll know how badly you need the money you're suing us for and have an idea of how long you can afford to wait before you'll have to settle for something less. It's an incredible advantage.

"If we need to, the bank can put its private detectives on your tail, find out if you're cheating on your wife or playing around with little boys. They'll even tap your telephone or bug your office if they have to. Probably half the illegal wiretapping in town is done for——[his law firm]. And all this at no cost to us; the bank'll do it as a favor.

"And if we really want to get nasty, we can ask the bank to squeeze you a little financially, call in your loans or dry up your sources of credit."

To return to Milbank Tweed: The Rockefellers treat lawyers the way a senior partner treats associates. They want answers, not advice. Robert Douglass, who served as Governor Rockefeller's counsel in Albany, once explained the process: "He gets an idea, and input from a variety of sources. Then he makes up in his mind what he wants to do." The lawyer's job is to provide the way to do it. "The worst way to approach Nelson Rockefeller is to say, 'You can't do it.' "

Significantly, in 1972 when Douglass—after nearly a decade of service to Nelson Rockefeller as assistant counsel, counsel and secretary—resigned to return to private law practice, he didn't return to his native Binghamton; he became a partner of Milbank Tweed.

Strangely, for all its close ties to the Rockefellers, Milbank

Tweed never represented the foundation of the family fortune —Standard Oil, whose legal business is mostly Sullivan & Cromwell's. The reason was the 1911 decree dissolving the oil trust. "It was very definitely Rockefeller policy that the law firm which represented them individually should not represent any one of the Standard Oil companies," Tweed noted.

But the bank's business more than made up for it and Milbank Tweed grew into one of the giants. Milbank, who died in 1949, was the undisputed boss. "A very practical lawyer," Tweed recalled. "In fact, he was more practical than he was a lawyer. He was distinctly a business lawyer and he was at his best as a negotiator and an arranger of business transactions. He was not a top-notch brief-writer or drafter of instruments."

Tweed, working from his deskless office, handled trusts and estates, devoting his private hours first to the Legal Aid Society, then to the Bar Association.

Hope, who died in 1956, was the tax expert and general counsel to Western Union.

Webb's specialty was real estate. He had represented the Rockefellers on their acquisitions of land for the Williamsburg restoration, the Grand Teton resorts and Rockefeller Center. But he never got along with Milbank. "Milbank," according to Tweed, "had to make himself a little objectionable at times and Webb was the fellow who just didn't like that sort of thing at all. He wanted to be absolutely free and independent."

After seven years of chafing under Milbank's authority, Webb left the firm to form a partnership with Chauncey Belknap. He took a substantial part of the firm's real-estate practice with him. Belknap & Webb also represented the Rockefeller philanthropies.

In 1947, the firm became Patterson, Belknap & Webb with the addition of former War Secretary Robert Patterson. He had been a member of Milbank Tweed's predecessor firms until his appointment to the federal bench in 1930.

In his history of the firm, Timothy Pfeiffer—Milbank Tweed's chief litigator—told of one case that illustrates the complex ties between the firm, the Chase and the Rockefellers.

During the 1930s, the Colorado Fuel & Iron Company went through a court-ordered reorganization. John D. Rockefeller, Jr., was both the chief stockholder and the chief bondholder. Milbank Tweed was counsel for the bondholders, and proposed that the Chase be made depository for the bonds, at a fee of $1 per each $1,000 worth of bonds, to cover the cost of the paperwork. "Mister Junior" showed up with one bond—worth $17 million!

A postwar returnee to Milbank Tweed was John Lockwood, who had served as Nelson Rockefeller's counsel in Latin America and at the State Department. He soon succeeded Thomas Debevoise as personal counsel to the Rockefeller family, dividing his time between Milbank Tweed's office at 15 Broad Street and the Rockefeller family's offices in Suite 5600 of the RCA Building. He handled the acquisition of the East River property that John D. Rockefeller, Jr., donated for the United Nations headquarters, as well as the legal aspects for the expansion of Rockefeller Center.*

Another postwar arrival was John J. McCloy, brought into the firm by Milbank when he fell out at Cravath. His initial tenure at Milbank Tweed lasted little over a year, and fifteen years passed before he returned. In 1947, he was named president of the World Bank; in 1949, High Commissioner for Germany; and in 1953, when Aldrich was appointed ambassador to Britain, chairman of the Chase. When he reached the bank's mandatory retirement age, he returned to become "of counsel" to Milbank, Tweed, Hadley & McCloy.

Putting Hadley's name on the shingle preserved the tie to the old Webb firm. The son of a Yale president, Morris Hadley excelled as a business-getter, garnering Aluminium, Ltd., American Brake Shoe Company and, before the war, a number of Japanese clients. In some unusually effusive prose, Pfeiffer said of him: "As a mathematical computer and repository of office financial data, his astonishing ability to analyze figures—

---

* But not all "personal" matters: "Tex" Moore of Cravath handled Nelson Rockefeller's divorce; Edward S. Greenbaum, "Happy" Rockefeller's suit for custody of the four children from her first marriage.

though he still counts up to ten on his fingers—and his capacious memory, make it quite unnecessary for the firm to rent IBM equipment."

In 1951, Aldrich started discussions about the Chase's acquiring the Bank of Manhattan. The Bank of Manhattan was amenable, but its counsel, Wilkie Bushby, of Root Ballantine, argued that under the bank's 1799 charter—originally issued to Aaron Burr to form a water company!—approval of *all* the Bank of Manhattan's stockholders was required. It was an impossible condition to meet. It was a contention with which the Chase's lawyers couldn't agree, but it blocked the merger. The more cynical suggested that Bushby was merely trying to keep from losing his firm's biggest client.

Three years later, McCloy became chairman of the Chase and resumed the merger talks. This time, he found a way around Bushby's legal roadblock—merge the Chase *into* the Bank of Manhattan. It seems curious that the high-paid legal talent at Milbank Tweed had not thought of that before. This time the merger went through, creating what was then New York's largest bank. Pfeiffer noted that the merger agreement was only seven pages long and didn't contain a single "and/or"!

Despite the legal formality, Chase was clearly the senior partner and it was obvious that its law firm, Milbank Tweed, would represent Chase Manhattan. But Dewey Ballantine—as the firm had then become—had such expertise, especially on matters relating to the charter, that even after the merger it continued to get a substantial portion of the bank's legal business.

"We use them for certain things," McCloy says, with a first-person plural that illustrates the closeness of client and counsel. "But the fundamental representation is Milbank Tweed."

Proprieties also played a part in the selection. The Bank of Manhattan's officers wanted its firm to retain a piece of the action as a symbol that it hadn't been totally submerged in the combination. In addition, Dewey, according to one account, made a personal pitch to the Rockefellers to keep some of the bank's business as his "admission fee" to the firm. Tweed noted that "it was partly through his efforts and partly through the standing and efficiency of the other partners that the Chase [Manhattan] Bank sent and still sends some of its business to that firm."

Over the years, Milbank had set policy while George Hite took care of the office. But as Milbank Tweed grew—currently fifty partners, one hundred associates—and the founders aged, it decided to put its management on a permanent basis. It created a five-man management committee, a policy committee for long-term planning, a partner in charge of the library and another in charge of recruiting, as well as a professional office manager to supervise the nonlegal personnel. With the bank's assistance, it also established a pension and retirement program that has become the model for the profession. The structure was complex, perhaps inordinately so.

"You talked about the management of the firm," an interviewer once asked Harrison Tweed. "I don't understand that part of it."

"Well, I don't, either," Tweed replied.

It's easy to understand. If anyone called the shots at Milbank Tweed, it remained the Rockefellers and Chase Manhattan. When the bank erected its sixty-story skyscraper—the first step in Chairman David Rockefeller's plan to rejuvenate the financial district—Milbank Tweed moved in with the first tenants. "The Chase wanted us to," Tweed explained, and the firm obeyed.

That's not unusual. A bank's influence is often so powerful that it determines the physical location of its law firm. It's no accident that Shearman & Sterling is in the Citibank building or White & Case in the Bankers Trust Annex. When Citibank moved a major portion of its executive offices to Park Avenue, Shearman & Sterling followed with a midtown office in the same building. Similarly, White & Case with Bankers Trust, Simpson Thacher & Bartlett with Manufacturers Hanover, etc.

"No law firm should ever be so committed to a single client that it loses its independence," one lawyer argues. Indeed, attorneys in a law firm's banking department come to resemble less independent advisors than glorified house counsels, often looked down upon by other lawyers, including those in their own firms. The cozy relationship between client and counsel is reinforced by the ease with which lawyers may move from the firm to the bank, from one payroll to another. Sometimes the only difference is the name on the paycheck. Associates in a law firm's banking department often spend several years working not only on bank business, but *in* the bank. Says one attorney from a firm with a banking client, "They're almost legal prostitutes."

Shortly after the turn of the century, Felix Frankfurter spent a brief apprenticeship as a Wall Street lawyer. But he was so appalled at what he termed the "boot-licking deference" of the attorneys to railroad robber baron E. H. Harriman that he ultimately retreated to Cambridge and the groves of academe.

Though some lawyers still speak of theirs as a "servile" profession, that sort of scene is not likely to be repeated in the executive suites of the 1970s. In fact, the opposite is more likely to be the case.

First, the days of the robber barons are gone. American business is no longer dominated by strong-willed titans like Harriman, John D. Rockefeller and J. P. Morgan, but managed by accommodating organization men who defer to the experts. Second, the role of the lawyer is much more important today; no corporation can make a move without first consulting counsel. Finally, quite often, the lawyers run the corporation.

Many of today's top business executives are former associates or partners in the firm that serves as the company's counsel. It's one of the easiest ways a law firm cements its relationship with a corporate client. As critic David Bazelon noted, the law firm " 'alumni' infiltrate the corporate client and thus ensnare it eternally for the firm."

When a large law firm becomes counsel to a corporation, a senior partner generally will go on its board of directors; a junior partner will become its general counsel; and its associates will go into the house-counsel's office. It's the old team still working together; only the titles have changed.

Sometimes the lawyers take over the reins of management directly, running the client corporation from their law offices. This is especially true in the communications and entertainment industries, where founding fathers couldn't cope with the crises of mushrooming growth or sudden financial retrenchment.

But in this era of corporate conglomeration, when business is more often a matter of merger, finance, foreign markets and government relations than of merchandising and production, lawyers who know their way around Wall Street and Washington are increasingly called upon to head old-line blue-chip businesses.

Robert Page, a name partner at Debevoise Plimpton, left the firm to become president of Phelps Dodge. George Dillon went from Shearman & Sterling to the presidency of Air Reduction. John Connor left Cravath for the presidency of Merck & Company before going on to become Lyndon Johnson's Commerce Secretary and later president of Allied Chemical. D. P. Kircher, of Winthrop Stimson, went on to become president of Singer. The roster of Sullivan & Cromwell alumni, as recorded by Arthur Dean, includes presidents of American Bank Note Company, Niagara-Mohawk Power, Marine Midland Bank and International Nickel. The list of lesser corporate officers who came from their companies' law firms would fill pages.

We've already noted the career of John McCloy—an example of the lawyer going from firm to client and back again, thus tying the bonds between the two tighter than ever. An even better example is U.S. Steel and White & Case.

In the encyclopedias, Irving S. Olds is listed as "American industrialist," but for three-fourths of his adult life he was a lawyer, a partner with White & Case. In 1938 "Big Steel" picked him to serve as its special counsel during the touchy investigation of the New Deal's Temporary National Economic Committee. Under Olds' tutelage, U.S. Steel came out of the inquiry with its stature undiminished—if anything, enhanced.

As *Fortune* noted: "The good-humored skill with which steel officials conducted themselves before the T.N.E.C. might serve as a model of how Big Business could defend its right to a profit and still be solicitous of the public interest. . . . There is no denying the favorable impression that the corporation made."

Olds also made a favorable impression on the company's directors. In 1940 he was named chairman and chief executive officer, succeeding Edward R. Stettinius. Upon his retirement in 1952, Olds returned to White & Case. Unlike most lawyers-turned-executives, he had never resigned from the firm, and remained with it until his death in 1963.

A few months after Olds made the shift from law firm to client corporation, he brought in a young White & Case associate who'd assisted him on the T.N.E.C. inquiry—Roger M. Blough. Blough's career is more typical of the lawyer-turned-executive. He started as general solicitor of U.S. Steel's Delaware subsidiary and over the years he rose through the upper echelons to general counsel in 1953 and chairman in 1955, to go down in history as the man who evoked John F. Kennedy's scathing comment, "My father always told me that all businessmen were sons-of-bitches, but I never believed it until now."

In 1969, Blough stepped down from the chairmanship and returned to White & Case—this time as a full and very senior partner. "The guessing," said *Forbes*, "is he earns nearly as much practicing law as he did presiding over a $5 billion industrial giant."

So, for the better part of thirty years, U.S. Steel has been run by White & Case lawyers. When Olds and Blough returned to the firm, the executives they appointed and promoted were in no position to gainsay their advice or to seek counsel from another law firm. U.S. Steel on occasion may defy the United Steelworkers or the United States government, but when it comes to a law firm, it's locked in.

6

The Care and Feeding of Corporate Clients—II

The most mysterious figure in any law firm is the business-getter. What he does is even more of a mystery. Sometimes it seems that he spends more time on the golf course than in the law office, but he's not out there to break par—he's there to make rain.

The business-getter—or "rainmaker" in law-office parlance —is the man responsible for landing new clients and keeping old ones from slipping off the hook. How he does it can rarely be described, not even by most lawyers, not even by the rain-makers themselves.

Most of it is chemistry. "Some people just naturally attract, inspire confidence," says Orison S. Marden, of White & Case. "I don't know how to explain it."

Though he may never crack a law book, the rainmaker is usually the most powerful person in any firm, commanding the corner office and demanding the biggest draw. Sometimes he's a back-slapping glad-hander; more often he's a crusty curmudgeon like Paul Cravath or General Boykin Wright, whom one lawyer described as "a guy you wouldn't choose to go on a camping tour with." Sometimes he's an out-front figure like Thomas E. Dewey; more often he's unknown to the general public. As one lawyer puts it, "Somebody you never heard about may generate a lot of business."

Had it not been for his friendship with Lyndon Johnson, Edwin L. Weisl, Sr., would have remained such an anonymous figure. In 1937, he went to a White House conference. At the end of the meeting, FDR suggested to an aide that he "take the young man over and introduce him to Lyndon Johnson."

The tall congressman from Texas and the dumpy, mustached Wall Street lawyer hit it off right away. In 1949, Weisl gave LBJ a bit of gratuitous advice that helped make the future President a millionaire: "*I* told Johnson to buy those television stations—you could have picked up one yourself in those days."

In the 1950s, Johnson gave Weisl a taste of the political spotlight, tabbing him to be counsel of the Senate Preparedness Committee. And in 1964, at the President's prodding, New York's divided Democrats named Weisl National Committeeman. When he died in 1972 at the age of seventy-four, the obituaries identified him as "key Democrat."

"Weisl would have been nothing if it weren't for Lyndon Johnson," one Wall Street lawyer insists. But few at Simpson Thacher & Bartlett would agree. For forty years Weisl was one of the most powerful rainmakers in the blue-chip bar. His power in the firm stemmed largely from two life-long friendships—with John Hertz, of taxicabs, rent-a-cars and later investment banking fame; and with Barney Balaban, the movie mogul—and from his ability to make new friends. "He always understood your problems," Lyndon Johnson says. "I would always come to Eddie first with any problem." One observer called him "the embodiment of discretion."

Weisl was born on Chicago's West Side, the son of immigrant parents, and worked his way through the University of

Chicago. After an apprenticeship in the U.S. Attorney's office, he joined a Chicago law firm in the mid-1920s. In 1930, he came to New York on a case involving the Atlas Corporation, and Atlas' president, Floyd Odlum, induced him to stay in New York as a member of "his" firm—Simpson Thacher & Bartlett.

Balaban, by that time, had leaped from running nickelodeons in Chicago to the presidency of Paramount Pictures, which became a Simpson Thacher & Bartlett client while Weisl served as the movie company's general counsel, director and chairman of the executive committee. Meanwhile, Hertz had left taxicabs, limousines and car-rentals to become a partner in Lehman Brothers, which also entered the firm's fold. Weisl wound up as a director of the One William Street Fund, operated by the giant investment house, and got to know Robert Lehman well enough to call him "my closest friend." In Chicago, Weisl had done some libel work for the Hearst newspapers. He renewed his links with the publishing empire in New York and soon wound up as counsel to Richard S. Berlin, president of the Hearst Corporation.

In the 1960s Weisl successfully thwarted two threats to his power base. The first, curiously, started with the man who had brought him to New York—Floyd Odlum. In 1960, the Hughes Tool Company needed a New York "green-goods" lawyer to handle a multi-million-dollar debenture. Odlum, who had served as chairman of RKO during Howard Hughes' dalliance as a movie-maker, suggested to the "bashful billionaire" that he retain Chester C. Davis, of Simpson Thacher & Bartlett.

Meanwhile, Lehman Brothers was serving as a financial advisor to TWA, which had been plucked from Hughes' control and placed under a three-man trusteeship. The airline was on the eve of its final falling-out with Hughes. Lehman Brothers suggested that there was a conflict of interest in its firm representing both Hughes and the investment house.

Weisl was not about to lose Lehman Brothers—even for one of the world's wealthiest clients. Davis was confronted with the choice of dropping his new client or leaving the firm. He decided to keep the client he'd never met. He resigned from the firm and set up shop across the hall. (Simpson Thacher & Bartlett was then located at 120 Broadway.) Maxwell Cox, then a Simpson Thacher & Bartlett associate who had assisted Davis, was given a leave of absence to complete the work on the offering. Five weeks later, when TWA filed its multi-million-dollar antitrust suit against Hughes Tool, Cox' temporary leave became permanent, and the firm of Davis & Cox has been busy ever since, most notably with exposing Clifford Irving's "auto-biography" of Hughes.

Davis' modus operandi is as unorthodox as that of his illus-trious client. "He'd fiddle around the office all day," says a lawyer who once worked with him, "then go off to Whyte's [a now-defunct restaurant] and toss off martinis like glasses of water. Then he'd come back to the office and toss out ideas for his assistants to work up overnight. Nine out of ten were no good, but that tenth one would be a dilly."

An even greater threat to Weisl's power base came in 1966 when Gulf + Western, the giant conglomerate whose list of acquisitions fills nearly two full pages in *Moody's Industrial Manual*, bought a controlling interest in Paramount and then merged the movie company into its corporate shell. Gulf + Western was represented by Joel Dolkart, of what was then Strasser, Spiegelberg, Fried & Frank, who had been general counsel to the conglomerate since its formation in 1958.

Again loath to lose a major client, Weisl succeeded in bag-ging a bigger game. The following year he persuaded Dolkart to join Simpson Thacher & Bartlett. "I switched and the client came with me," he said. And Weisl went on the Gulf + West-ern board.

Only the very rare lawyer—like Weisl, Wright or Colonel Joseph Hartfield, of White & Case—proves to be a potent rain-maker. In recent years, the most successful rainmakers have made their contacts in government service. Roswell Gilpatric, of Cravath, and Cyrus Vance, of Simpson Thacher & Bartlett, are prime examples.

The breed possesses qualities that take years to develop and can't be spotted by a hiring partner. No young lawyer—no matter how wealthy or well connected—is going to bring in U.S. Steel, Jersey Standard or Chase Manhattan as a client. The most that can be expected of him is a small corporation with a potential for growth or the estate of a rich relative. As a rule, the larger the firm, the less emphasis it places on the business-getting potential of the young lawyers it hires. As the blue-chip bar becomes more institutionalized, forging the complex links that lock a corporate client to its law firm, it becomes more of a meritocracy.

But there'll always be room for a rainmaker.

In our glimpse of Weisl's career we have seen some of the ways lawyers get, hold and sometimes lose corporate clients.

As to getting clients, first and foremost is the personal bond. Often it's a blood-tie. Time-Life's link to Cravath is probably less dependent on Harold Medina, Jr.'s, success in defending libel suits than on the fact that "Tex" Moore is Henry Luce's brother-in-law.

"The institutional client is a myth," one Wall Street lawyer insists. "Dig deeply into any long-standing attorney-client relationship and you'll find a blood-tie somewhere."

His stress on consanguinity seems exaggerated. Louis Auchincloss, an astute observer of social mores, suggests that it still holds true, but only for Jewish firms. "Our Crowd" families, he says, are more clannish than white-Protestant ones, except in the South.

Surely, personal friendship is as—if not more—important as kinship in the choice of a lawyer. The bonds may stem from college, as with John D. Rockefeller, Jr., and Albert Milbank. Or from the Army: "Wild Bill" Donovan served in General Pershing's Mexican campaign with a future president of Eastman Kodak; years later Donovan Leisure became counsel to the camera concern. Or from residential proximity: George Kennan, the renowned Russian expert, lived next door to Edward S. Greenbaum in Princeton, New Jersey, and retained him to represent Svetlana Stalin.

Second, the lawyer may be recommended by another lawyer

or by a satisfied client, as with Odlum and Hughes. This is especially true for "specialists." Antitrust experts such as Robert Bicks, of Breed, Abbott & Morgan, or Milton Handler, of Kaye Scholer, are constantly being called in by other lawyers. "We can't take all the cases that have been submitted to Handler," says a Kaye Scholer partner.

Success on one matter may spur calls on others. In 1947, Frederick Livingston, of Kaye Scholer, successfully mediated a threatened strike at a New Jersey factory. When a corporate officer he'd dealt with there shifted jobs and encountered labor problems at his new plant, he again called on Livingston. Another successful mediation, and Livingston got a call from another company nearby which was negotiating with the same union. "We can trace a whole school of clients from that one case," a partner notes.

On occasion, a corporate client operates on the old principle, if you can't beat 'em, join 'em, by hiring the lawyer who bested him the last time around. TWA President Charles Tillinghast, Jr., a lawyer himself, was so impressed when John Sonnett, of Cahill Gordon, deposed him in one case that he retained him and his firm to handle the airline's antitrust action against Hughes Tool Company. Sonnett won a treble-damage judgment of $145 million.

Law firms, of course, are not supposed to solicit clients, but of course they do. The solicitation may range from a casual comment over cocktails to a presentation almost as elaborate as those whipped up by advertising agencies. "The litigation department once stopped for a few weeks," a former Cravath associate recalls, "while they compiled a record of every antitrust case they'd ever handled—so they could land GM."

Once it lands a client, a law firm will go to great lengths to keep it from slipping off the hook. It forges the institutional bonds, putting its alumni in the client's front office. Its lawyers develop personal ties with company officers. Minor matters, as Harrison Tweed once noted, "are considered and discussed by a junior partner and a subordinate corporate officer. The relationship between them is almost precisely the same as that between the old-fashioned general practitioner and his client-friend of long standing. . . . It generally happens that as the corporate officer goes up in the hierarchy so does the lawyer. Frequently, the close business and legal association and the personal intimacy exist for twenty-five years or more." In other words, Milbank Tweed has a few friends at Chase Manhattan.

Although blue-chip firms rarely take such cases off the street, they will handle matrimonial matters and personal-injury suits for officers of client corporations. They prefer to farm out such business to specialists or to "satellite" firms of former associates, but often a client insists that *his* firm handle the matter.

Sometimes this work is done gratis. Even when there is a fee, it seldom compensates for the time and effort involved. The chief of litigation at one Wall Street firm recently had to spend a week out of town trying a medical malpractice suit on behalf of a client's ninety-year-old mother!

Out-of-town clients may have to be entertained. Virtually every law firm has one lawyer who never brings in any business or does any legal work. "Good old Joe's" only asset, it seems, is a hollow leg—an ability to sit at the bar at P.J. Clarke's or "21," Baltusrol or Blind Brook and match a tippling vice president drink for drink, dirty joke for dirty joke.

Visiting clients will be treated to lunch or dinner or taken to Broadway shows. Breed, Abbott & Morgan, like many firms, buys season boxes for the Jets, Knicks and Ranger games for use by out-of-town clients. During the day, while the men are talking business, the clients' wives will be entertained at tea by the partners' wives or taken on Fifth Avenue shopping tours.

If the wives aren't along, the law firms may provide female companionship; usually such matters are discreetly handled by a senior clerk. "Why not?" said one lawyer, surprised that I should ask about what amounts to pimping. "Advertising agencies do it. The biggest corporations do it at sales conventions. Why not law firms? If you look on a law firm as money, business, clients, you wouldn't think anything of it."

Despite these efforts, law firms do lose clients. In this age of conglomeration, the most common way is through corporate merger. One attorney calls them "the biggest single risk to law firms today." Many small and medium-sized firms have gone under when their biggest clients were swallowed by corporation-consuming conglomerates. Even big firms can be hurt. When Mack Trucks was absorbed by Signal, the West Coast conglomerate, Kaye Scholer lost its biggest client. "It was a jolt," a partner admits. But he—like most corporate lawyers—takes the problem of mergers philosophically: "You win some and you lose some." To the layman, the most surprising thing about mergers is that a law firm will willingly cooperate down to the last signature on the last dotted line in the complex legal process that does away with a major source of its income, like a clergyman suggesting that his wealthiest parishioner convert to another faith.

A firm can also lose business when personnel change—either at the firm or the client corporation—and the personal bonds that long linked the two dissolve. The new president of Acme Acquisitions, Inc., couldn't care less if the founder grew up with Daniel Lord or Algernon Sullivan; he'll give the company's legal business to *his* boyhood buddy or college classmate.

Sometimes a law firm loses a client when it gets caught in a conflict of interest, as Simpson Thacher & Bartlett lost Hughes Tool, or Cravath lost Honeywell when the company joined with the other six of the "seven dwarfs" of the computer industry in an antitrust action against IBM.

It can lose a client when it gets caught on the losing side of a corporate power-struggle, as Davis Polk did when Kirk Kerkorian took over MGM.

It can lose a client when a lawyer leaves and takes it with him, as Strasser Spiegelberg lost Gulf + Western, though lawyer shifts in the blue-chip bar are even rarer than those of clients.

Finally, no client will stay long with a firm if it doesn't get good service—and that means good advice. Here are two examples of what can happen when a client follows his lawyer's advice, and when it doesn't. Same client, same counsel: First Boston Corporation and Sullivan & Cromwell.

In May, 1953, Vice President Adolph H. Wenzell went on loan from First Boston to advise the Budget Bureau on financing a $100 million electric plant to be operated by the Mississippi Valley Generating Company—the so-called "Dixon-Yates" contract. He remained on First Boston's payroll, collecting $10 a day for "subsistence" plus transportation expenses from Uncle Sam.

Nine months later, when it became apparent that First Boston would handle the project's financing, the question of possible conflict of interest arose. Wenzell called Arthur Dean, Sullivan & Cromwell's "chairman." Dean, who was leaving town, referred him to John Raben, now the firm's No. 2 man. They met on February 26, 1954. Raben advised Wenzell to quit as a Budget consultant "forthwith and in writing." He repeated the advice again and again in the following weeks, but for some reason Wenzell did not resign until April 12, when, as the courts later ruled, he "discarded his Budget Bureau hat . . . and resumed his role as a First Boston vice president."

As a result of this conflict of interest, the $100 million contract was canceled.

Second case: In March, 1970, representatives of First Boston went to Philadelphia for the closing of a $120 million loan to the Penn-Central Railroad. With them went a myopic, thirty-three-year-old lawyer from Sullivan & Cromwell, William J. Williams, Jr. But Williams' eyes were sharp enough to spot some startling discrepancies in Penn-Central's financial statements.

Williams had studied the Penn-Central's financial statements and concluded that "there was a risk, perhaps a significant risk, that some time within the next one or two years that the railroad could end up in bankruptcy whether they obtained $120 million or not."

In Philadelphia, Williams started questioning David Bevan, the railroad's financial vice president, about the figures. "My impression was that . . . he was being evasive," he later told the

S.E.C. Bevan's impression was that Williams was a pain in the caboose. A few days later he came to New York, conferred with Arthur Dean and asked that Williams be taken off the Penn-Central matter. Dean declined.

Williams, meanwhile, had reported his findings to Dean. The Sullivan & Cromwell chairman instructed him to tell First Boston that the law firm would not sign the offering unless the Penn-Central's financial statements were amended to show the true facts.

This the Penn-Central was unwilling to do. Balked in its effort to find private financing, the railroad was forced to seek a government-guaranteed loan. When that fell through, it filed for bankruptcy.

Insiders had long known that the line was in trouble. But for the outside world the Penn-Central's slide into bankruptcy started with a few questions from a myopic young lawyer.

There is a classic comment about Elihu Root which has been variously attributed to Thomas Ryan, William Whitney, J. P. Morgan and other robber barons: "I have had many lawyers who have told me what I cannot do. Mr. Root is the only lawyer who tells me how to do what I want to do."

But lawyers are cautious creatures. Sometimes they *will* tell a client, "You can't do that!" And sometimes a bull-headed client will go ahead and do it anyway, retaining other counsel who will go to the wall for him. Sometimes corporations go "shopping" for such a counsel, and several blue-chip firms have acquired reputations for taking cases and approving courses of action that more cautious lawyers have rejected.

The most dramatic example of counsel caution and client switching in recent years occurred with Lord, Day & Lord and *The New York Times* over publication of the Pentagon Papers.

On Monday, June 14, 1971, an impressive array of legal talent was lunching at the University Club. There was Alexander Bickel, a professor of constitutional law at Yale; James Goodale, a senior vice president and in-house counsel of *The*

New York Times; and attorneys from Cravath; Cahill Gordon; Hawkins, Delafield & Wood; and Pillsbury, Madison & Sutro, the San Francisco giant.

They had spent the morning at the *Times* office working on the joint *amicus curiae* brief that the mass media would file in the Earl Caldwell case. Caldwell, the *Times*' San Francisco correspondent, was resisting the Justice Department's effort to compel him to testify about Black Panther activities. Caldwell claimed a newsman's "privilege" of protecting his sources of information.

Cravath represented CBS; Cahill Gordon, NBC; Hawkins, Delafield & Wood, ABC; and Pillsbury, Madison & Sutro, the *Times*, which had retained local counsel in the West Coast case. To add prestige and avoid intramural argument, the attorneys decided to bring in an academic authority to write the brief and argue the appeal. It was the same pattern the paper pursued when Herbert Wechsler, of Columbia, was retained to appeal a libel suit brought by the Birmingham, Alabama, police chief. His argument in *Sullivan* v. *New York Times* elicited a landmark decision, in which the Supreme Court ruled that public officials are virtually libel-proof. This time, Bickel was the academic authority, brought in by Floyd Abrams, of Cahill Gordon, who had been his student at Yale Law some dozen years before.

As they relaxed over lunch, the conversation turned to other topics—especially the *Times*' publication of the Pentagon Papers, which had started the day before. Bickel praised the paper for its action, then added: "If the Department of Justice tries to clamp down on you, I hope the hell you fight it to the hilt."

Midway through the meal, Gene Roberts, the paper's national news editor, arrived with a message for Goodale: The Department of Justice *was* about to clamp down: government action to halt publication of the controversial documents appeared imminent. Official word didn't come until seven thirty that night in a telegram from Attorney General Mitchell to the *Times*' president, Arthur Ochs Sulzberger:

I have been advised by the Secretary of Defense that the material published in the New York Times . . . contains information relating to the national defense of the United States and bears a top secret classification.

As such, publication of this information is directly prohibited. . . .

Moreover, further publication of information of this character will cause irreparable injury to the defense interests of the United States.

Accordingly, I respectfully request that you publish no further information of this character and advise me that you have made arrangements for the return of these documents to the Department of Defense.

"Punch," as Sulzberger was known to everyone at the paper, was in Paris, so Executive Vice President Harding Bancroft delivered the reply. As *Times Talk*, the paper's house organ, put it:

He called Robert C. Mardian, assistant attorney general in charge of the internal security division.

"We refuse to halt publication voluntarily," Bancroft told him politely. Mr. Mardian's reply was an equally polite, "thank you."

Actually, it wasn't quite that simple. The decision climaxed weeks of bitter battle between the *Times* and its law firm, Lord, Day & Lord, and within hours would lead to an open break.

Like the paper itself, the *Times'* legal representation was a family affair, passed on to the son-in-law. Alfred Cook had represented Adolph Ochs when Ochs bought the paper in 1896 and remained counsel to it. In 1922, a young Yale Law graduate named Louis M. Loeb joined Cook's firm—Cook, Nathan & Lehman—and soon afterward married the boss' daughter.

In time, Loeb was assigned to handle various legal matters for the paper. He likes to tell one story on himself: He was sent to attend a meeting of the *Times*' stockholders. "Mr. Ochs came into the room and looked around. Then he said, 'There's nothing of any importance coming up today because Mr. Cook sent Mr. Loeb here today.' His daughter never let me forget it."

By 1941, Loeb was spending a half-day at the *Times*, the other half at his law office. In 1947, Cook announced his retirement and Loeb started looking for another position. "Cook had all the business," Loeb recalls. "He never planned for the future of the firm. His attitude was *'après moi, le déluge.'*" A Yale classmate invited Loeb to join Lord, Day & Lord. He did, taking the *Times* with him as a client.

In time, the *Times*' legal business grew so much that Loeb placed a Lord, Day & Lord associate, James Goodale, as the paper's full-time in-house counsel. A private phone connected Loeb's office on Lower Broadway with the *Times*' executive suite, bypassing two switchboards. Loeb's proudest boast is that in the twenty-three years that he and Lord, Day & Lord represented the *Times*, it never lost more than six cents in a libel suit.

The dual association made Loeb a part of the city's Legal Establishment. In 1956, he became the first Jew to head the Bar Association. His idea of getting away from it all was to board the *Queen Mary*, sail to Southampton and return without debarking, remaining incommunicado for two weeks. By 1971, he was getting away from it more and more; at seventy-two, he was ailing and considering retirement.

On the surface, it looked like the ideal client-counsel relationship—the good, gray *Times* and an "Our Crowd" attorney in one of New York's oldest law firms. It *was*—until the Pentagon Papers.

About six weeks before Mitchell's telegram, the *Times* told Loeb and Lord, Day & Lord that it had come into possession—never mind how—of top-secret documents detailing America's involvement in Vietnam. It asked for a legal opinion as to whether or not they could be published.

"We put the best brains in the office to work on it," Loeb says.

Soon afterward, Herbert Brownell, the former Attorney General and Lord, Day & Lord's senior partner, Loeb and John W. Castles 3d, the firm's chief litigator, met at the *Times* offices with the paper's brass to deliver its legal opinion.

"We told them," Loeb says "that they were running the risk of being criminally sued and it was our advice that the *Times* should not knowingly participate in a breach of the law. We advised them that they should not publish and that they should apply to have the material declassified."

There was even talk at Lord, Day & Lord that the firm had a legal obligation to report what it considered an impending violation of the law—possible publication of the purloined papers—to the authorities. But no one at the firm actually went that far.

After the meeting, "Punch" Sulzberger told Managing Editor A. M. Rosenthal that he would make no decision on whether or not to publish until he read the extracts being prepared by Neil Sheehan and a team of *Times* reporters holed up at the New York Hilton.

One of those most opposed to Lord, Day & Lord's advice was its alumnus, Jim Goodale. "We had a great disagreement between lawyers on the subject," he recalls. "My opinion was that the material was publishable and that we could win any case. Their opinion was to the contrary. We had a terrific difference of opinion, a battle royal. I was going crazy. I had a terrific desire to see this thing published. It was a point of principle. But it seemed to me I was going to lose somehow. I was strongly considering an alternative choice of a career."

At the beginning of June, Goodale took a week off. "When I came back, I found a rush to go to press. At the end of the week, I got back into it again. I read all the articles and I felt more strongly than ever that it would have to be published."

At Goodale's prodding—and that of Abe Rosenthal and Washington bureau chief Max Frankel—the vacillating "Punch" Sulzberger finally decided to disregard the advice of Lord, Day & Lord and gave the order to publish.

"I told Loeb on Friday that the series would start on Sunday," Goodale says. It was one of his proudest moments.

When Mitchell's telegram arrived, Bancroft called Loeb with the news. The attorney continued to chart a cautious course. "I told him that I would be surprised if the *Times* didn't comply with the request from the Department of Justice," Loeb says. Goodale's recollection is that Loeb didn't cite legal reasons, only "the public interest." "We disregarded that. We didn't need a law firm to tell us what 'the public interest' was."

The *Times'* executives placed a call to Sulzberger in Paris. Over the speaker phone, Bancroft relayed Loeb's advice to halt publication. To some present it sounded as if he were seconding the motion. Rosenthal, fearing "Punch" might agree, nudged Goodale in the ribs. "For Christ sake, say something!" he whispered. Goodale got on the line and argued the case for continued publication. He apparently convinced Sulzberger.

"Okay, go ahead and publish," "Punch" told them.

By this time, the first-edition deadline was approaching. While Bancroft phoned Mardian with the paper's decision, Goodale and the editors spent most of the next hour drafting a front-page statement announcing the *Times'* defiance of the government's request:

> The Times must respectfully decline the request of the Attorney General, believing that it is in the interest of the people of this country to be informed of the material contained in this series of articles.
>
> We have also been informed of the Attorney General's intention of seeking an injunction against further publication. We believe that it is properly for the courts to decide. The Times will oppose any request for an injunction for the same reason that led us to publish the articles in the first place. We will of course abide by the final decision of the courts.

Once the presses were rolling, Goodale turned to the problem of defending the paper against the inevitable government court action, certain to come the next morning. He called Loeb at home, told him of the paper's decision and asked him to alert Castles to be ready to go to court. Loeb suggested that Goodale speak to Brownell first.

In the meantime, Brownell had received another phone call —from John Mitchell. The Attorney General said he hoped that the *Times* would comply with the government's request. But, if it didn't, he continued, he hoped that Brownell's firm wouldn't take the case. He pointed out that it might be personally "embarrassing" because the executive order under which the government was acting had been drafted by Brownell when he was Attorney General and there was a memo in the department's files that the order was still "valid, legally binding and enforceable."

Goodale phoned Brownell, and reported afterward: "He [Brownell] said it was 'shocking' that we hadn't obeyed the telegram"—apparently the regard of one Attorney General for the edicts of another, though Brownell's private opinion of Mitchell's performance at Justice was unprintable. Then he said, 'We can't represent you.' "

It was the biggest shock of the day. Like a church elder nabbed in a vice raid, the nation's most prestigious newspaper had to embark on a midnight manhunt for legal counsel. Goodale immediately thought of Alexander Bickel.

"I think we can get Bickel," he told Bancroft. "I'm sure we can if Floyd Abrams will come in on it."

Abrams picks up the thread of the narrative: "At twelve thirty that night I got a call from Jim Goodale asking if I knew where Bickel was and asking if we would be willing to work together on what looked like a major battle with the government to suppress publication of the series. I told him that I did not know where Bickel was and that I would be happy to take the case, but that that was something that I would have to discuss with my partners in the morning."

Bickel had checked out of the Yale Club and neither Goodale nor Bancroft could locate him. Then they recalled that newsmen have well-deserved reputations as skip-tracers. Half the *Times*' city room was impressed into the effort. A few phone calls to New Haven and to Palo Alto, California, where

Bickel was spending his sabbatical, and the errant law professor was tracked down at his mother's home on the Upper West Side. It took just twelve minutes. The next morning Rosenthal posted a notice on the pillar beside their desks: "God bless night rewrite."

Bancroft called Bickel, who agreed to join with Abrams on the case. The law professor then called his former student to make arrangements.

"At about one fifteen," Abrams continues, "I picked up Bickel and we came down here [Cahill Gordon's office on Pine Street] and picked up a few books containing the statutes which we thought the government might act under. We spent the night here and prepared a memo setting forth our views. I received clearance to take the case at eight thirty that morning."

A few hours later, when the case of the *U.S.* v. *New York Times, et al.*—twenty-two officers, editors and reporters were named as co-defendants—was called, the paper was represented by Alexander Bickel and the firm of Cahill, Gordon, Sonnett, Reindl & Ohl, Floyd Abrams "of counsel."

To some it seemed strange that the Establishment *Times* would be represented by a firm with the image of a bunch of tough, scrapping, up-from-the-street-corner Irishmen. "We weren't hiring Cahill Gordon," Goodale explained afterward. "We were hiring Floyd Abrams, who knew the First Amendment and who was in a large corporate law firm."

The rest is history. The *Times* lost the first round, as Judge Murray Gurfein issued a temporary order halting further publication of the documents until the case was decided. Abrams called in two other Cahill Gordon partners—William Hegarty and Lawrence McKay—and backstopped the front-office trio with seventeen associates. Then they embarked on a frantic round of hearings, arguments and appeals. On June 30, just fifteen days after the legal skirmishing began, the U.S. Supreme Court, in a precedent-setting 6-to-3 decision, denied the government's plea to prohibit publication of the Pentagon Papers.

The series resumed, and the *Times'* management finally had a respite to reappraise its relationship with Lord, Day & Lord. "There was a short period of time when the relations were pretty unpleasant, to put it mildly," Loeb says.

"We had pretty much concluded here that we wanted to use specialty lawyers," Goodale says. Lord, Day & Lord was dropped as general counsel, though it continued to handle the paper's corporate and tax work. Cahill Gordon was signed on to handle local litigation. Labor relations, copyrights, etc., were farmed out to other firms.

But the old, cozy, familial relationship of the *Times* with Lord, Day & Lord was gone—even more so with Loeb's retirement. On January 1, 1972, Loeb became "of counsel" to the firm; by fall, he would be relocated in Southern California.

As for the *Times'* new litigator, Floyd Abrams, the Pentagon Papers case was a milestone in his brief career. Framed on the wall of his office is the stereotype matrix of the *Times'* July 1 issue, its eight-column banner headline announcing his Supreme Court victory. On the shelf below are the books in the case: the one-volume edition of the Pentagon Papers issued by the *Times*; the four-volume version released by Alaska Senator Mike Gravel; the complete edition put out by the Government Printing Office; and the two volumes of briefs and pleadings in the case. On his desk is a more frivolous momento—a button that says, "Free *The Times* XXII."

7

"As My Lawyer, Dick Nixon, Said the Other Day . . ."

It was Richard Nixon's fifth crisis—the "Kitchen Debate" with Nikita Khrushchev. For Donald Kendall, it was an even greater crisis—not for the fate of the free world, but his future with the Pepsi-Cola Corporation.

Kendall, the new president of Pepsi-Cola International, had opened a soft drink kiosk at the American Exposition in Moscow in 1959, but he was fielding flak from the home office about the expense. He feared the episode might end his career in carbonation.

"The night before the exposition opened," he recalled, "Tommy Thompson [U.S. Ambassador Llewellyn Thompson] gave a reception for the Vice President at the embassy. I was invited as one of the exhibitors. I met Nixon going in the door. I'd known him from before. We'd worked together at a couple of meetings for Eisenhower's People-to-People program. I told him my predicament. We had to get some publicity out of this or I was dead.

" 'Don't worry about it, Don,' he said. 'I'll bring Khrushchev by and we'll get a Pepsi in his hand.'

"The next day, Nixon brought Khrushchev by to the Pepsi kiosk. We had Russian-speaking girls who offered him a Pepsi from New York, then one from Moscow. I asked him which he liked best. Naturally, he said the one made in Moscow. And he drank about five more to prove his point. Our slogan at that time was 'Be Sociable.' We got front-page publicity all over the world, 'Khrushchev learns to be sociable.' The publicity was unbelievable. It saved my job."

Most people remember the 1959 Moscow exposition for the Nixon–Khrushchev debate. Donald Kendall remembers it as the time when a Russian Communist saved his capitalist hide. And he never forgot his debt to the middleman—Richard Nixon.

When Nixon joined a Wall Street law firm in 1963, Kendall gave it the business of Pepsi-Cola International. Soon afterward, when Kendall moved up to the presidency of the parent company—which had diversified into peanuts, potato chips and truck rentals and renamed itself PepsiCo, Inc.—Nixon's firm got all the concern's legal business. Perhaps even more important for Nixon's political future, Pepsi footed the bills for the overseas trips that made him a foreign-policy "expert."*

Pepsi-Cola was the only major client Nixon personally brought into the firm. But he hadn't been hired to hustle clients. Nor had he been hired for his legal expertise. Despite his fourteen years of governmental service, his experience at the bar was minimal: a few years as a small-time, small-town lawyer before World War II, a few months with a corporate firm in Los Angeles between his presidential defeat in 1960 and his "last press conference" of 1962. Nixon was brought into the firm as a "public partner," a sort of $200,000-a-year-plus piece of window-dressing. Even at that price it was cheap advertising.

The public partner is a relatively recent concept for the blue-chip bar. For decades Wall Street law firms have produced

---

* Those who handled the account also got a fringe-benefit—a steady supply of soft drinks and "noshes" in the office.

men who went on to make their mark in government or politics; Elihu Root, Charles Evans Hughes, John W. Davis; and in recent years, John McCloy, John Foster Dulles and John Mitchell, to name but a few.

By contrast, the public partner comes *from* government or politics to the big-time bar. He comes in at the top, usually to a firm that has started to slip. A firm that is riding high has no need to recruit high-priced talent and promote it over the heads of present partners. The public partner's arrival is almost always heralded by a shake-up of the shingle, with the new man's name coming first. What good is having a public partner if he isn't advertised?

Equally prominent men may languish unheralded in other firms. How many people know that Herbert Brownell is at Lord, Day & Lord? Or Arthur Dean at Sullivan & Cromwell? In such solidly established firms, it isn't necessary to advertise the stars. Nor, strictly speaking, are such men "public partners"; they have merely returned to the fold after a hiatus of government service. When David Peck stepped down as presiding justice of the Appellate Division and returned to Sullivan & Cromwell, his name disappeared into the list of thirty-two partners. When his successor, Bernard Botein, joined a smaller midtown firm, it was promptly renamed Botein, Hays, Sklar & Herzberg.

The public partner isn't expected to play an active role in the management of the firm or to handle many legal chores. He isn't expected to bring in clients, but he is expected to be available to consult with them. It even helps if he keeps a hand in politics or civic projects. Every time he gets his name in the papers it's another advertisement for the firm.

In a smaller setting, an ex-mayor or a congressman with a night-school degree from Loophole College of Law can pass muster as a public partner. But on New York's "fast track," as Nixon once termed it, only someone on the level of a senator or Cabinet member or above is truly eligible. The most prominent examples are three defeated Republican presidential candidates—Willkie, Dewey and Nixon.

In 1963, the firm of Mudge, Stern, Baldwin & Todd was a

Wall Street wallflower, solid and respectable, but somewhat staid and old-fashioned. It had the lineage of a thoroughbred, its genealogy filling two full pages in the office-manual. The firm was founded in 1869 by Simon H. Stern and evolved over the years into Mudge, Stern, Williams & Tucker, which merged in 1955 with the almost equally hoary firm of Baldwin, Todd, Rose & Cooper.

Although long one of Wall Street's leading law factories, Mudge Stern had managed to keep out of the public eye. Until Nixon joined, it had no name partner, no politician or public personality familiar to the man in the street, nor even one especially active in the councils of the bar. The only partner who had achieved a reputation outside the office was Henry Root Stern, Jr., who had headed the State Board of Social Welfare under Governor Dewey.

"We're like the lady who only wants her name in the papers twice—when she's born and when she dies," Randolph H. Guthrie, one of the present senior partners, once said. He admits now that he should have added a third occasion—"when she marries."

In the opinion of many lawyers, Mudge Stern had become a legal backwater, losing out on new business to more glamorous and more aggressive firms. But if a suitable suitor could be found. . . .

The marriage-broker was one of Mudge Stern's oldest and biggest clients—Elmer Bobst, the retired chairman but driving force of Warner-Lambert Pharmaceutical Company. Known as "the Vitamin King," Bobst was then nearing eighty, but still remarkably active., He had taken a fatherly interest in Nixon since his vice-presidential days. They had met at a savings bond dinner in New Jersey. Bobst was chairman, Nixon the guest speaker.

"I referred to him as 'Mr. Vice President,' " Bobst recalls.

" 'Look,' he said, 'your name is Elmer. My name is Dick. Let's cut out the "Mr. Vice President." ' "

"I liked him right away. I found out a week or two later that he was coming to New Jersey for a vacation. He'd just started to take an interest in golf, so I had him made an honorary member of my club. We played golf together, took trips on my boat. We had a very pleasant time. He came for another summer."

"Uncle Elmer," as Julie and Tricia called him, remained close to Nixon. "Losing the election [in 1960] was a terrific shock," he says. "I invited him and Pat and another couple on our yacht the day after the Inauguration. He just wanted to get away."

After another electoral defeat two years later, Bobst again came to Nixon's rescue. "Their [Mudge Stern's] senior partner died. I felt the firm ought to have some new blood. Then came the thought of Mr. Nixon"—who had just been defeated for governor of California and was looking around for greener pastures.

The marriage was arranged and the firm of Nixon, Mudge, Rose, Guthrie & Alexander was born. As a former Vice President, presidential nominee and protégé of client Bobst, Nixon naturally came first. Then Mudge, to preserve the link with the past. The order of the remaining names was determined by drawing numbers from a hat; Nixon held the hat.

Third place went to Milton C. Rose, a courtly, old-worldly gentleman who headed the firm's trusts and estates division. Then Bob Guthrie, an earthy South Carolinian descended from the Randolphs of Virginia who managed the corporate accounts and who was the chief architect of the firm's expansion over the coming decade. And finally, John H. Alexander, the firm's tax expert—trim and taciturn, fastidious in appearance and matinee-idol handsome. The name of founder Stern lapsed into limbo.

Nixon settled into a twenty-fourth-floor corner office overlooking New York Harbor. Other offices in the firm were designed in Danish modern; Nixon's might be described as 1930s Oriental gee-gaw. It was (or rather *is*, since it has been preserved, untouched and unused) a museum of mementoes—"a sanctuary for a President-in-exile," Jules Witcover called it. On the desk is an inscribed pen set, the gift of President Eisenhower; on the ledge behind, autographed photos of Queen Elizabeth, Prince Philip, Belgium's King Baudouin, the Shah of Iran, Nehru and others; on the wall opposite, signed photos of Ike, Herbert Hoover and Albert Schweitzer. One cabinet is filled with engraved gavels, one bookcase with elephant statuettes. A case containing ornately carved oriental junk lines a side wall.

The new senior partner did not have to drum up business; his very presence attracted clients. "The corporation executive has an almost childlike enthusiasm for celebrities," one partner explains. Businessmen flocked to the firm, some simply for the prestige of having a former Vice President participate in their business discussions, some just for the thrill of being able to boast, "As my lawyer, Dick Nixon, said to me the other day. . . ."

Nixon himself remarked about this phenomenon when he was practicing law in Los Angeles. "I never realized how easy it is to make money," he told a visitor. "I just got twenty-five thousand dollars for telling a bunch of stupid jerks something they could have learned from the newspapers."

It seems that the officers of some company wanted to open operations in France, but were concerned about political conditions there. They sought Nixon's advice. The former Vice President made a pose of pondering the problem for a week or so, then rendered his opinion. Shorn of excess verbiage, it was: France will remain stable as long as de Gaulle's in power.

Most of Nixon's work for the firm was not strictly legal, but business—advising clients on dealings overseas or negotiating with foreign governments. During his nearly six years with the firm, he tried only one case.

The suit, which Nixon argued only at the U.S. Supreme Court level, involved the delicate issue of the right of privacy versus freedom of the press. Significantly, in view of both his previous and later dealings with the fourth estate, Nixon pleaded for privacy. It was anything but the "strict construction" he has espoused as President, arguing against a freedom engraved in the Constitution and for a "right" that isn't.

The case, *Time, Inc.* v. *Hill*, dated back to the mid-1950s.
Joseph Hayes had written a play, *The Desperate Hours* (it
later became a successful movie starring Humphrey Bogart
and Fredric March). It was a fictionalized account of an actual event—escaped convicts holding a family hostage in their
suburban Philadelphia home. During the play's out-of-town
tryout, *Life* magazine posed the actors in the house. But the
incidents in the play were far more sensational than those of
real life and the father, James J. Hill, sued. After two trials in
the New York State courts, the Hill family was awarded
$30,000 damages. Time, Inc., handled as always by Cravath,
appealed. At this point, Nixon was retained to represent Hill.

The issue was the right of privacy versus freedom of the
press. But after two hearings, the high court ruled on a nar-
rower issue: the wording of the judge's charge to the jury. Six
judges voted to send the case back for a new trial, three to
uphold the award. The new trial never came off since an out-of-
court settlement was arranged, with Time paying part of Hill's
legal costs. It can be said that Nixon lost the battle but won
the war; the Court denied his argument, but he got the money.
It's a curiosity of history that the opinion supporting Nixon in
the only case he ever argued before the Supreme Court was
written by Abe Fortas, whose promotion to Chief Justice he
vehemently opposed.

Nixon's arrival on Wall Street coincided with his firm's conglomeration; it had started diversifying in the mid-1960s. In
1963, it absorbed the Wall Street firm of Dorr, Hand, Whit-
taker & Watson, chiefly railroad lawyers; in 1964, the Washington firm of Becker & Greenwald, admiralty specialists; and
in 1966, Caldwell, Trimble & Mitchell, a small firm in the
highly lucrative field of municipal bond certification. With this
last a sixth name was added to the shingle—that of John N.
Mitchell. In five years, Nixon Mudge swelled from 57 lawyers
to 105.

Even with a public partner like Nixon, the firm remained
essentially nonpolitical. Unlike rival firms headed by men
adept at threading a way through the labyrinths of govern-

ment, it did not try to exercise clout or throw its weight in Washington. It stuck to the law books, discreetly advising its corporate clients and administering its estates, and tried to keep its name out of the papers.

It was hard. For a while Nixon tried to pull his share of the load. He had been brought in as a lawyer, but he soon became bored by the practice of law. He had been brought in as a name, not as a candidate or a potential President, but there was a vacuum in the Republican party and Nixon soon stepped in to fill it.

"It was the greatest surprise to any of us here that we had anybody who went into politics, much less the Presidency," said Bob Guthrie. "We don't know what to do about it. We're still trying to adjust to it."

When Charles de Gaulle stepped down as President of France, the joke in New York legal circles was that he would become a partner at Paul Weiss. It wasn't as far-fetched as it sounded. No law firm in New York is so studded with political talent as the institution commonly called "Paul Weiss."

Though its antecedents can be traced to the nineteenth century, the modern firm came into being in 1945 when Louis S. Weiss and John F. Wharton joined forces with Randolph E. Paul and Lloyd K. Garrison. Paul, Weiss, Wharton & Garrison had only thirteen lawyers, but even then it evinced a political prominence that eclipsed many of its Wall Street rivals.

Paul, who died in 1956, was a tax expert and former general counsel to the Treasury. Weiss, who died in 1950, was active in liberal causes and chairman of the New School's board of trustees. Garrison, former dean of the University of Wisconsin Law School and chairman of the War Labor Board, went on to head New York City's Board of Education. Wharton, now "of counsel" and virtually retired, was a prominent theatrical lawyer.

From the start, Paul Weiss was innovative and scored a number of "firsts" in its incipient years. In 1949, it was the first major Wall Street firm to move to midtown. It was the first to take in a woman partner—Carolyn Agger, now Mrs. Abe Fortas, who joined the Washington office in 1946. It was the first to hire a black associate.

The firm did not get its big spurt until 1950 when it took in a new senior partner—Simon H. Rifkind. A short, dark, mustached man with bushy brows, he may, as one observer has noted, "resemble a rather timid chipmunk," but for four decades he has been a giant on New York's legal scene.

He started as an assistant to Senator Robert F. Wagner and became a junior partner in his firm. "Si Rifkind was the legal luminary and workhorse," a former associate there recalled. "He was the only one who worked on Saturday. Senator Wagner never did any work. Occasionally he held hearings as a referee in some case that a friendly judge gave him. But his major contribution was to produce business. With Wagner a lot of it was of a political character."

One episode from Rifkind's service with Wagner assured him of a footnote in history. He was one of the last persons to see Judge Joseph Crater, whose disappearance in 1930 remains one of the great unsolved mysteries of all time.

The incident had a humorous epilogue forty-one years later when the New York Police, making a routine follow-up in "the disappearance of Joseph Force Frater [*sic*]," sent a form letter to the Bar Association asking the whereabouts of "Simon Rifkin [*sic*], Attorney, formerly of 120 Broadway, New York City, complainant who filed the Missing Persons Report." Snorted Rifkind: "If they can't find me, how could they ever find Crater?"

In 1941, at Wagner's behest, President Roosevelt named Rifkind a federal district judge. He served with distinction, but stepped down in 1950 complaining that he was "unable to maintain a reasonable standard of living" on a judge's $15,000 salary. As a partner in the renamed firm of Paul, Weiss, Rifkind, Wharton & Garrison, he would do far, far better.

One attorney describes Rifkind as "one hundred per cent lawyer—he eats, drinks, breathes the law; he probably even dreams the law." Unlike most senior partners at comparable firms, Rifkind excels as a courtroom battler. He defended white-collar criminal cases, headed President Kennedy's railroad arbitration panel, represented Mrs. Kennedy in her suit to prevent publication of William Manchester's *Death of a President* and again, after she became Mrs. Onassis, her action against a *paparazzo*.

Though his politics are solidly Democratic, Rifkind possesses the true advocate's ability to argue either side of a case. He boasts that on the same day he went to two different courtrooms to argue opposite sides of identical motions—and won both!

"He's initially very skeptical," says a lawyer who once assisted him. "But as he gets into a case more and more, he comes to believe that his client is one of the most persecuted and vilified men in history. He winds up believing in the client's case more than the client."

He also knows how to use practically every courtroom trick that's ever been devised. The associate recalls sitting beside Rifkind during an appellate argument. Opposing counsel scored a telling point. Rifkind responded by sitting up with a look of shocked surprise. He grabbed a yellow legal pad and scrawled an instruction to his aide:

"Look through the record like you're looking for something, then hand it to me."

The associate delved into his briefcase and came up with a document. It could have been the lawyer's laundry list, for all anyone knew. Rifkind scanned it, then turned to the opposing counsel with a look of utter contempt and finally leaned back with a smile of complete satisfaction.

"The judges knew what he was up to," the lawyer says. "He wasn't fooling them. There was nothing in the record that contradicted what was said. But it was a great sideshow and they loved to watch it. And it distracted the judges just when our opponent was making his most important point."

Once, when Rifkind was on the bench, a lawyer objected that a complaint had been copied word-for-word from one previously filed.

"Was it a good complaint?" Rifkind asked. "You wouldn't want him to copy a bad complaint, would you?"

As a lawyer, Rifkind has shown no compunction against borrowing someone else's telling tactic—no matter how unlikely the source. An associate recalls Rifkind's closing argument in a criminal case: "He cupped his hands in front of him and said, 'You know, liberty is like a little bird that you can hold in your hands. You can feel its heart beat. You can either let it free to fly'—and he spread his hands and looked up at the ceiling—'or you can crush it to death'—and he kneaded his hands together."

The associate had wondered at the time how Rifkind came to use such a strange analogy. The answer came a few nights later when he was watching a 1930s gangster melodrama on the *Late Late Show*. In the movie's climactic scene, attorney Adolphe Menjou pleaded with the jury for Ann Sheridan's life: "A young girl's liberty is just like a little bird's. . . ."

Rifkind became Paul Weiss' driving force—an astute litigator, an ace business-getter, an able administrator. Paul Weiss' roster of regular retainers came to include Revlon, Kinney Services (now Warner Communications), the New York *Post*, Field Enterprises and Twentieth-Century Fox.

In 1957, Rifkind pulled off a spectacular coup for the firm—a Chicago office headed by Adlai Stevenson. New York, Washington, Chicago, it looked as if Paul Weiss was on its way to becoming the General Motors of the legal world. But the expansion was short-lived. The Chicago firm of Stevenson, Rifkind & Wirtz was wiped out by the New Frontier. Stevenson went to the U.N. and Willard Wirtz to the Labor Department. Of Chicago's non-name partners, Newton Minow became chairman of the F.C.C. and William McCormick Blair ambassador to Denmark.

"I regret that I have but one law firm to give to my country," Stevenson had quipped.

With Paul's death and Stevenson's departure, what was left of the Washington office—Stevenson, Paul, Rifkind, Wharton & Garrison—was merged into the Washington firm of Arnold, Fortas and Porter. Paul Weiss later opened another office in the capital.

Still Paul Weiss grew and prospered. From thirteen lawyers

in 1945, the ranks swelled to 110 by 1970; the firm grossed about $10 million a year and moved from its modern Madison Avenue office to an even plusher one at 345 Park Avenue.

But there was an ominous cloud on the horizon. Paul Weiss had become a one-man show and that one man—Si Rifkind—was nearing seventy. Many younger lawyers wondered what would happen when he was gone. A few found positions with a more certain future.

Paul Weiss averted the deluge by garnering a galaxy of legal and political stars. First, Morris B. Abram, the Atlanta attorney who had argued the successful Supreme Court challenge to Georgia's system of counting votes by county-unit. Perhaps even more important than Abram's legal acumen was his presidency of the American Jewish Committee, which gave him contacts with potential clients across the country. Then, Theodore C. Sorensen, counsel to the late President Kennedy. And later, former Attorney General Ramsey Clark.

It should have been talent enough to dazzle any firm. But in 1967, Paul Weiss picked up an even more glittering star—former counsel to the United Steelworkers and the AFL-CIO, former Secretary of Labor, former Supreme Court Justice, former U.N. ambassador—Arthur J. Goldberg.

Abram, Sorensen and Clark had been fitted in without much to-do. In current listings, Clark is the fifth-ranked partner—behind Rifkind, Garrison and long-time members Howard Seitz and Adrian DeWind; Abram is sixth; Sorensen eleventh. But Goldberg, it turned out, had an ego as big as the Bronx. He came to Paul Weiss on the understanding that he was not expected to recruit clients and that he would have time for civic projects; Rifkind would remain the firm's force. But Rifkind had been a mere district judge, Goldberg a Supreme Court justice; he was not about to be ranked beneath a judicial inferior. Accordingly, the firm was renamed Paul, Weiss, *Goldberg*, Rifkind, Wharton & Garrison.

The new arrival made it clear that he was to be known as "Justice Goldberg." The plates on other partners' offices said "Mr. Clark" or "Mr. Rifkind"; the one on Goldberg's said "Jus-

tice Goldberg." When he ran for governor in 1970, his haughty
demeanor prompted some observers to dub him "the Jewish
Pope" and others to scoff that he campaigned like someone
running for the Supreme Court. Eventually, Goldberg tried to
laugh off such charges. He'd tell audiences that he'd asked his
wife:

"Dorothy, do you think I'm stuffy?"

She supposedly replied: "Of course not, Mr. Justice."

There are those at Paul Weiss who could believe it actually
happened.

Rifkind got revenge in small ways. The telephone operators,
who once answered "Paul Weiss Rifkind," reverted to the time-
honored "Paul Weiss." Rifkind himself managed to show a visitor around the plant, pointing out everything from the library
to the cafeteria, without showing him Goldberg's office or even
mentioning the justice's name.

With so much political talent aboard, it was inevitable that
some partners would wind up on the ballot, but for a few years
it seemed that *everyone* at Paul Weiss was running for something.

Abram seemed solid to be the Democratic Senate candidate
in 1968, but he got caught in the crossfire between Senator
Robert Kennedy and President Johnson. Unable to reconcile
his Vietnam views to both men, he pulled out of the race,
resigned from the firm and took off to Massachusetts and the
presidency of Brandeis University. After a tempestuous two-
year term, he returned to Paul Weiss and tried to enter the
1970 Senate sweepstakes, but it was discovered that he'd let
his New York residency lapse.

Instead, the State Committee's nod went to Ted Sorensen.
But the former JFK aide discovered that the Kennedy magic
works only for those with the Kennedy name; he placed a sad
third in the primary.

Goldberg got the gubernatorial designation, but barely
squeaked through the primary and lost disastrously to Nelson
Rockefeller in the fall election.

Less famous partners kept busy on other fronts. DeWind

managed the Kennedy-backed campaign of Judge Samuel Silverman for Manhattan Surrogate in the 1966 Democratic primary. Silverman, a former Paul Weiss partner, made a late entry into the race that caught Rifkind flat-footed; he'd just signed an endorsement of his opponent. Silverman won, but soon got bored by the routine of probating wills and returned to the Supreme Court.

Edward N. Costikyan, leader of Tammany Hall during Mayor Wagner's "reform" period, later managed two losing local campaigns. Costikyan, curiously, is the only major figure at Paul Weiss who went *from* the firm to politics, not vice versa.

The most stunning electoral coup was pulled off by a Paul Weiss lawyer whose tie to the firm did not come out in the campaign. In the 1972 Democratic primary, Elizabeth Holtzman, a Paul Weiss associate, upset Brooklyn Congressman Emanuel Celler, the dean of the House of Representatives.

Two other Paul Weiss associates won Assembly seats on the Upper East Side. And, if that wasn't enough, two Paul Weiss partners even wound up running against each other—DeWind as a McCarthy delegate from the "Silk Stocking" district in the 1968 primary, Sorensen on the Robert Kennedy slate. DeWind won.

It seems a wonder any of them ever had time to practice law. What law they squeezed in often was of no financial benefit to the firm. The stars took on several celebrated cases free or for nominal fees. Clark helped defend the Berrigan brothers in the Kissinger-kidnap plot. Goldberg successfully appealed the draft-dodging-conspiracy conviction of Yale Chaplain William Sloane Coffin, pressed the Alaska Eskimos' multi-million-dollar land claim against the federal government, argued Curt Flood's challenge to baseball's reserve clause and won the Democratic party's case for keeping a slate of McCarthy electors off the New York ballot in 1968.

But some civic projects paid off. Mayor Lindsay asked Goldberg to mediate a pay dispute among the city's police, firemen and sanitation workers. It was assumed that he'd donated his services, but he submitted a bill for $25,000 for the three days' work. The sanitation union balked at paying its share, and Goldberg ultimately settled for half.

Goldberg got the assignment because the city needed someone of sufficient stature to awe the warring unions. But sometimes a public partner's political posture can corral clients, even the most unlikely ones.

In 1965 General Motors sicked private detectives on Ralph Nader, until then an obscure do-gooder. It was an obvious effort to uncover incriminating information that might offset the charges the consumer crusader made in his book *Unsafe at Any Speed*. But it rankled a Senate subcommittee taking Nader's testimony about auto safety. The most irate members were the chairman, Connecticut Democrat Abraham Ribicoff, and Robert F. Kennedy. GM President John M. Roche was haled before the panel.

He showed up with his new attorney—Ted Sorensen. GM and a New Frontiersman! Would Abbie Hoffman hire Herbert Brownell? But GM obviously thought it would get a more sympathetic hearing represented by a prominent Democrat than by a typically conservative blue-chip corporate counsel. And who better to assuage the anger of Kennedy and Ribicoff than their former colleague?

Except it didn't work. Sorensen didn't say a word at the hearing, while Ribicoff and Kennedy barely acknowledged his nod of greeting. He sat silently as Roche was forced to apologize to the subcommittee and to Nader. GM eventually paid Nader a settlement of $450,000.

Abram, Sorensen, Clark and Goldberg came into the firm with the understanding that they would have time for civic projects. But others who got caught up in the political whirl had to make their own arrangements about finances. When he was with the firm, Assemblyman Peter A. A. Berle took a leave of absence during Albany's legislative sessions. In describing his own accommodation, Costikyan said:

> My income suffered. Time spent on politics is not compensible, as is time spent by a partner on his clients' affairs. Overworked partners cannot fail to take into considera-

tion the frequent absences of a junior on political gambols. "A voice on the other end of the telephone" is the way one key partner described me. My share of the firm income was fixed accordingly—although fairly, since my partners were prepared to "carry me" in my political venture to some extent.

Moreover, to avoid any criticism once I was county leader, I made an arrangement with my firm so that I would not share in any fees involving dealings with the City of New York—another cut off the top. . . .

There was no corresponding increase in clients as a result of political activity. Most prospective clients, I assume, who heard of me through politics, must have assumed I was a full-time politician. In any event, I had little extra time available to take on new matters.

Periodically there's an undercurrent of rumbling among Paul Weiss juniors that their work subsidizes the stars, though it would seem that the paying clients should be the ones to complain. In any event, the young men no longer have to worry about subsidizing Paul Weiss' brightest star. In June, 1971, Goldberg left the firm to set up practice in Washington. "In reappraising how I can best apply my professional time and energies, I have decided to free myself from responsibilities associated with the position of senior partner of a large and busy firm in New York," he explained.

If there was a final showdown at Paul Weiss, it remains "behind closed doors." One lawyer ascribed Goldberg's departure to a case of "Potomac fever"—a desire to be back at the center of political power. Since his rout by Rockefeller, he had become a political has-been in New York; in Washington, he could be a giant again.

Despite campaign disclaimers, Goldberg was never truly a New Yorker. He told one political crony that he "hated" the city. Whenever possible he'd slip away to his Virginia farm. Nor had he really fitted in with the firm. "He didn't like all this fuss and bother, keeping time-sheets and that sort of thing," one lawyer says. "He wanted to run his own peanut-stand."

With Goldberg gone, Paul Weiss quickly reverted to its old name. "You never saw anybody move so fast as they did in getting his name off everything," says another lawyer in the building. "There was a general jubilation among the partners." Goldberg had never been a "rainmaker" and there are no indications that Paul Weiss' billings suffered once he left. In fact, the firm has swelled since his departure—from 110 lawyers in 1970 to 138 in 1972, 45 partners and 93 associates. About the only client Goldberg took with him was Curt Flood's ultimately unsuccessful challenge to baseball's reserve clause.

An attorney who specializes in defending airline accident claims called a partner at Mudge, Rose, Guthrie & Alexander not long after Richard Nixon became President to inquire about a job with the firm. But Mudge Rose has no airline business, he was told. The attorney replied that the word around town was that Mudge Rose was about to become counsel to Eastern Airlines.

The partner decided to check out the matter with his seniors. He found that Eastern *had* approached Mudge Rose, not to become its general counsel, but to handle a highly controversial and hotly contested transpacific route application before the Civil Aeronautics Board. Mudge Rose did not take the case.

The incident illustrates the problem that has plagued the firm since one of its partners became President and another the Attorney General. It has boomed with an almost unasked-for affluence and is forced to turn away prospective clients, especially those who come seeking clout in Washington.

In January, 1969, the first and sixth names came off the shingle and the firm became Mudge, Rose, Guthrie & Alexander. In addition to Nixon and Mitchell, it lost Leonard Garment, its chief of litigation, who became a White House assistant, and several associates to the lower ranks of the Administration.

The name may have been changed, but along Wall Street Mudge Rose was still called "the Nixon firm" and the presidential presence colored many of its actions. As Guthrie puts it, "We don't want to do anything to embarrass the President."

"We have a problem," he continues. "We obviously don't want to refuse to handle the matters of clients because of problems with the Administration. On the other hand, we don't want to hold ourselves out to clients, either substantially or optically, because of our relations with the Administration. Generally, we don't take on any job relating to the government from a new client."

But Mudge Rose's successes with government on behalf of some *old* clients raised eyebrows in political circles.

Two months after taking office, Mitchell's Justice Department dropped out of an antitrust action against El Paso Natural Gas, one of Mudge Rose's oldest clients. Solicitor General Erwin Griswold, a Johnson Administration holdover, insisted that the decision not to continue the case was his, and that it had been made before Nixon and Mitchell took office. But William M. Bennett, who had forced the case against El Paso, first as a member of the California Public Service Commission, then as a "consumer representative" in a class action, attributed the Justice Department's withdrawal to El Paso's involvement with the Nixon firm. Between 1961 and 1967, he said, El Paso paid Mudge Rose fees of more than $770,000.

Then there was the abortive $200 million government loan to save the Penn-Central Railroad from bankruptcy. Although Mudge Rose had handled some matters for the railroad before —mostly foreign financing—it was obviously called in because the Penn-Central's management thought the firm had an "in" with the Administration. Guthrie was introduced at the line's board meeting as "a member of the Nixon firm" and "close to the White House." Although Transportation Secretary John Volpe insisted that the line sever its ties to Mudge Rose, he supported the loan. However, when congressional opposition developed, the Administration backed down. Representative Wright Patman, the Texas populist who was instrumental in blocking the loan, pointed out that Mudge Rose was also counsel to Investors Diversified Services. The Minneapolis mutual fund was a major Penn-Central stockholder, and, before his election, Nixon was an IDS director.

The next eyebrow raiser was Warner-Lambert's merger with Parke, Davis & Company. Richard McLaren, then head of the Justice Department's antitrust division, urged that the merger be disallowed. The decision went to Mitchell, who disqualified himself because his former firm was counsel in the case. Deputy attorney general Richard Kleindienst thereupon overruled McLaren and let the merger go through. Because of McLaren's continued objections, the case was later shifted to the Federal Trade Commission, and a final judgment is still pending.

And, finally, there was the marked increase in the firm's municipal bond business. Since Nixon's election, Mudge Rose added agencies in Kentucky, Nebraska, New Jersey, West Virginia, Washington, D.C., and the Virgin Islands. It also picked up a $150 million Tennessee Valley Authority bond issue, its first T.V.A. account. Some of the new business was brought in by attorneys hired away from Hawkins, Delafield & Wood, but some of the shifts—especially on the first issues let out by the new Republican administrations in Kentucky and New Jersey— seem to have been politically inspired. Though Mudge Rose's performance is probably no better and no worse than that of other bond-certification specialists, there were many politicians who reasoned that it couldn't hurt to be represented by the former law firm of the President and the Attorney General. As William H. Cannon, the new head of the bond section, put it: "The Democrats had it before, the Republicans have it now. That's the ball game—politics, I guess."

The biggest bond bonus of all was the Postal Service issue. In July, 1971, it was disclosed that Mudge Rose had been named counsel for the Postal Service's first $250 million issue. The fee for the "preliminary" legal work was estimated at $100,000. According to one account, if the firm remained counsel for the entire $10 billion authorized in postal bonds, the fee could run as high as $2.5 million.

One of the eyebrows that arched highest at this news belonged to Morris K. Udall, the Arizona Democrat who headed the House Postal Service Subcommittee. "Surely, somewhere among the 250,000 lawyers in the country, there is someone else who can handle this," he said. "And surely with all its other business, this barefoot firm in New York can survive without this particular multi-million-dollar contract."

Though Mudge Rose was retained not by the Postal Service, but by the underwriters, Udall's subcommittee found that "an appearance of impropriety exists at the very least. . . . [Mudge Rose] should have been excluded from consideration, if only for appearance's sake."

Guthrie continues to insist: "We don't want to get into an atmosphere that's political—we're strictly professional lawyers." He sees lobbying as an area in which the firm has no desire to acquire expertise and he has no intention of making Mudge Rose the firm to see in Washington, D.C.

But the image persists, among both lawyers and laymen. Says one attorney: "You're a client and you've got a problem with the Maritime Commission. You're sitting in Guthrie's office. All he has to do is pick up the phone and call Washington. . . ." It may not be true, but such a reputation can't hurt business. As a younger partner pleaded, "Don't write that we don't have any clout—that would be just as bad."

"Of course, they're political," says a partner in another Wall Street firm. "You can't do a job for your clients unless you use your contacts, pull a few strings and throw your weight around now and then. They may not be political in the same sense as Paul Weiss or Royall Koegel or Covington & Burling, but when you have both the President and the Attorney General come out of the same firm, it can't help but be political. They may say they aren't, they may try not to be, they may bend over backwards so it won't seem like they are—but that's simply recognition of the fact. It's like being Jewish. You can convert and call yourself a Catholic or an Episcopalian, but if people still think of you as Jewish, then you're Jewish. People think of them as a political firm, so they are."

Political or not, there's no question that the firm's business has boomed in the years since Nixon went to the White House.

Mudge Rose expanded to encompass five of the top six floors at 20 Broad Street. Even so, space was so short that the firm's computerized accounting offices and real-estate section had to be housed around the corner. It also maintains offices in Washington—at 1701 Pennsylvania Avenue, a block from the White House—and in Paris. From 105 attorneys when Nixon left, it swelled to 120—40 partners and 80 associates. Despite its successes, there was a general feeling along Wall Street that it may have sacrificed quality for quantity, that its business burgeoned faster than its ability to handle it.

"That's a problem," Guthrie concedes, "and that's one of the reasons we look closely at new business. I dare say, if we had really wanted to, we could have doubled the size of the firm. But there's no particular merit in being big. We just want to do a good job. We're not hungry. We do very well anyway."

The 1968 election may have been good for business, but it presented Mudge Rose with some top-level personnel problems. Of the three name partners left, Rose was already edging into retirement, doing much of his work from his farm in Massachusetts. Guthrie and Alexander remained active.

Among other things, Alexander headed the presidential Task Force on Business Taxation. Though he was a former law partner, he suffered the same fate as others named to head presidential commissions—he was ignored. His report was completed in April, 1970, but not printed until September and not released until December, and then "without comment" from the White House.

Both Guthrie and Alexander are past sixty-five and looking forward to retirement someday. Though the abilities of the remaining partners are not disparaged, none is considered weighty enough to match the array of former judges and Cabinet officers who head Mudge Rose's Wall Street rivals.

There is no question of Nixon's returning to the firm after his White House tenure. "It would be *infra dig*," Guthrie says.*

---

* The only *ex*-President who worked as a Wall Street lawyer was Grover Cleveland, who served as counsel to Davis Polk's predecessor firm between his two administrations.

Nor is Mudge Rose looking for another name, another celebrity from the outside to become Nixon's successor as public partner. That would be playing second-fiddle to a ghost.

Thus, the future lies with the other departed partner. With the 1972 election coming up, Nixon needed someone to manage his reelection campaign. Who better than Mitchell, who so coolly handled the chore in 1968? It was arranged that Mitchell would resign, return to Mudge Rose—not to Wall Street and the bond business, but to the Washington office, one floor above Nixon's campaign headquarters—and run the campaign.

Another factor in Mitchell's return was money. Ever since her arrival in Washington, the tart-tongued Martha Mitchell had been poor-mouthing about how hard it was to make do on the Attorney General's $60,000 salary. With hubby back in private practice, she would have no cause for complaint; Mitchell used to boast that he made more money at the firm than Nixon.

But Mitchell's partial pull-out from politics did not satisfy Martha. After her celebrated flight to the Westchester Country Club and another series of post-midnight telephone calls in which she claimed she was "a political prisoner" of the GOP, Mitchell accepted her ultimatum and resigned as campaign manager—though some political insiders insist his resignation had less to do with domestic crises as with his involvement in bugging the Democratic National Committee's headquarters. He returned—supposedly full-time—to Mudge Rose, but one observer noted, "There were no callers waiting to see him outside, and the telephone remained still."

Nor was Mitchell's return eagerly accepted by some members of the firm. Over the opposition of many juniors, his partnership was "railroaded" through by Guthrie. But, given the touchy political situation, his name did not go back on the shingle, at least not immediately.

Some of the young lawyers undoubtedly felt that cutting Mitchell in for a seven- or eight-point slice of the pie would reduce their own draws. But politics may have also played a part in the process. In 1968, by one partner's estimate, there were as many lawyers from the firm working for various Democratic candidates as Mitchell had recruited to work for Nixon. They may have feared that his return would make the firm too political.

John Mitchell had left the firm in 1969 a virtual unknown. He returned to it a very public personality—and a very political one. With Mitchell doing business a block from the White House, Mudge Rose—or Mudge Mitchell, or Mitchell Mudge —more than ever could be "the firm to see."

8

The Workers Are
the Means of Production

In February, 1968, a notice appeared on the bulletin board in the *Harvard Law Review* office:

> Q. Why do they call it the going rate?
> A. Because if no one else matches it, we are all going to Cravath.

In that month, Cravath, ever playing the pacesetter, hiked the "going rate"—the salary paid to starting associates—from $10,500 to $15,000. For the previous few years, West Coast firms had been outbidding Wall Street and Park Avenue for the law schools' cream-of-the-crop. Almost everyone in the blue-chip bar believed that a raise was overdue, though few were prepared for such a quantum jump. Cravath insisted that the hike was designed not to meet the West Coast competition, only the soaring costs of living in New York. Within a few weeks the other firms followed suit, lest they saw everyone "going to Cravath."

Two years later Cravath raised the going rate to $16,000 and there's talk that it may soon go to $17,500. At the present base, associates can expect automatic raises to $19,000 within two years.

"Most expensive training in the world," snorts Randolph H. Guthrie, of Mudge Rose. "It's too goddamn much to pay them, because they don't know anything."

It may be high, but few who have had the opportunity to scan a law firm's balance sheets would agree that associates are overpaid—at least not in terms of what they produce. Associates are the foot-soldiers of the legal army, the dogfaces who burn the midnight oil doing the dirty work of scouring through the law books and polishing the boilerplate, while their seniors enjoy the luxury of two-hour lunches at the Down Town Association and of catching the 5:15 to Westport or Old Westbury.

A Simon Rifkind may bill at $250 an hour or more, but the lowly associates are the real money-makers of any law firm. An associate is expected to produce 1,600 billable hours a year; his time is billed to the client at anywhere from $40 to $75 an hour. At $50 an hour, one associate's annual exertion produces $80,000 in income, five times his starting salary. By contrast, a partner who produces 1,000 billable hours at $100 an hour brings in $100,000, barely enough to cover his own draw. As one former Paul Weiss associate put it, "The workers not only don't own the means of production—they *are* the means of production."

The apocrypha of legal literature is filled with horror stories about the exhausting hours associates once had to put in. Harrison Tweed's is classic:

"I remember a time shortly after I came to the office [Byrne & Cutcheon], when on a Friday afternoon [senior partner James Byrne] gave me a memo to write on a question of law which seemed to be very difficult. He said, 'I would like to have it at nine o'clock Monday morning' . . . so I went to work.

"On Monday morning, Mr. Byrne sent for me and said, 'Do you have the memo, Tweed?' I said, 'Mr. Byrne, I am sorry, I have not had time to finish it.' He looked at me and said, 'Did you work all day Saturday?' I said, 'Yes.' 'Did you work all day Sunday?' I said, 'Yes.'

"He glared at me and asked, 'What time did you go home on Friday night?' I replied, 'Three o'clock in the morning.' 'What time did you go home Saturday night?' I told him that I had quit at two o'clock in the morning. Then came the final, 'What time did you go home Sunday night?' And I had to confess that I had done so at eleven o'clock.

"He pounded the desk and said: 'Don't tell me that you didn't have time to finish that memorandum. Tell me the truth —that you wanted to go home early Sunday night!' "

Surely such stories have been embellished over the years, and the incidents are certainly funnier in retrospect than they were at the time.

Such herculean labors are also largely a thing of the past, though night and weekend work is still the norm rather than the exception at most firms. Sullivan & Cromwell maintains a midtown hotel suite for associates whose night labors cause them to miss the last train from Grand Central or Penn Station. A few firms still have reputations for being "sweatshops," most notably Cravath and Paul Weiss. According to a former Paul Weiss associate, senior partner Simon Rifkind believes in a "total-immersion" theory—"You'll never be a good lawyer unless you spend five years totally immersed in the law."

David Bazelon, who served briefly at Paul Weiss, recalled "the most grating line" from his years there: On the rare days that he was able to leave the office at the normal hour of five thirty, a colleague would invariably come along with his arms full of papers and ask, "What's wrong—half-day today, Dave?"

But the associates' work-load has fallen greatly throughout the blue-chip bar. As late as five years ago, associates were expected to produce 2,000 billable hours a year. The target is now down to 1,600 and the actual output is even less. According to one survey, an associate in a Wall Street firm averages only 1,493 billable hours. The fall-off is one of the reasons for the recent growth of the blue-chip firms. In a firm with one hundred associates, the difference in output between 2,000 and 1,600 is enough to occupy twenty-five lawyers.

The reduced work-load is only one of the changes of the past decade in the role of associates. They stem largely from the values of the Kennedy and post-Kennedy years. If the Eisenhower Administration marked the era of the "organization man," the years since JFK's Inaugural have been accented by individual idealism, sometimes to the point of anarchy. The change permeated all segments of society and was reflected even in its most conservative profession—the law.

The 1960s saw a turning away by the younger generations from the traditional paths to glory and the time-honored standards for success. "*Ask not what your country can do for you; ask what you can do for your country.*" Thousands responded by entering the Peace Corps, joining the civil rights movement or enlisting in the War on Poverty. Millions more sympathized. By 1970, noted Mark Green, an alumnus who joined Nader's Raiders, Harvard Law School's "legal heroes were neither Arthur Dean nor Dean Acheson, but Ralph Nader and William Kunstler." The brightest graduates of Harvard, Yale, Columbia and other law schools were no longer content to slave eighty hours a week on behalf of U.S. Steel or Standard Oil. If they had to put in such long labors, they preferred to do it for causes they believed in.

By the mid-1960s the blue-chip bar encountered difficulty replenishing its ranks. Even those who came to Wall Street and Park Avenue were no longer willing to sacrifice their private lives and leisure time to the cares and concerns of Kuhn Loeb or Chase Manhattan, no matter what the future financial rewards. They wanted "jam today."

Once again, the blue-chip bar was forced to respond to the temper of the times. The higher going rate—no matter what Cravath's explanation—was one result. So was the cut in working hours and the increase in *pro bono* work, a change caused not so much by the newfound idealism of those at the top of the blue-chip bar as the pressures from below. In some firms associates were even given a voice—if not a vote—in management.

The change showed most clearly in the patterns of recruitment. In the past, the law factories had been content to sit back and wait until the law school graduates came down from Cambridge, New Haven and Morningside Heights, introductory letters in hand, and made the rounds of the Wall Street offices. Now virtually every firm has a hiring partner (or hiring committee), much of whose time is devoted to seeking out and seducing new associates. Each year they make the round of campuses—usually in tandem with an associate who is a recent alumnus of whatever school they're visiting—to state the case for Cadwalader, Chadbourne or Cravath.

The prospects are wined and dined and tempted with all the wiles of the legal Delilahs. A Merrill Lynch report noted the case of "a businessman who recently invited his lawyer for lunch [and] was turned down because the lawyer was taking the client's son to lunch. The son, a second-year law student at Columbia who was *magna cum laude* at Harvard, worked for the lawyer this summer and was 'more important.' "

Second-year students are lured to the law offices for jobs as summer interns in the hope that they'll be impressed enough to return permanently after graduation. But summer internship is a two-edged sword, since the interns return to campus and feed the student grapevine with tidbits of information that make up the word-of-mouth mosaic about which firms rank high and which low.

Currently, Cleary Gottlieb and Paul Weiss (despite its reputation as a "sweatshop") rank high because they're liberal in politics, relaxed in atmosphere and active in *pro bono* work. Equally important is the fact that both firms are expanding. Whether a firm is going up or down or standing still is always an important consideration in where to apply; an expanding firm has more openings for partners.

Sometimes a firm can pull gaffes in its recruitment effort. Kaye Scholer once turned off many Columbia students—

including law review editors—when it advertised "law review only." And Randolph Guthrie didn't help Mudge Rose's cause when he touted prospects on the opportunity of socializing with Martha Mitchell.

In its talent search the blue-chip bar is also casting further afield. A decade ago the nets were spread little beyond Harvard, Yale and Columbia and, in the case of some "white-shoe" firms, Virginia. Now hiring partners regularly probe the talent pools at N.Y.U., Georgetown, Cornell, Chicago, Stanford and such state schools as Michigan, Wisconsin and California. However, graduates of "local" law schools such as Brooklyn Law and St. John's are still scorned.

"We're now interviewing all over the country," says Cyrus Vance, of Simpson Thacher & Bartlett. "We're getting associates from all over the country. We never did in the past tap these sources of talent. Now all the big law firms do this."

They've also changed their pitch. "When you interview now," says a recent Fordham Law graduate, "instead of telling you about the firm teas and how long it takes to make partner, they tell you about their *pro bono* projects."

The stress on *pro bono* work, of course, is part of the blue-chip bar's response to changing conditions. Its continued emphasis may be a sign of its slowness in gauging the changes. Another shift in student attitudes is clearly in the making.

The idealism of the 1960s is fading. A generation which witnessed the death of its dreams in the murders of Martin Luther King and Robert Kennedy, which suffered the savage repression of Chicago and Kent State, which saw the peace movement fade into feebleness while the war still raged, which found the dream of Woodstock transformed into the nightmare of Altamont—such a generation no longer took up the cudgels for the cause . . . any cause.

Also, as the job market in industry and education tightened, law school enrollment swelled—from 41,499 in 1961 to 94,469 in 1971. Applications to law schools grew even faster: Harvard Law gets 8,000 a year for 500 openings. Throughout the 1970s, according to the Bureau of Labor Statistics, the nation's law schools will be graduating twice as many attorneys as there will be openings for them.

How this will affect the blue-chip bar's patterns of recruitment remains to be seen. Certainly, they'll be more able to pick and choose, culling the cream-of-the-crop and further enhancing their position at the peak of the Legal Establishment.

The effects are already showing in the law schools. Mark Green, the "Nader Raider" who hailed the dedication of 1970's law school students, observed sadly two years later: "The tide of change now seems only a trickle, and the longevity of law student activism has equaled that of the Nehru jacket . . . most [law school graduates] still go to work for corporate law firms when that moment of career decision arrives. They talk like Danny the Red but go the way of Oliver Barrett IV."

In 1921, John J. McCloy graduated from Harvard Law and returned to his native Philadelphia to find a job. His problem was that he'd grown up on the wrong side of the Main Line.

"The Establishment wouldn't take me," he recalls from the perspective of more than fifty years. "My mother's hero was George Wharton Pepper [the archetype of the "Philadelphia lawyer"]. When I tried to get a job, I was advised by Mr. Pepper that he thought it was pretty difficult to break into the law in Philadelphia, that it was a 'family town,' a 'closed corporation.'

"I didn't get an offer in Philadelphia. So I went down to the old Market Street station and took the first train to New York. All I had to do was tell them what my grades were and I had offers from the best firms in New York City."

Boston and Philadelphia law firms have always been more "social" than those in New York. But Wall Street was not without its own restrictions.

"It did not take me many days to discover that the doors of most New York law offices in 1899 were closed, with rare exceptions, to a young Jewish lawyer," Joseph M. Proskauer recalled in his memoirs. "Fifty years have elapsed since then and I am happy to record that there has been a distinct improvement in the situation."

Even though 60 per cent of the lawyers in New York are Jewish, throughout most of the century the blue-chip bar has been a WASP enclave. Occasionally a Jewish name would pop up on the rosters of partners—Leo Gottlieb at what was then Root Clark; Eustace Seligman at Sullivan & Cromwell and Edwin Weisl at Simpson Thacher & Bartlett. But by and large the Wall Street law offices were as "restricted" as their senior partners' country clubs. The city's bar was rigidly segregated into "Jewish" and "gentile" firms. Jewish graduates of Harvard, Yale or Columbia law schools might be accepted as associates in the gentile firms, but almost never promoted to partnership.

A Kaye Scholer partner recalls: "A partner at Davis Polk would come to Ben Kaye and say, 'There's a first-class associate in our firm who I think should be a partner, but my partners don't agree with me. His name is so-and-so. Why don't you give him a call?' Half-a-dozen of our partners in the forties came from the big downtown firms."

"We benefited for years from anti-Semitism," says a senior partner at another Jewish firm. "We couldn't get a better recommendation for a man than that he'd been turned down solely because of anti-Semitism. We kind of regret the absence of it now."

The racial and religious barriers erected by the blue-chip bar fell in the postwar decades. The action salved the conscience, polished the image and benefited business, especially so since Jewish firms like Kaye Scholer and mixed firms like Paul Weiss were attracting clients that once gravitated to Wall Street's gentile law factories.

"Our clients include a large number of corporations that ten or fifteen years ago wouldn't have come to a Jewish firm," says a Kaye Scholer partner.

So Jews became partners and . . . and nothing happened. The old excuse evaporated—that clients wouldn't confide in a Jewish lawyer. It turned out that corporate clients couldn't care less if their counsel was named Pincus or Pinkney, as long as they got good service.

In 1964, the *Yale Law Journal*, at the behest of the Anti-Defamation League of B'nai B'rith, prepared a study of discrimination in the New York Bar. Among its findings:

> The Jewish law graduate still faces significant employment discrimination, but far less than he would have a generation or even a decade ago....
>
> Religion was of little relevance to the job-hunting success of those at the very top of their class....
>
> Client prejudice was a marginal consideration at most, and a rapidly disappearing one....
>
> The opinion was unanimous that straight-forward prejudice has been on the wane for years and will continue to decline in importance.

The prediction was borne out, so much so that in the eight years since the ADL has not found the subject worthy of further scrutiny.

The change struck hardest at the Jewish firms, which saw the graduates they once attracted going to the previously prejudiced gentile law factories—and staying there. To remain competitive, they had to achieve a modicum of racial balance by recruiting gentile lawyers. It wasn't easy. As the Yale study noted: "Once a firm becomes known as 'Jewish,' almost all of the gentiles and many of the Jews will not apply to it for work."

Alan Stroock recalls a few years back when a blond, Nordic-looking Harvard Law graduate with a name like "Squires" applied at Stroock & Stroock & Lavan: "His credentials were perfect. The interview was ideal. We wanted him and he wanted us. I kept thinking to myself, 'Our first Christian!' As he was getting up to leave, he said, 'There's just one thing, Mr. Stroock—I'll need two days off at Rosh Hashona.'"

Since then, Stroock & Stroock & Lavan, like most Jewish firms, has acquired several gentile associates and partners. There has been a tendency for Jewish firms to bring in gentile

politicians in recent years: William vanden Heuvel at Stroock;
Paul Curran at Kaye Scholer; former Police Commissioner
Vincent Broderick (temporarily) at Phillips Nizer; Senator
Goodell at Roth, Carlson, Kwit, Spengler & Goodell; and for-
mer Nassau County Executive Eugene Nickerson at what is
now Nickerson, Kramer, Lowenstein, Nessen & Kamin.

Jews, of course, were not the only victims of the bar's discrimination. Vanden Heuvel, a Donovan Leisure associate in
the 1950s, remembers "Wild Bill" Donovan's "telling me that
one of the reasons he founded his own firm was the prejudice
against Catholics that he encountered among the Wall Street
firms."

Although the barriers against Catholics fell long before
those against Jews, the percentage of Irish and especially Ital-
ians in the blue-chip bar has remained miniscule, primarily
because the products of parochial-school education receive little impetus to attend the first-rate "national" law schools. One
Italian lawyer (who works for the city) insists that St. John's
in Brooklyn is "better" than Harvard Law. But until it is—or
until Wall Street *thinks* it is—the blue-chip bar will continue
to be "prejudiced."

The *Yale Law Journal* originally planned to probe all racial
and religious discrimination in the New York bar. It sent ques-
tionnaires to six hundred Yale Law graduates from 1951 to
1960 who had worked in New York. But "there were no Ne-
groes and too few Catholics among the respondents to make
meaningful comparisons possible."

For blacks and Puerto Ricans the old pattern of exclusion is
now reversed. Virtually every major firm is actively trying to
recruit at least one "token" minority member. But the pool is
too small, and the few blacks and Puerto Ricans who hold law
degrees show little inclination toward corporate practice. As
far as can be determined, there is only one Puerto Rican partner in a blue-chip firm—Congressman Herman Badillo at
Stroock. And only one black—Amalya Lyle Kearse at Hughes,
Hubbard & Reed. (She's also the first black—of either sex—to
win a national bridge championship.) "She's not here because
she's black," said the firm's senior partner, Orville H. Schell, Jr.

"She's not here because she's a woman. Amalya is in this firm because she's good."

The hottest campaign on the discrimination front in the law involves not Jews or Catholics, blacks or Puerto Ricans, but women. In 1971, nine women law students and recent graduates of Columbia and N.Y.U. filed a sex-discrimination complaint with the city's Commission on Human Rights against ten law firms, including such pillars of the Legal Establishment as Cravath, Shearman & Sterling, Sullivan & Cromwell and Winthrop Stimson. At the same time, the commission announced that it would investigate forty-five other firms to determine if a general pattern of sex discrimination existed.

Of the 3,926 lawyers listed in the fifty-five firms, 161 were women; of the 1,409 partners, nine were women. According to the complainants, the discrepancy was not accidental. Diana Blank charged:

> Some firms refuse to grant interviews to some of the highest ranked women in the class while seeing and hiring men with lesser qualifications.
>
> If the firms do agree to interview women, most of the questions asked stress plans for marriage and babies rather than professional capabilities and dwell on the drawbacks of being a woman lawyer.
>
> If job offers are made to women, many firms impose the condition of agreeing to work in "women's areas" of law such as wills and estate planning or "blue sky" work.

One of the group reported that she was told by Shea, Gallop, Climenko & Gould—a political firm highly favored by those dealing with city agencies—"We'd hire you right away, Mrs. B——, if you weren't a woman." Roth Carlson allegedly told one applicant they "did not hire women lawyers, because they would go off and get married"; Senator Goodell lamely replied that he was in favor of women's lib.

All the firms denied the charges, yet to be adjudicated. A spokesman for Cravath called them "utterly unfounded and based on a complete lack of understanding of the facts."

Curiously, when the Human Rights Commission heard a sex-discrimination complaint against Citibank, the defense was headed by Richard Troy of Shearman & Sterling—itself one of the subjects of a pending sex-discrimination complaint. One spectator called it "a case of the pot calling the kettle white."

According to the Bureau of Labor Statistics, only about 3 per cent of the 270,000 lawyers in the United States are women. But their ranks are swelling and feminist pressure is bound to grow. According to estimates, women constitute about 10 per cent of the law school class of 1974, and the percentage can be expected to increase even more in subsequent years. At N.Y.U., one of the more militant schools, women already constitute nearly a quarter of the law school's enrollment.

Some firms accused of sex discrimination have been barred from recruiting at several campuses. Michigan, for example, barred Royall Koegel—one of the ten defendants in the New York action, with only one woman associate among its ninety-five lawyers.

After a year-long investigation, the Human Rights Commission issued its findings of the first firm studied—Royall Koegel. It found a "pattern and practice" of discriminatory recruitment, hiring, promotion and treatment of women attorneys. Its report read:

> Almost without exception [Royall Koegel] has rejected women applicants for permanent and summer employment although women with qualifications equal to and better than the male applicants have applied.
>
> [Royall Koegel] has failed to advance women to partnerships although men with equal or inferior tenure and experience to the women have been so promoted.
>
> [Royall Koegel's] interviews are conducted in such a manner as to express a preference for men and to discourage women.
>
> [Royall Koegel], since 1965, has restricted its female representation to one division, trusts and estates.
>
> [Royall Koegel] pays the initiation fees of several part-

ners in a club that excludes women [The Sky Club atop the Pan Am Building].

Privately, a partner at one Wall Street firm admits that his firm—like most—was reluctant to take women. "It's because of the clients. We had some Japanese clients who came to the office and we assigned a woman associate as part of the team to work with them. They came back to us and said, 'Very sorry, we do not want women lawyers.' "

Another Wall Street lawyer agreed: "A client is willing to be coddled by a lady nurse, but he will not want to be told what to do by a lady lawyer. I think this will break down in the next five or six years. It's breaking down now."

So the old stereotype of the WASP Wall Street lawyer is changing. "The best thing to be today," says one highly placed partner, "is a black, a woman, and on a law review, and you can write your own ticket with any law firm in the United States—north of the Mason-Dixon Line."

The legendary turn-of-the-century lawyer Walter S. Carter —"collector of young masters and progenitor of many law firms," in Otto Koegel's phrase—was the first to recruit top graduates of the best law schools to serve as what were then called "law clerks." But "Carter's kids" lasted only a year or two before they went off on their own.

It took Paul Cravath, a "Carter kid" himself, to institutionalize the process, while Emory Buckner gave the "kids" the name "associates." Under the Cravath system—adopted by virtually every other firm—the associate's apprenticeship initially lasted about ten years. It is a time of testing, to determine if he possesses those intangible qualities that produce a partner. The moment of truth, when the associate is tapped for partnership, may be the most traumatic event in a lawyer's career, leading, as Louis Auchincloss observed, to "a life-time of anticlimax." But only one in five completes the course.

First, the successful candidate has to show that he can handle the work. Surprisingly, some of the brightest law school graduates can't "hack it" in the big-time bar. "It's the lack of ability to come to a decision," says an associate at Breed, Abbott & Morgan. "Often there's no clear-cut answer to a problem, but you have to resolve it the best you can. We had one guy who could never decide anything. It was always, 'on the one hand, this . . . on the other hand, that.' He couldn't decide whether to sign a letter personally or with the firm name, whether it should be 'yours truly' or 'sincerely yours.' "

Second, the associate must be able to get along with clients. "That's the primary concern of the firm," the associate continues, "how clients react to a man. Another type of personality problem is the guy who is thoroughly knowledgeable, but who lacks the ability to inspire confidence in his judgments. A fellow who lacks confidence is socially effete."

Yet the converse qualities can be equally dangerous, because they irk the associate's seniors. "Super-achievers are not made partners," the associate explains. "But they go on to make good elsewhere. It's because of the firm's unwillingness to take in a guy who moves too fast. They don't want to rock the boat."

A senior partner at another Wall Street firm agrees: "The most important thing is how well clients respond to a man. We're very concerned about the playback of clients and we're also concerned very much about internal relations."

Perhaps the easiest way for an associate to move up the ladder rapidly is to have a "rabbi," a senior partner who takes the newcomer under his wing, gives him important assignments and promotes his cause in the partners' councils. In firms without antinepotism rules, the "rabbi" is often the associate's father, uncle or in-law. Where there's no blood-tie, there's the mysterious chemistry of personality. The process can continue long after the junior has achieved his partnership.

At Sullivan & Cromwell, John Foster Dulles was Arthur Dean's "rabbi." Whitney North Seymour, Sr., now senior partner at Simpson Thacher & Bartlett, started as the protégé of

Thomas Thacher. At Webster Sheffield, "Beth" Webster, who sired only daughters, found a surrogate son in John Lindsay.

The career of Cyrus Vance is even more illustrative. Edwin L. Weisl, Sr., served as his "rabbi" at Simpson Thacher & Bartlett. When Weisl, who had cultivated a friendship with Lyndon Johnson during the New Deal days, was named counsel to the Senate Preparedness Committee which Johnson formed in the post-Sputnik backlash, he brought Vance along as his assistant. The Weisl–Johnson combination promoted Vance to general counsel of the Army in the Kennedy Administration. When Johnson became President, Vance was named Deputy Defense Secretary, and he went on to serve as LBJ's troubleshooter in Korea and Cyprus and as Averell Harriman's second-in-command at the Paris peace talks. As a result, he returned to the firm in 1969 a very commanding public figure.

Finally, there's the element of luck. A new associate may have the ill-fortune to get assigned to doing routine research or to a dead-end case where he never gets a chance to demonstrate his abilities and attract the attention of an influential partner. He may get caught up in a mammoth antitrust action only to find that the firm has no place for him once the case is concluded. Or he may join a firm that suddenly loses a major client and enters into a period of retrenchment or decline.

The process of promotion and weeding-out is seldom direct. The associate who won't be promoted to partner isn't called into a senior's office and told, "Jones, you're not going to make it here at Wickerwalder." Instead of telling the lawyer to look elsewhere, the senior partners will slip the word to smaller firms or to client corporations that there's a young lawyer available and to make him an offer.

Subtle hints will be dropped at the office. The unsuccessful associate will be shifted to routine assignments and housed in an out-of-the-way office. When Simpson Thacher & Bartlett was at 120 Broadway, the associates who were moving up got assigned to an office overlooking the street, while those who were not wound up on the airshaft and the word would spread through the firm, "——got the shaft."

The most dramatic hint is in the paycheck. "At the end of the third year," one lawyer explains, "you can go from nineteen thousand dollars to twenty-five thousand. That's a sure sign that you're doing well. Or you can go from nineteen to nineteen, which is the message that you've got to look elsewhere."

"When a firm decides that a man should not be a partner, he already knows it," another lawyer says. "There's a mutuality in that decision."

But sometimes there's no message, especially for the associate nearing the end of his apprenticeship. The limbo when a man is neither washed out nor promoted can be excruciating.

In such cases, he can leave. The associate at Breed, Abbott & Morgan observed that no new partners had been made since 1968 and saw no prospect of there being any in the immediate future. He left for a smaller midtown firm that promised him a partnership within two years.

He can wait . . . and hope. Orison S. Marden, later president of the New York City, New York State and American bar associations, joined White & Case as an associate in 1929, but wasn't promoted to partner until 1946.

Or he can wait without hope. The "failures who stay" are the permanent associates, men who have mastered a narrow specialty, who are too expert to replace, but who lack the prerequisites of partnership and the ambition to strike out on their own. For some reason, most of the permanent associates seem to be Irish. Perhaps it's because of the racial and religious prejudices that once pervaded most Wall Street firms. Perhaps it's because of the bureaucratic nature of the breed—men who seek security and who are satisfied to remain in a routine, repetitive job.

In its 1964 firm history, Shearman & Sterling lists thirteen permanent associates, men who "have been with us for a long time, and they have been, and are, invaluable to us in bringing to the firm special qualifications and competencies. They are experts, 'specialists' in their particular fields." It's the sort of condescending language a southern matron might use to describe the colored servants.

Permanent associates are a dying breed. They are being phased out by attrition at most firms, because they are models of failure who disrupt a law office's social structure. "The new associates never say 'hello' to them," one lawyer says. "It's very difficult for an associate to work with them. Their feeling is, 'If they can't help themselves, they can't help me.' "

They tend to be looked down upon—or overlooked—by both partners and new associates. At one firm there is a permanent associate who handles labor relations. According to a senior partner, "At the time he should have been made partner, he lacked the social and scholastic credentials, having gone to Fordham and having a rough style." That wouldn't bar him today, but, "Now they know he won't leave."

On one occasion when a senior associate left the firm, there was a good-bye party for him at the office. During the revelry, a partner clapped another associate on the back, "Now you're the senior associate here."

"No, there's ——," the lawyer replied, naming the permanent associate.

The partner snapped: "I'm not talking about the fixtures on the wall."

Some associates find that the regimented life of the law factory is not for them, and depart for smaller firms, for academe, for business or government. Some never had any intention of staying; they became associates at Cravath or Sullivan & Cromwell as part of their training, like taking postgraduate courses, or to acquire assets when they apply elsewhere.

"If you felt that way about the firm, why did you come here in the first place?" an associate in Louis Auchincloss' *Powers of Attorney* is asked.

He replies: "For the resale, my friend, for the resale."

The institutionalization of the blue-chip bar has affected associates in several ways. The period of apprenticeship has shrunk from ten to about seven years. The cut reflects the associates' other years of apprenticeship—the Army, graduate studies, judicial clerkships and government service. Even more, it's a reaction to the unwillingness of 1970s' law graduates to remain underlings until they're thirty-five or forty.

Selection and promotion have become less haphazard. In the past, firms sometimes hired a lawyer whose grades didn't measure up to standard on the hunch that he might be a "sleeper." If he didn't work out, he could always be let go in a year or two. With starting salaries at $16,000, few firms are willing to take such chances today.

Similarly, decisions as to whether or not to promote an associate were often made on the whim or word of one or two partners. Now formalized review procedures are the rule at virtually every firm. One of the most elaborate is at Kaye Scholer. "I felt," says managing partner Frederick Livingston, "that if I'm going to specialize in labor relations for clients, we ought to have good labor relations here at Kaye Scholer. So we established a personnel committee.

"We closet ourselves in a hotel suite for two days and review every associate at the end of the year. For the man's first two years, it's a semiannual review. Then we call in the person for an interview. We tell him our evaluation—what he's doing right, what he's doing wrong, what he can do to improve himself. The office manager does the same thing for the nonlegal personnel. It's a very time-consuming process, but we think it's very worthwhile."

The number of associates at every firm would be even greater were it not for the recent introduction of "executive assistants," "legal assistants," "paralegals," "paraprofessionals" —each firm has its own term for them. Most lawyers flippantly refer to them as "paratroops."

They don't drop out of the sky—they come from Smith, Vassar and Radcliffe. Their function is in flux and each firm is feeling its way finding uses for them. Basically, they function like *Time* researchers, taking over many of the nonlegal chores otherwise handled by junior associates. So far, their numbers are small—from five to a dozen at each firm.

"It's an elevated nothing," says Miss S——, who worked as a

paratroop at Simpson Thacher & Bartlett. "We're paid less than a beginning secretary"—$125 a week, as opposed to a legal secretary's $145. "There's nowhere to go. It's for girls right out of college who don't know what to do. Some of them plan to go to law school. An awful lot of the girls went in with the intention of meeting some handsome attorney."

But so far no office romances have developed for Miss S——'s fellow paratroops—other than an incompleted pass at the water-cooler. The resisting paratroop was transferred to another department. "They [the lawyers] lead very protective lives and if they're going to fool around, they're smart enough to fool around outside the office," she notes.

As for the work, "It's a lot of garbage"—compiling the bound-volumes, the permanent collection of documents in each case; digesting testimony; culling through corporate files for relevant documents—"nothing that requires great talent. If we're doing nothing, we're sent to accounting or proof-reading."

The use of paratroops is bound to increase—if only for economic reasons. Better to pay a girl $125 a week than a lawyer $500. And it frees the associate for the legal work he was trained to do.

9

A Lot Goes on
Behind Closed Doors

A sociologist, as James T. Farrell once observed, is a man who spends $50,000 of an institution's good money to find the location of a whore-house. To produce a book called *Lawyers' Ethics*, a sociologist named Jerome Carlin spent a lot of the Russell Sage Foundation's good money to tell us that a lot of New York lawyers are shysters.

He tells us who they are—not by name, but by sociological stratification. The shyster is most likely to be a "lower-echelon lawyer," Jewish, of lower-class origin, a graduate of a low-ranked school, an individual practitioner or in a small firm, and with lower-class clients.

By contrast, Carlin continues, the "elite" lawyer—most likely a WASP in a large firm with blue-chip clients—is "the best-trained, most technically skilled and ethically most responsible." Carlin's findings were based on interviews with 801 private practitioners selected roughly at random in Manhattan and the Bronx.

The same pattern prevails in the records of the Grievance Committee of the Association of the Bar of the City of New York, the official arm of the Appellate Division for investigating lawyers' misconduct. In 1970–71, the committee received 2,215 complaints against approximately 1,800 lawyers, almost all of them small practitioners.* Except for volume—up about 10 per cent a year each year since World War II—the pattern did not differ from that of the past.

But the figures do not answer the question: Is the blue-chip bar really any more ethical than the street-corner practitioner?

John Bonomi, the tough, former Kefauver Committee counsel who heads the Grievance Committee's staff, stresses that the figures indicate only that the blue-chip lawyer—because of his kind of practice—is less likely to get caught. "There may be a lot of unethical conduct that goes on behind closed doors that we don't know about." He adds that the only way to uncover it would be to filch files or tap telephones. "The cure might be worse than the disease."

Even Carlin, who generally lauds the ethics of the blue-chip bar, issues his own caveat: The blue-chip lawyer may appear more ethical because he can buck the dirty work to someone else. He notes one lawyer's comment: "I've been shocked by members of the large firms who bring clients here and suggest I should fix this thing—talk to the cops or the judge. It's these 'respectables' who suggest that we go in and try to put in the fix. . . ."

The figures may also reflect the built-in bias of the blue-chip

---

* The disposition of these cases illustrates the near immunity attorneys enjoy. Of the 2,215 complaints, 810 did not allege misconduct, while most of the remaining 1,405 were settled by notifying the lawer and letting him mollify his client. The committee took action on 266 complaints against 239 lawyers; of these, 184 were sent a "letter admonition," 8 referred directly to the Appellate Division for disciplinary action, hearings held on 47; of these, 19 were admonished, 16 recommended for disciplinary action by the court, 7 dismissed, 5 pending. Of the 52 cases prosecuted in court, 6 attorneys were disbarred, 10 suspended for varying periods, 2 censured, 1 dismissed, 33 pending. Yet the New York Grievance Committee is the most vigorous in the nation, with a disbarment rate three times the national average! As a recent American Bar Association study noted, it "processes the great majority of disciplinary matters in a highly efficient manner with a professional staff, formulated procedures, progressive policy and adequate financing."

bar. The Association of the Bar of the City of New York *is* New York's Legal Establishment and its Grievance Committee is more likely to get tough with those it considers "shysters" than with backsliders of its own ilk. The committee is well aware of this. In 1967, then-chairman William Piel, Jr., noted that he had tried to broaden "the base of committee membership by including more single practitioners, members of small and medium-sized firms and lawyers engaged in public service." But few lawyers outside the large law factories have time to spare for the arduous Grievance Committee service. Significantly, Piel himself is a partner at Sullivan & Cromwell.

The belief that there is a double standard of discipline in the bar is widespread—and with good reason. Consider these two statements:

1. There are so few trial judges who just judge . . . who rule on questions of law and leave guilt or innocence to the jury. And Appellate Division judges aren't any better. They're the whores who've become madams. . . .

I would like to [become a judge]—just to see if I could be the kind of judge I think a judge should be. But the only way you can get it is to be in politics or buy it—and I don't even know the going price.

2. I shudder to think what a Martian astronaut . . . would think of our courts and what goes on, or does not go on, in them. As to the judges, what would he think of certain of them, in theory elected by the public but in fact hand-picked by political leaders for purely political purposes irrelevant to merit?

The language of the first may be more vivid, but their import is the same. The first was made by Martin Erdman, a Legal Aid Society lawyer who works in Manhattan's Criminal Courts Building. As a consequence, he was censured by the Appellate Division. The second was made by Francis T. P. Plimpton, then president of the Bar Association, at the association's Centennial Convocation. Naturally, no action was taken against him.

It's just the double standard. As Joseph Borkin defined it in *The Corrupt Judge*:

> . . . the selective application of the Canons, with one code for the Brahmins of the law and another for its lesser servants, with a soft impeachment for knavery on the grand scale and a swift, harsh discipline for the fumblings of the petty shyster.

Or, as one lawyer says, "John Foster Dulles got away with things another lawyer would have been disbarred for." Unfortunately, he did not elaborate.

Almost any lawyer can relate one horror story from personal experience. A New York City commissioner tells of an incident from his days in private practice, a case involving a partner at one of Wall Street's largest and most respected firms—"one of those Social Register WASPs with numerals after his name." In a matrimonial dispute, the Wall Street lawyer had advised his client, the scion of a wealthy Texas family, "to get out of town to avoid service." Advising a client to flee the court's jursidiction is a breach of the canons.

"If certain guys had done that whose families hadn't come over on the Mayflower, I know what they'd be accused of," the commissioner says. "To me, something like that from a guy who's a leader of the bar was unforgiveable. I've never forgotten it."

But few who tell such tales are willing to back them up, to allow the use of their own names or to supply a sworn affidavit that enables us to identify those they talk about. Fewer still file a formal complaint with the courts or the Grievance Committee. As a result, we're left with little more than rumor, gossip and innuendo.

That's why the case of *U.S.* v. *Greater Blouse Assn.* is so interesting. It provides a rare glimpse of what goes on behind the closed doors of the Legal Establishment, a peek at a bit of legal maneuvering that may seem trivial to the layman and—

most important—a look at the way the blue-chip bar blinks its eyes at the possible failings of its own.

U.S. v. *Greater Blouse* was an antitrust action. In 1959, the Justice Department filed suit against women's apparel contractors' associations in New York and Pennsylvania, a local of the International Ladies Garment Workers Union and some of the corporate and union officers, charging conspiracy to fix prices and restrict trade. Five years later, the government came into court and said that, after reviewing the evidence, it doubted that it could prove the case "beyond a reasonable doubt," and moved to dismiss the indictment.

In a surprising turnabout, one of the defendants—the Slate Belt Contractors Association of Eastern Pennsylvania—objected. Its attorney, John W. Castles 3d, of Lord, Day & Lord, explained why:

"It was Slate Belt that was victimized by the criminal conduct which is alleged in this indictment. . . . During the four- or five-year period—almost five years now since this indictment has been pending—there has been no price-fixing in the blouse industry, nobody has been telling Slate's people who they must sell to and who they must not sell to. . . . The threat to Slate Belt from the government's sudden decision to abandon its grand jury action is very serious. Slate Belt is faced with the reimposition of this system."

Judge Edward Weinfeld reserved decision. After the hearing, Castles returned to his office on Lower Broadway and conferred with Lord, Day & Lord's senior partner, Herbert Brownell, who had been the Attorney General when the Greater Blouse investigation started. Brownell decided to secure support for Slate Belt's position that the prosecution should be continued from three attorneys who had worked under him at Justice on the case.

First he called Robert A. Bicks, the former assistant attorney general in charge of the Antitrust Division who had become the rising star at Breed, Abbott & Morgan. Bicks agreed to file the affidavit Brownell requested. Next Brownell called Ronald

S. Daniels, one of the two trial attorneys originally assigned to the case. Daniels, then with the midtown firm of Townley, Updike, Carter & Rogers, also agreed, and went downtown to Lord, Day & Lord's office to help Brownell line up the third attorney—Lawrence Gochberg, then in private practice in Stamford, Connecticut.

Daniels phoned Gochberg and introduced Castles. As Gochberg recalled it, Castles asked him "to furnish him with an affidavit" stating that "at the time of the indictment in this case there was sufficient evidence to support the allegations of that indictment" and that "Slate Belt had cooperated with the government during the investigation. . . ." Brownell later came on the line and confirmed the request, adding that "he could see no impropriety in my [Gochberg's] fulfilling it."

But Gochberg, it seems, had more than a lawyer's usual sense of caution. He put three conditions on his cooperation— first, that he get an okay from John J. Galgay, head of the Antitrust Division's New York office; second, that Brownell put his request in writing; third, that Daniels get an opinion from the Bar Association.

That evening, Gochberg called Galgay at his home in suburban Hartsdale. "Galgay made it crystal clear that whether or not I gave such an affidavit was entirely my responsibility," he said.

Four days later, Gochberg continued, "Galgay in open court, in effect, confirmed my conversation with him. He stated that the only objection the government had to my affidavit, as well as the affidavits of [Bicks and Daniels], was that the affidavits were irrelevant." Meanwhile, Brownell sent the letter:

> As a former government official, I understand your reluctance to become involved in this matter. However, I believe that you owe a duty to the court as well as to my client, which cooperated with you during the investigation, to bring certain facts to the court's attention at this time.
>
> I have reviewed the affidavit which you intend to give and I am convinced that it is in no wise improper.

Daniels, as requested, called Thomas Ramseur, Jr., a partner of White & Case who was a member of the Bar Association's Committee on Professional Ethics (which renders advisory opinions), and got the green light to go ahead.

The affidavits were filed. But three weeks later, during a conference in chambers, Judge Weinfeld "questioned the[ir] propriety," since their subject matter was "obviously based upon information and knowledge derived by each attorney during his service as an attorney of the Department of Justice."

In another turnabout, the government now objected to submission of the affidavits, contending that the information in them was "confidential and privileged."

Meanwhile, Ramseur informed Ralph Colin, chairman of the Ethics Committee, of the advisory opinion he had rendered. Colin was aghast. "I informed Mr. Ramseur," he wrote Judge Weinfeld, "that I seriously questioned the correctness of the views which had been expressed by him to Mr. Daniels and seriously questioned whether Mr. Daniels should have supplied the affidavits to the defendants in the action."

Colin suggested that the Ethics Committee file an *amicus curiae* brief supporting the government's contention that the affidavits violated client-counsel privilege. Judge Weinfeld replied that "while the Court makes no request for a brief . . . any brief which the committee desires to submit will be received."

Lord, Day & Lord—at this point acting less as counsel for Slate Belt than as counsel for itself—objected to intervention by the Ethics Committee while the motion was pending. And the Bar Association's Executive Committee voted to bar the Ethics Committee from filing the brief. At the time, Herbert Brownell was president of the Bar Association.

The association's official explanation was that it would be a "departure from the established practice of the association" to file an *amicus curiae* brief without a formal request for one. In protest, Colin resigned as chairman of the Ethics Committee. "I believe in following precedent," he said, "but not blindly."

In his decision allowing the government to drop the prosecution, Judge Weinfeld said:

The submission of these affidavits by former attorneys of the Department of Justice, used in opposition to the government's motion, raises a serious and substantial question of propriety. However, it is unnecessary to decide the question, since the issue presented by this motion is the current status of the matter, not its status upon the return of the indictment, and on this issue the affidavits are without relevancy.

We'll leave it to grammarians to parse the subject of the first sentence and determine if the judge's question was directed at those who supplied the affidavits or those who filed them, or both.

Judge Weinfeld pointedly filed all the correspondence concerning the affidavits in the court record—thus providing a fully documented account of how the blue-chip bar protects its own. Brownell and his former assistants escaped without inquiry, leaving only an unanswered question in an unpublicized case.

We shouldn't find it surprising to find the blue-chip bar engaged in such shaving of the corners of the canons. After all, Brownell insisted that he did nothing wrong and at least one member of the Ethics Committee agreed with him. What is shocking is to find the blue-chip bar engaged in outright corruption—Louis Levy's "loan" to Judge Manton or Hoyt Moore's admitted bribery on behalf of Bethlehem Steel.

It can be argued that both cases were products of another era, a period when both business and the bar were more free-wheeling, more attuned to the spirit of laissez faire and the-public-be-damned, less likely to be deterred by outside scrutiny or internal inhibitions.

John Bonomi insists that a Moore case today would not escape the Grievance Committee's scrutiny. And David Dorsen, New York City's Deputy Commissioner of Investigations, doubts that such conduct could escape notice in today's moral climate.

"In the old days," Dorsen notes, "a partner could count on an associate to keep his mouth shut. But now the Nader influence is making itself felt. Now they've got to keep it to themselves—which is very hard—or else do it straight."

Perhaps so. But it didn't deter Ben Javits in the most flagrant case of corruption to strike the blue-chip bar in years.

Benjamin A. Javits was born in 1894, the son of an immigrant janitor on the Lower East Side. By the time his brother Jacob, ten years younger, came of age, Ben was the force in the family, going to law school at night, working by day as a bill collector. He made enough money to move the family out of the slums, first to Brooklyn, then to the Upper West Side.

"Ben was utterly relentless in his determination that both of them were going to make it big," said one observer. "Ben gave Jack the drive. He gave him the objectives, the ambition and the conviction that he could really be somebody. If Jack is Cinderella, then Ben is the fairy godmother."

When Jack finished law school in 1927, he joined Ben in the partnership of Javits & Javits on Lower Broadway. Their specialty was corporate reorganization, a highly profitable field in the depression years. After serving in World War II, Jack got involved in Republican politics and was elected to Congress in 1946. Through the years the firm prospered. By 1954, when Jack was elected New York's Attorney General, Ben had become a millionaire.

Upon assuming state office, Jack withdrew from the firm. The official explanation was that it would be a conflict of interest for him to practice privately while serving as the state's No. 1 lawyer. But the estrangement between brothers became apparent when Jack was elected senator in 1956. Instead of returning to Javits & Javits, he teamed with some colleagues from the Attorney General's office to found his own firm, with offices in the Seagram Building.

Javits, Trubin, Sillicocks & Edelman also did well. Although Javits—in the tradition of many "public partners"—gave the firm little more than the use of his name, he derived a substantial income from it, enough so that his entire Senate salary went for staff and expenses.

Among the firm's major clients was the First National City Bank, for which it handled mortgage closings—not the small ones, which were the chore of the bank's house counsel; not the multi-million-dollar ones, which were the concern of Shearman & Sterling; but the medium-sized ones. Javits' firm represented Citibank on thirty such closings in 1968, the loans averaging $160,000 each; seventeen in 1969, average $230,000; and nineteen in 1970, average $158,000.

"Deals like these are plums," said one lawyer, "and banks often choose lawyers they want to reward."

The "Nader Raider" panel studying the bank called them "political contributions in disguise." It noted that as a senator, Javits had consistently supported legislation sought by the bank. After the report was released, Javits announced his withdrawal from the firm and his retirement from practice.

Ben's firm, which had moved uptown to Rockefeller Center, remained Javits & Javits, but the junior Javits was now Ben's son, Eric. By 1961, when Lewis Rosenstiel called him for help, Ben was edging into retirement.

Rosenstiel was the multimillionaire founder and chairman of Schenley Industries. On November 30, 1956, he married for the fourth time. His bride was a blond divorcée thirty years his junior—Susan Lissman Kaufmann. One judge later described her as "a woman with an insatiable desire and hunger for money with an appetite that could neither be satisfied or appeased."

Rosenstiel was certainly in a position to try. He had assets of about $25 million and an annual income of more than $1 million. He and Susan settled into a life of what another judge termed "Byzantine luxury"—a twenty-eight-room Manhattan townhouse, an eighteen-hundred-acre Connecticut estate, an eighteen-room winter house in Florida, trips to Europe and all the luxuries of life.

But by 1961 the marriage had palled. Rosenstiel called in his old friend, lawyer and business confidant Ben Javits. He told Javits that he "couldn't take it anymore and would have to get rid of her."

"I told Mr. Rosenstiel that—first place, I didn't want to take the case," Javits testified later. "It was a lot of work. I didn't want to work and I tried to settle it. He wouldn't stand for a settlement. I thought he was very foolish about that and I told him it would be exceedingly expensive. He agreed. 'It doesn't make any difference. I will spend five million dollars, ten million, whatever it is! Spend it!' "

Until the law was liberalized in 1966, the only ground for divorce in New York was adultery—a situation that forced thousands to obtain "quickie" divorces in Mexico, as Susan Rosenstiel's first husband, Felix Kaufmann, had done.

Javits retained Mrs. Mae Korn—his former secretary who had earned her law degree at night—and sent her to Juarez to inspect what came to be called the "Kaufmann decree." She reported back that she thought there were grounds for setting aside the decree, thus providing the legal basis for Rosenstiel to obtain a New York annulment. But the Mexican court battle was bound to be lengthy, and Susan Rosenstiel, who had already retained Louis Nizer, was certain to fight it.

Ben Javits found a quicker way. In January, 1962, a "Samuel Goldsmith" filed a third-party action in Juarez to set aside the 1954 divorce of Felix and Susan Kaufmann. He claimed to have been a creditor of theirs who was defrauded by the divorce. Other than a notice on the courthouse bulletin board, no word of the action went out. Not until months later did Mrs. Rosenstiel learn that under the terms of this "Goldsmith decree" she was still legally married to Felix Kaufmann. Javits planned to keep the "Goldsmith decree" secret until the annulment action was well underway, so that Nizer and Mrs. Rosenstiel wouldn't have time to challenge it in the Mexican courts.

At this point, Rosenstiel became disturbed at Javits' handling of the case. He asked for an accounting of the more than $400,000 he'd advanced. Javits sent him the records with a handwritten note attached:

Dear Lew, since you are so inquisitive, here's my book-keeper's sheet, but please return it. It does not look good for your files. It should stay in mine.

Soon afterward, Rosenstiel dumped Javits and retained Roy Cohn. He also filed suit against Javits to recover $410,000 in fees and disbursements. The record of *Rosenstiel* v. *Javits* disclosed that Javits' agents had laid out more than $33,000 in legal and "public relations" fees and "charity" contributions to various Mexican officials, including the Attorney General of Chihuahua, to obtain the "Goldsmith decree." Some of the transactions were incredibly complex, so their real nature would not show on Javits & Javits' books.

When asked about the payments, Javits said, "All I can tell you is that I was told this is the way to do business in Mexico."

It took an *amparo* action in the Mexican federal court and the open intervention of the U.S. State Department to have the "Goldsmith decree" set aside. "Goldsmith" finally surfaced, but his signature did not jibe with that of the person who originally filed the papers in Juarez. There's doubt that he ever existed; neither Kaufmann nor Mrs. Rosenstiel had ever heard of this supposed "creditor" of theirs.

With Javits out of the picture, *Rosenstiel* v. *Rosenstiel* started its tortuous progress through the courts and spawned a series of acrimonious actions which continue to clog the calendars more than a decade later. Along the way, the state Court of Appeals handed down a landmark decision upholding the validity of Mexican divorces in New York, and Nizer was awarded the largest fee ever given an attorney in a New York matrimonial action—$360,000. (On appeal, it was trimmed to $288,000.)

Rosenstiel's suit against Javits was allowed to lapse; eventually, there was an undisclosed out-of-court settlement. But a new proceeding against the aging and ailing attorney had started. On October 30, 1964, after hearing one of the appeals in *Rosenstiel* v. *Rosenstiel*, Presiding Justice Bernard Botein referred the allegations against Javits to the Grievance Committee. It says something about the bar's willingness to protect its own that none of the lawyers or judges previously involved in the case saw fit to blow the whistle.

Meanwhile, Eric Javits was having his own problems with the authorities. A handsome man who liked to hobnob with high society, he harbored political ambitions, but he was badly beaten his first time out—a race for the Republican state senate nomination in the "Silk Stocking" district. (His wife, Stephanie, could have won a Jacqueline Kennedy look-alike contest. One report of Mrs. Kennedy's frugging at a Palm Beach nightclub went out over the wires when in reality it was Stephanie.)

Eric got involved as a go-between in setting up one of the bribes in the State Liquor Authority scandal. Although he co-operated with the district attorney, he had to call two press conferences in an attempt to explain his role. "I was never a party to any bribe attempt or scheme," he insisted. "I was not guilty of any improper conduct. It was not clear to me that any bribe was going to take place."

The Grievance Committee apparently took him at his word. Father Ben was not so fortunate. The hearing in his case did not get underway for four years—first because of the pending litigation, then because of Javits' illnesses.

The ailing attorney did not appear at the initial hearings. He had suffered cancer of the pancreas, a herniated diaphragm, a heart attack and pneumonia. He was seventy-five, completely retired from practice and living in Florida. He could have accepted the easy "out" by resigning from the bar, but he chose to fight.

In May, 1969, he took the stand at the Grievance Committee's hearing room in the Bar Building to deny the charge that he "attempted to perpetrate a fraud upon the courts of Mexico and the United States by paying moneys to Mexican public officials and a Mexican national in order to improperly obtain and subsequently defend a nullification of a Mexican divorce decree."

Gulping pills for his heart condition and gasping for breath,

Javits insisted that whatever happened in Mexico was the responsibility of another attorney—Sol Rosenblatt, a divorce specialist who shared space in the Javits & Javits suite. "I delegated the whole Mexican situation to him," he insisted. Rosenblatt was not available to contradict him: He had died the previous year.

The Grievance Committee did not accept Javits' explanation. Nor did the Appellate Division, which in January, 1971, by a 4-to-1 vote, suspended him from practice for three years. The relatively light punishment was meted out because of his "general standing and good reputation . . . at the bar and in the community, and also due to his advanced age, his demonstrated ill health and his purported retirement from the active practice of law."

The dissenting vote was cast by Justice James B. M. McNally, who held that Javits should have been disbarred. "I find no mitigating circumstances," he said. "[Javits] knowingly embarked on a course of professional misconduct in compliance with the demands of his client. He was motivated solely by monetary interest."

From Florida, Javits called the decision "unjust, unfair and improper." He appealed for reinstatement, but both the New York Court of Appeals and the U.S. Supreme Court turned a deaf ear.

We can only speculate on what the judges would have done had the attorney involved been some street-corner practitioner.

10

The Green-goods Counsel
as the Big Board's Cop

"When attorneys act like businessmen, they have to be treated like businessmen."

The comment was uttered offhand by Judge Jack Weinstein during a courtroom colloquy. But it—and the case he was hearing—illustrate the most dramatic step in decades in policing the blue-chip bar, and, through it, the nation's securities markets.

To paraphrase Karl Marx: A specter is haunting Wall Street —the specter of *BarChris, Leasco* and *National Student Marketing*.

To the layman—indeed, to most lawyers—*Escott* v. *BarChris Construction Corp., Feit* v. *Leasco Data Processing Equipment Corp.* and *S.E.C.* v. *National Student Marketing Corp.* are obscure, if not unknown, cases. But to those who deal in "green-goods" they are as important as *Brown* v. *Board of Education* was to southern school superintendents, *Baker* v. *Carr* was to rural-dominated state legislatures or *Mapp* v. *Ohio* was to police vice patrols. So far, none of these decisions has been engraved in stone by the Supreme Court, but even so they've made the blue-chip bar shake in its white shoes.

Their effect has been to set a new standard of conduct for securities lawyers. Their lash strikes at the Legal Establishment's Achilles heel—its well-padded pocketbook.

BarChris involved a company that built bowling alleys. With the advent of automatic pin-spotters in the late 1950s, bowling boomed and so did Bar-Chris' business. To raise funds for its expanding enterprise, it went public and offered stock. Later it issued debentures. When a sizable number of its customers defaulted on payment, Bar-Chris went bankrupt. Several stockholders sued, contending that the company's registration statement had a number of inaccuracies and material omissions.

In a long (sixty-four pages) but extraordinarily lucid opinion for a complex stock case, the late Federal Judge Edward McLean—once a name partner at Debevoise Plimpton—ruled that there *were* inaccuracies and material omissions. What's more, he found that those at fault included not only Bar-Chris' officers and directors, but its underwriters and accountants—as well as its lawyer. None, he found, exercised the "due diligence" required by law to make the stock registration statement as accurate as humanly possible.

The blue-chip bar read with concern Judge McLean's comments on the lawyer's role:

> Grant became a director of BarChris in October 1960. His law firm was counsel to BarChris in matters pertaining to the registration of securities. Grant drafted the registration statement for the stock issue in 1959 and the warrants in January 1961. He also drafted the registration statement for the debentures. . . .
>
> Grant is sued as a director and as a signer of the registration statement. This is not an action against him for malpractice in his capacity as a lawyer. Nevertheless, in

considering Grant's due diligence defenses, the unique position which he occupied cannot be disregarded. As the director most directly concerned with writing the registration statement and assuring its accuracy, more was required of him in the way of reasonable investigation than could fairly be expected of a director who had no connection with this work. . . .

I find that Grant honestly believed that the registration statement was true and that no material facts had been omitted from it. In this belief he was mistaken. . . .

It is claimed that a lawyer is entitled to rely on the statements of his client and that to require him to verify their accuracy would set an unreasonably high standard. This is too broad a generalization. It is all a matter of degree. . . .

There were things which Grant could readily have checked which he did not check. . . .

Grant was obliged to make a reasonable investigation. I am forced to find that he did not make one. After making due allowances for the fact that BarChris' officers misled him, there are too many instances in which Grant failed to make an inquiry which he could easily have made which, if pursued, would have put him on his guard. In my opinion, this finding on the evidence in this case does not establish an unreasonably high standard in other cases for company counsel who are also directors. . . .

Bar-Chris was hardly in the big leagues of American industry. In 1960 its sales were $8.5 million. Nor was its law firm—Perkins, Daniels, McCormick & Collins—up among the giants of the blue-chip bar. It was merely another of many midtown firms which had handled a new stock issue during the big bull market of the early 1960s.

If that were all there were to it, it wouldn't be worth our while—or Wall Street's concern. But Judge McLean's decision had far-reaching implications. To many, it reversed the traditional pattern of legal practice. If a defense lawyer in, say, a murder case forgot to question a key witness, his client got the electric chair—but the attorney would still get his fee. Under Judge McLean's ruling, if a corporate counsel—especially one who was an officer or director of the company—slipped up in a securities case, he was as liable as any other officer, even if the others had duped him. His duty in a stock registration, the judge found, was not so much to his corporate client as to its potential investors. His duty was not so much, in Elihu Root's old dictum, "to keep his client out of court," as to keep his client honest.

It was a doctrine that the Securities and Exchange Commission came to pursue with a vengeance in the coming years— not only against securities lawyers, but against underwriters, accountants and even public relations men.

Within a few weeks after *BarChris* was decided, one legal publisher rushed into print with a pamphlet warning Wall Street:

> A succession of recent cases has swept the financial community into a turmoil—and the end is not yet in sight. BarChris, Law Research and Texas Gulf and related cases write radically new law that may expose you to perpetual jeopardy....
> Who's affected?—Everybody....
> Who's next?—There's no way of telling....*

The pamphlet summed up the effects of *BarChris* and the other decisions in a single contrapuntal sentence: "You must know what you are disclosing—you must disclose what you know."

The legal implications of the next major securities case to affect the blue-chip bar were less far-reaching, at least initially, but its target was far more important—Robert Hodes, a partner of Willkie, Farr & Gallagher. Dapper, a product of Dartmouth College and Harvard Law, Hodes (who pro-

---

* Neither *Law Research*—despite its name—nor *Texas Gulf* affected lawyers as lawyers.

nounces his name to rhyme with "Rhodes") had spent twenty years with the firm and had become the tenth-ranked partner on the letterhead. He was general counsel and a director of Leasco Data, the stock-market *wunderkind* of the late-1960s, a Long Island firm that started with computer leasing, then moved to Park Avenue and embarked on a conglomeration spree.

Among the concerns it acquired was Reliance Insurance Company. When Leasco took over the insurance concern, one of its early acts was to liquidate Reliance's "surplus surplus" of more than $38 million. For Leasco it was a windfall profit. But it provoked a stockholders' suit, brought in the name of Dudley Feit, a contentious Brooklyn textile buyer who held two hundred shares of Reliance stock. He named Leasco, three of its directors—including Hodes—its accountants and under-writers for failing to disclose their intentions to liquidate the surplus surplus.

The case was incredibly complex. The decision of Brooklyn Federal Judge Weinstein ran 128 pages and his formula for recovery reads like an equation for a space shot. Weinstein, a former Columbia Law professor, exonerated the accountants and the underwriters, but found Leasco and its directors liable. Relying heavily on *BarChris*, he noted:

> Defendants' registration statement was . . . misleading in a material way. While disclosing masses of facts and figures, it failed to reveal one critical consideration that weighed heavily with those responsible for the issue—the substantial possibility of being able to gain control of some hundred million dollars of assets not required for operating the business being acquired.
>
> Using a statement to obscure, rather than reveal in plain English, the critical elements of a proposed business deal cannot be countenanced under the securities regula-tion acts. . . .

As for the lawyer's role in this not-to-be-countenanced manipulation, Judge Weinstein went on:

Hodes . . . was involved in the discussions leading up to the exchange offer for Reliance shares as early as the fall of 1967 and was constantly involved in the deal throughout both the preliminary and execution stages of the transaction. He, or a representative of his law firm, attended all meetings and was consulted on all matters pertaining to the acquisition. He was directly responsible for preparation of the registration statement and initiated all of the research regarding reorganization of Reliance and separation of its surplus surplus. . . . Hodes was so intimately involved in this registration process that to treat him as anything but an insider would involve a gross distortion of the realities of Leasco's management.

Eventually, a complex schedule of payments was adopted under which Leasco would have to shell out only $110,000 to the cheated shareholders. Feit's attorney, a solo practitioner named Sidney B. Silverman was awarded a fee of $225,000, to be paid by Leasco—which shows that it can be as profitable to take on the Establishment as to be part of it.

But the question of *who* would pay remained open. After the trial, Leasco announced that it would assume the then-still-to-be-determined liability of Hodes and the two officer-directors. At this point the S.E.C. stepped into what had heretofore been a private dispute, objecting that such a course would be unfair to Leasco's shareholders, already clobbered by the stock's drastic drop on the Big Board.

Some indication of the importance of this proceeding to the blue-chip bar can be gleaned from Leasco's decision to retain as "special counsel" on the still-pending S.E.C. motion one of Wall Street's leading litigators, David Peck, of Sullivan & Cromwell.

The third case echoed like an anarchist's bomb blast through the canyons of the financial district. On February 3, 1972, the S.E.C. filed a forty-six-page complaint in the District of Columbia District Court against National Student Marketing Corporation, charging it with perpetrating "a fraudulent scheme . . . in 83 separate transactions."

Wall Street insiders knew that government action against National Student Marketing was bound to come sooner or later. For nearly four years the company had been one of the highest-flying operations around in what one of its officers later termed "the funny money game." National Student Marketing started as a small concern catering to business efforts to penetrate the growing "youth market," but it too soon embarked on an orgy of conglomeration that sent its stock soaring like a V2 rocket—and crashing with as great an explosion.

National Student Marketing's stock opened at $6 a share in April, 1968, and reached a peak of $144 in December, 1969. By the time the S.E.C. filed its suit, the stock had been bounced from the Big Board and was down to $2.25 bid on the over-the-counter market.

What made the action against National Student Marketing "extraordinary" and "unprecedented," in *The Wall Street Journal*'s terms, was the new standard of conduct the S.E.C. sought to set for corporate counsel.

To drive the point home, the commission named as defendants not only the company and its officers, but the auditors and the lawyers—and their law firms as well! What's more, one of the firms cited was the nation's sixth largest and one of Wall Street's most prestigious—gray, gentlemanly White & Case. And the White & Case partner singled out was as blue a blood as can be found in a Wall Street law office—Marion Jay Epley 3d, the thirty-five-year-old son of the former Texaco president and board chairman.

The chief charge against Epley and White & Case involved a so-called "comfort letter" from the auditors attesting that the books and finances were in proper order—a prerequisite to National Student Marketing's acquisition of Interstate National Corporation, an insurance company, on October 21, 1969. Because of their vast cash resources, insurance companies are prime targets for ingestion by carnivore conglomerates. White & Case represented National Student Marketing; Lord, Bissell & Brook, of Chicago, the other law firm cited by the S.E.C., was counsel to Interstate National.

According to the S.E.C., about an hour before the closing was completed, the auditors informed White & Case and Epley, the partner assigned to National Student Marketing matters, that they wished to add another paragraph to the comfort letter. The appended paragraph indicated that National Student Marketing's financial picture was not as rosy as previously painted.

"White & Case, Epley and Davies [John G. Davies, National Student Marketing's vice president and general counsel] failed to inform the other persons present at the closing of this additional paragraph," the S.E.C. said.

About an hour *after* the closing was completed, the complaint continued, the auditors called again and "informed defendants White & Case and Epley that [they] wished to add still another paragraph to the comfort letter. . . .

> In view of the above mentioned facts, we believe the companies should consider submitting corrected interim financial information to the shareholders prior to proceeding with the closing."

In less polite language: Don't cinch the deal until you put out the straight scoop.

Again, the S.E.C. charged, "defendants White & Case and Epley made no effort to communicate the contents of this final version of the comfort letter to the representatives of Interstate who had been present at the meeting."

Instead, the complaint continued, "White & Case . . . issued an opinion at the direction of the defendant Epley stating that all steps taken to consummate the merger had been validly taken. . . ."

The core of the complaint was contained in a subsequent paragraph. The S.E.C. said that White & Case should not have issued the opinion and that, if the companies had persisted in the merger, the attorneys' and their law firms' proper course was "to cease representing their respective clients and, under the circumstances, *notify the plaintiff Commission concerning the misleading nature of the . . . financial statements.*" (My italics)

Long before there was a decision—indeed, even before a motion was made—one law professor hailed the case as a "landmark."

The S.E.C.'s mimeograph machines were kept busy churning out copies of the complaint in what quickly came to be called "the White & Case case." One lawyer called it "the best-read document since *Gone With the Wind.*" A legal publisher distributed thousands of copies to lawyers as a public service, and a bit of advertising.

Law schools and bar associations held hastily called seminars to discuss the ramifications of the case. One Wall Street law firm distributed copies of the complaint to all its lawyers, with the implied caveat. White & Case convened an extraordinary meeting of all its fifty-six partners to discuss the action.

The firm denied the charge, but otherwise declined public comment on the case. Its counsel, the Washington firm of Arnold & Porter, filed motions with the court to have the action against White & Case severed from the other defendants and to have the case shifted from Washington to New York, where presumably both lawyers and judges are more familiar with the complexities of securities law, and more sympathetic to its practitioners.

Not only is the target in the White & Case case far more prominent than those of either *BarChris* or *Leasco*, its legal implications for the blue-chip bar are much more sweeping:

First, unlike the previous cases, it does not charge a lawyer in his capacity as a corporate officer or director, but solely as a lawyer.

Second, it names not just the lawyer, but his firm. All fifty-six White & Case partners—most of whom had nothing to do with National Student Marketing and knew nothing of its affairs—are made responsible for the actions of one.

Third, the complaint—if upheld by the courts—could set a precedent exposing law firms to a rash of damage suits from irate stockholders. No firm dealing in "green-goods" would be immune. Indeed, within two weeks of the S.E.C.'s complaint White & Case was named in a stockholders' suit against National Student Marketing. And the word around Wall Street was that the S.E.C. would throw meat to the wolves, with several more cases against blue-chip firms ready to file if its action in *National Student Marketing* was upheld.*

Fourth—and this is apparently the S.E.C.'s chief aim—it could reverse the traditional pattern of securities practice, making the corporate counsel less a legal advisor and confidant than an "expert"—like an auditor—responsible not so much to his client as to the investing public.

"What we're saying," said S.E.C. Commissioner James J. Needham after the case was filed, "is that in the securities area we have always relied on the bar and feel they have a special responsibility in the securities area, just as accountants and other professionals do."

It was a long step beyond keeping the client honest; it was hauling him in if he got out of line. Many securities lawyers saw the suit as one shot in the S.E.C.'s campaign to make the blue-chip bar Wall Street's policeman. And they wondered what it would do to the traditional attorney-client privilege.

"Attorneys are not above the law," said one "green-goods"

---

* In a case filed too recently to report its ramifications, Willkie, Farr & Gallagher got hit again by the S.E.C. in November, 1972. Three of its lawyers—partners Allan F. Conwill and Raymond W. Merritt and associate John S. D'Alimonte—were named as defendants in a civil suit against Robert Vesco, the wheeler-dealer who succeeded Bernie Cornfeld as head of the faltering Investors Overseas Services. According to the S.E.C., the three Willkie Farr lawyers "lent their skills to facilitating and executing defendant Vesco's schemes to mulct the [I.O.S.] funds" of $224 million. S.E.C. Commissioner Philip A. Loomis called it "one of the largest securities frauds ever perpetrated" and intimated that criminal prosecution was likely to follow the civil action. Willkie Farr issued a statement defending the three lawyers: "It is unfortunate that the commission afforded [them] no opportunity to be heard prior to the institution of the action. The firm expresses its complete confidence in the [ir] professional and personal integrity."

lawyer. "But on the other hand, attorneys should not play the role of secret agent 007 for the Securities and Exchange Commission."

Though the S.E.C. denied this intention, the potential targets were doubtful. One lawyer said, "It is fair to say that at the very least the complaint contains what the commission considers to be the standard of conduct that will be demanded of the securities bar."

And that standard is: When investors rely on an attorney's opinion and certification, "the attorney's responsibilities cease to be solely to his client and run to these third parties."

The net result, many lawyers fear, will be to make the blue-chip bar supercautious, more selective in accepting corporate clients, less ready to commit their law firms to certifying their clients' good conduct.

"It's going to cause a lot of trouble for the Legal Establishment," says one Wall Street lawyer. "No lawyer is going to be able to give independent advice if he's going to be watching out for his own skin. It's going to change the whole system of securities practice. And the securities business is the heart of the Legal Establishment."

11

The Public Servant
as Private Lawyer

There is something about the practice of corporate law that seems to drive men out of it. Not just the associates who never make partner, but those at or near the top of the profession.

Consider the cycle: A lawyer joins a firm at about age twenty-five and spends the next five to ten years striving to make partner; for the next fifteen to twenty years, he's a junior partner, moving up, making money; then at about age fifty, his children grown and gone, his home in the suburbs paid for, he surveys his situation, finds his work repetitive and routine and wonders whether he really wants to spend the rest of his working life drafting indentures.

Of course, many—if not most—lawyers stay the course, but they still seek other outlets. When the bug bites, some take up writing or painting or golf. Some seek a place on the bench or in academe. Some dabble in business. Some become brahmins in the bar associations. Others take out their frustrations in drink or women. But most lawyers seek out some form of public service.

"Certain branches of corporate law are deathly dull," says Roswell Gilpatric. "I don't know how I could have stood it for forty years if I hadn't left the firm several times."

A contrary view is expressed by Francis T. P. Plimpton: "I never got bored with an indenture in my life. There's a challenge in polishing those things, in honing the language. There's a fascination about it. There's almost a glory in working all night to get out a registration statement."

Glory or not, when the call came, Plimpton jumped at the chance for public service, leaving his firm for four years to serve with Adlai Stevenson—briefly his law school classmate at Harvard—at the United Nations. "I wouldn't have missed it for anything. I wouldn't do it over again."

There are many reasons why lawyers, more than most men, and corporate lawyers, more than most lawyers, are so suited to public service.

First, they're drawn to it. Their daily lives are devoted to the decisions of government, to dealing with government officials, to interpreting the laws and regulations. For any lawyer who has ever said to himself, "I could draft a better regulation than that off the top of my head," the chance to do so is irresistible.

Second, as Arthur Dean has noted, "Lawyers can more readily than many effect total, temporary or partial withdrawal from the daily routine to attend to public affairs." A shopkeeper or factory foreman can't. But in a large law firm, others can pick up the load if a lawyer wants to devote half his hours to politics or public affairs. And if he wants to go off to Washington for four years, the firm and its clients will still be there when he gets back.

Third, lawyers come well equipped for government service. Cyrus Vance notes that law is a profession "in which people are trained to take a great mass of facts, sift them, marshal them—that's the sort of thing that tends to be useful in the executive branch of government."

No lawyer in the nation has had as distinguished a career in public service as John J. McCloy. And none has written more eloquently on the qualities of what he termed "the extracurricular lawyer":

> The lawyer who has faced the give and take of the courtroom, who has debated before the appellate court with lawyers of equal skill and resourcefulness, or who has run the gamut of conferences with counsel for opposing sides has usually had a rich background with which to face . . . public life.

McCloy listed several of the attributes that so qualify a lawyer for public service: He's an "expert in relevancy much more likely to come up with the right answer in any given situation." He's acquired "competence in oral and written expression." He is accustomed to working irregular hours—and so is his wife. But, above all, he's adept in the art of compromise:

> He has learned to gauge human emotions and to make due allowance for them, for in his practice he has seen them flare and subside; his training has taught him the practical necessity at least of assessing the other side's point of view if not of conceding its merit; it has similarly given him the ability to judge what are the important and what the less significant facts of a situation. . . . All these facets of the lawyer's experience are useful to him in promoting compromise and thus in enhancing his value; for no one, I venture to say, who has had government or business experience can fail to recognize how necessary a part compromise plays.

The lawyer deals with the world as it is, not as he would wish it. It gives him patience—an especially useful tool in threading the labyrinths of government or prodding a lethargic bureaucracy. Businessmen, McCloy notes, are used to giving orders, and when they come into government "become discouraged because they can't just press a button."

Finally, many lawyers go into government because they feel a sense of obligation. "In our generation," says Cyrus Vance, "a great many of us had a conviction that we ought to spend a portion of our career in government service."

Or McCloy again: "My father on his deathbed told my mother two things—I should study Greek and I should become a lawyer. He had a feeling that a lawyer is a public servant. I think that had something to do with my feeling that at some stage in my career I should go into government. I'm sure I had a richer life by reason of my public service."

Parallel with this sense of obligation, though, is another quality most lawyers disdain to discuss—an instinct for power. Louis Auchincloss, who professes no desire whatsoever to go into government, offers a six-word explanation for the periodic exoduses of the McCloys and Deans, Vances and Gilpatrics to government service: "They want to rule the world."

Rule it they do. Though Richard Nixon—hardly typical of the breed—is the only man who made the leap directly from Wall Street to the White House, the lesser ranks of government have long been filled with partners from New York's corporate law firms.

Joseph Kraft, the Washington columnist, observed:

> One of the few authentic traditions in American politics arises out of the well-known love affair between the Republican Party and the Wall Street lawyers. From Theodore Roosevelt through Dwight Eisenhower there has been no Republican Administration in which men from the big downtown firms did not play a major role. From their ranks came four of the eight secretaries of state during the period—Elihu Root, Charles Evans Hughes, Henry Stimson and John Foster Dulles. So fixed was the tradition that whenever the Democrats felt obliged to look bipartisan, they automatically reached for a Wall Street lawyer.

Though power in the Republican party has tended to shift in recent years from the eastern Establishment's "old money" to the oil and aerospace wealth of the West and Southwest, the tradition still holds in the Nixon Administration. William P. Rogers is the fifth GOP Secretary of State to come out of a New York law firm.

The list of New York lawyers on temporary or part-time service in government is even longer. Whenever the President, the governor or the mayor needs someone for a special task, they almost automatically reach for a Brahmin of the Bar.

When President Nixon needed someone to review business taxes, he picked his old law partner John Alexander. When Governor Rockefeller needed someone to review the state's antidiscrimination laws, he picked Eli Whitney Debevoise, of Debevoise Plimpton, the son of the Rockefeller family counsel; when the subject was school finances, the choice was Manly Fleischmann, a name partner at Webster Sheffield.* When Mayor Lindsay needed someone to investigate possible breeches of ethics by city officials, he called successively on Cloyd Laporte, of Dewey Ballantine; Bruce Bromley, of Cravath; and Francis Plimpton.

When Rockefeller and Lindsay appointed rival commissions to investigate city-state relations, both were headed by Wall Street lawyers—Lindsay's by William vanden Heuvel, of Stroock & Stroock & Lavan; Rockefeller's by Stuart Scott, of Dewey Ballantine.

For the appointing authority, such selections give the panels not only competence, but the aura of above-the-battle impartiality—living symbols that the chips will fall where they may. Of course, many of those named to such panels are aware of what the appointing authorities expect and gear their reports accordingly; but all too often to satisfy the authorities, the panelists actually are as independent as they appear.

---

* Perhaps because he touches two bases, Fleischmann is often called upon to serve on state panels. A Buffalo resident, he divides his time between one of that city's leading law firms and Webster Sheffield in Rockefeller Center.

Consider the report of the commission Governor Rockefeller appointed to investigate the 1971 rebellion at Attica State Prison. Robert McKay, Dean of N.Y.U.'s law school, chaired the panel (academic lawyers are also prized for such special assignments) while Arthur Liman, of Paul Weiss, served as its chief counsel. Its report was highly critical of Rockefeller's conduct in the rebellion's bloody suppression.

For the lawyers who receive such appointments, the part-time posts can become major stepping stones in their professional careers. Two illustrations:

The late James B. Donovan was a senior partner of Watters & Donovan (now Donovan, Donovan, Maloof & Walsh), a medium-sized Wall Street firm specializing in trial work for insurance companies. A Brooklyn native, Donovan had attended Fordham and Harvard Law, had served as general counsel under "Wild Bill" Donovan (no relation) in the O.S.S. and had assisted Justice Robert Jackson in the Nuremburg war crimes prosecutions. Though he made a comfortable living, he could hardly have been reckoned one of the giants of the Wall Street bar.

Then in 1957, Donovan was appointed by the court to defend Colonel Rudolf Abel, the highest-ranking Soviet spy ever captured in the United States.* "In my time on this Court no man has undertaken a more arduous, more self-sacrificing task," Chief Justice Warren said of him.

Donovan diligently defended the Soviet agent, arguing Abel's appeal all the way to the Supreme Court, where he lost a 5-to-4 decision. Abel was sentenced to thirty years in prison.

Donovan had spent the better part of three years on the case. He donated his $10,000 fee to charity, and his firm lost some clients because of his defense of a "commie spy." But the

---

* Abel had asked the court for "counsel recommended by the bar association." Brooklyn Federal Judge Matthew T. Abruzzo called upon the Brooklyn Bar Association, which picked Donovan—as much, it seems, for his unblemished patriotism as for his legal expertise. Although a large number of Wall Street lawyers live in Brooklyn—Brooklyn Heights is only one subway stop from the office—Donovan was one of the few who belonged to the Brooklyn Bar Association, which is composed mainly of clubhouse hangers-on who practice in the borough.

case also served as a launching pad for Donovan's wider career in public service and a more lucrative law practice. In 1962, he was called upon by President Kennedy to negotiate with the Russians for the exchange of Abel for U2 pilot Francis Gary Powers. Later that year, he again answered JFK's summons to negotiate with Fidel Castro for the release of sixty-seven hundred prisoners from the Bay of Pigs invasion. As a result of his sudden fame, he received the Democratic senatorial nomination that year. Though he was roundly trounced by Jacob Javits, he remained in the public eye and in public service. Mayor Wagner appointed him to head New York City's Board of Education. In a few years he had leaped from relative obscurity to become a Brahmin of the Bar, so much so that he was honored by being "roasted" by the Bar Association—New York's, not Brooklyn's. Donovan died in 1970 at the age of fifty-four.

Second illustration: In 1970, after *The New York Times* published reports of widespread corruption in the New York Police Department, Mayor Lindsay appointed a five-member commission to investigate. To head the panel he picked a sixty-one-year-old lawyer named Whitman Knapp, a name partner in the medium-sized Wall Street firm of Barrett, Knapp, Smith & Schapiro. In the press and the popular mind the panel quickly became known as the "Knapp Commission" and its chairman a familiar figure, often seen shielding his eyes from the glare of the TV lights behind tinted glasses.

Though he had been active in the Bar Association, until his appointment by Lindsay, Knapp was unknown to the general public. Like many local lawyers who later rose to prominence, Knapp—Yale College and Harvard Law—started his legal career in the district attorney's office under Thomas E. Dewey and Frank Hogan. He soon rose to head the D.A.'s appeals bureau and earned a footnote in legal history for making what's believed to be the shortest argument ever before the U.S. Supreme Court.

The year was 1948. The case involved the obscenity prosecution of Edmund Wilson's *Memoirs of Hecate County*. When it was his turn to argue, Knapp stood before the justices and spoke just three sentences:

> The statute on which the judgment rests is valid. A reading of the book by this court will demonstrate that the finding of obscenity is reasonable. I therefore submit that the judgment should be affirmed.

No questions. The Court split, 4-to-4, thus upholding lower court verdicts that the book was obscene and, although sold openly, it's still legally banned in New York State.

After a slow start, the Knapp Commission struck pay dirt, astounding even jaundiced observers with the widespread extent of police corruption. Though most of the panel's work was done by its chief counsel, Michael Armstrong—on leave from Cahill Gordon—Knapp got the glory—and the reward. Even before the commission's final report was issued, President Nixon nominated him for a federal judgeship.

A private lawyer's public service can also benefit his clients. Consider the career of Lawrence E. Walsh: "Judge" to acquaintances, "Ed" to friends, Walsh is a thin, wiry man, a self-professed "square." He was born in Canada, raised in Queens, educated at Columbia and Columbia Law. He, too, started in the district attorney's office under Dewey, and much of his future success can be traced to the friendships he forged there.

After a few months as an associate at Davis Polk, he followed Dewey to Albany in 1943 and for the next decade held a variety of state jobs—assistant counsel and counsel to Dewey, counsel to the Public Service Commission and first director of the Waterfront Commission.

In 1954, with Dewey leaving office, Walsh was named to the federal bench. Though he served only three years, he still retains the title "judge." He resigned in 1957 when William P. Rogers, a colleague from the Dewey days in the D.A.'s office, was appointed Attorney General and brought Walsh to Washington as the Justice Department's No. 2 man.

In 1961, Walsh returned to Davis Polk—this time as a full-fledged partner. But few lawyers in New York remained as busy with extracurricular activities. He quickly developed what one lawyer termed "a reputation for knowing and doing exactly what was expected of him." In the wake of the State Liquor Authority scandal, Governor Rockefeller named him to head a panel to recommend revisions in the alcoholic beverage laws. Mayor Lindsay picked him to head a commission to study the Police Department; it recommended the ill-fated Civilian Review Board. The state's chief judge, Stanley Fuld—another colleague from the D.A.'s office—picked him as special prosecutor in the impeachment of a tainted judge.

Walsh's outside activities picked up after Nixon's election. His old friend Rogers became Secretary of State and tabbed Walsh to assist Henry Cabot Lodge at the Paris peace talks. At the same time, Walsh was chosen to head the American Bar Association's committee on the federal judiciary. In this post, he passed on all of Nixon's judicial nominations. It brought him into almost daily contact with his successor as deputy attorney general, Richard Kleindienst—an interesting assignment for a lawyer who defined his area of specialization at Davis Polk as "any matter relating with the Department of Justice once it got above the routine level."

Walsh estimates that the A.B.A. assignment takes up more than a third of his time—about seven hundred hours a year. "If I work eighteen hundred hours that makes up for it," he says. "I get about one thousand billable hours a year. Mr. Davis' idea of public service was that each person is expected to give ten per cent of his time to public service. I made up for those who don't."

Walsh's A.B.A. assignment also brought him into the cockpit of political controversy, for his panel approved Nixon's nominations of both Haynesworth and Carswell for the Supreme Court. Although Walsh admits that his approval of Carswell "disappointed a number of my friends," he continued to defend his action long after the Senate rejected the nominee.

"There is a defense of Carswell," he says, "but I'm tired of stating it."

But he stated it often enough to earn some due bills from the Administration. He wasn't long in cashing them.

In 1969, Whitney North Seymour, Jr., became U.S. Attorney for the Southern District of New York. As his executive assistant he named John M. Burns 3d. Although a Democrat, Burns had a long association with Mike Seymour, having managed his successful campaign for the state senate and his losing race for Congress, as well as having served as Seymour's legislative aide in Albany.

In the U.S. Attorney's office, Burns soon staked out his area of specialization—water pollution. Using a little-enforced provision of the Refuse Act of 1899, he racked up a startling record—a $5,000 fine against Consolidated Edison; a $25,000 fine against Transit-Mix Corporation; another $25,000 fine against Kay-Fries Chemicals. Soon the figures started escalating. Washburn Wire Company was fined $125,000 for polluting the Harlem River, though the fine was suspended pending a clean-up. Standard Brands was fined $215,000 for polluting the Hudson—and this time the penalty stuck.

Then, in October, 1970, Burns took on General Motors, accusing the auto company of dumping toxic wastes into the Hudson from its Chevrolet plant in Tarrytown.

GM does not retain any one law firm as its general counsel. It hires attorneys as the occasion demands. When it had to deal with John Mitchell's Justice Department, it showed up with Lawrence Walsh, of Davis Polk. Walsh had represented GM only once previously—on the legal aspects of GM's 1970 annual meeting in which the management slate was challenged by Ralph Nader's "Project Responsibility."

"I didn't even know at that time who Lawrence Walsh was," Burns says. He soon found out.

As Burns remembers their first meeting, from the outset Walsh was "very abrasive."

"Is this the policy of John Mitchell?" he asked.

"I don't know," Burns replied. "But his office has approved similar prosecutions in the past."

"Do you mind if I check with him?"

And a few minutes later: "Is this the policy of Dick Kleindienst?"

Burns said it was.

"Do you mind if I go see him?"

Seymour had disqualified himself from supervision of the GM case because his former firm, Simpson Thacher & Bartlett, had represented the auto company on occasion. In fact, while the case was pending Ross Malone, GM's general counsel, was arranging a testimonial dinner for Seymour's father.

The younger Seymour named his chief assistant, Silvio Mollo, Acting U.S. Attorney for the GM case. Burns and Mollo seldom saw eye to eye on the action. According to Burns, Mollo, practically a career assistant who specialized in criminal cases, considered water-pollution cases a waste of the office's resources. When he gave Walsh two extensions of time on the case, Burns protested, "That's not our policy." But Mollo replied, "That's when you're dealing with a different kind of lawyer."

A few days later, a Davis Polk lawyer arrived in Burns' office with a memorandum on the case and "an oral message that Walsh was on his way to Washington to give it to Dick Kleindienst."

Burns checked with his superiors in Washington and was told the case against GM was "the best case they'd ever seen." Then Burns wrote a letter to GM Chairman John M. Roche—the man who had to apologize to Nader—complaining about Walsh's threats to use "political influence to interfere with the pollution investigation." The letter went on:

> At least once before, GM attorneys assumed no one would be willing to lay his career on the line to see that the General Motors Corp. complied with rules of behavior applicable to all others, and Mr. Nader's discoveries . . . seriously injured the corporation's image.

Please be advised that there are many in this office who would also lay their careers on the line to insure that this office treats General Motors exactly the same as any other firm.

Little did Burns know then how prophetic that would be.

Walsh went to Washington—though he insists that "I never spoke with anyone above the level of the career people." It seems strange. Can a former deputy attorney general wander through the Justice Department offices on an out-of-town visit without paying at least a courtesy call on his successor, especially one with whom he was in almost daily telephone contact? Could Cyrus Vance or Roswell Gilpatric return to the Pentagon and speak with no one above the rank of major?

In any event, the result of Walsh's visit was clear. Burns was ordered to drop the criminal action against GM and work out a civil settlement. Reluctantly, Burns did so. Throughout the evening of Friday, January 8, 1971, he and Walsh negotiated the terms of the agreement. This time, Burns says, Walsh was "very charming and pleasant."

The settlement was signed at 10 P.M. Burns brought the document to Seymour's office. Seymour took it and handed Burns his walking papers. Burns asked that he be allowed to remain in office until the GM case was concluded; Seymour refused. For a while, Seymour insisted that Burns had resigned; later he admitted that he'd been fired—though the exact reasons were never disclosed. More than a year later, when Burns was running unsuccessfully for Congress from a Hudson Valley district, Seymour made a speech criticizing "certain publicity-seeking, self-styled conservation spokesmen." Burns claimed the speech was cleared with the Administration as part of the campaign against him.

Burns—who returned to a small Wall Street securities firm, Spear & Hill—blames Walsh for his ouster. "It's such a heavy-handed way to do it," he says. "But then you don't get a reputation for being tough by being discreet."

Walsh denies that he had anything to do with Burns' ouster

—though he later admitted that when he went to Washington he carried a letter to Kleindienst complaining about the New York assistant, but never delivered it.

"There was never any effort to have him fired," he insists. "He was his own worst enemy. It was his high-handed approach. His problems may have arisen from this lawsuit, but it was his own conduct that brought them on."

Walsh says he was as surprised as anyone that Burns was fired. "We signed the decree with Burns and I had no expectation that he wasn't going to handle the case from then on."

Nearly two years later, the question of whether GM complied with the decree remains open. The irony, according to Burns, is that it would have cost GM only two dollars a day to meet federal antipollution standards at the Tarrytown plant.

Walsh's next case involved one of Davis Polk's oldest and biggest clients—ITT. As a result of columnist Jack Anderson's disclosure of the now-famous Dita Beard memo, ITT's antitrust settlement was headline news for months. This is not the place to recapitulate all the threads of the complex plot, only Walsh's small but significant role in the settlement.

Davis Polk had been ITT's outside counsel for more than fifty years, but, as ITT started its sweeping conglomeration in the 1960s, it began using other firms, especially those that had represented the subsidiaries it absorbed.

ITT's acquisitions had received the green light from the Johnson Administration, but they came under a heavy attack from the dedicated trust-buster appointed by Nixon and Mitchell—Richard McLaren. He filed suit to dissolve three recent ITT mergers—with Grinnell Company, Canteen Corporation and Hartford Fire Insurance. By April, 1971, the first of the cases—Grinnell—was ready for argument before the Supreme Court.

Davis Polk was not ITT's counsel in the antitrust actions; that task was handled by the Washington firm, Covington & Burling. But ITT feared that an adverse ruling on Grinnell might set a precedent affecting its more important acquisition of Hartford Fire. So it hired another gun—Lawrence Walsh.

In his dozen years at Davis Polk, Walsh had handled only one other ITT matter. As with GM, it was inspired by Ralph Nader—a threatened suit to block the Hartford Fire merger. The suit never materialized, and when the government began its antitrust action, other counsel handled it.

Walsh, Fritz Schwarz, the firm's senior partner, and associate Guy Sturve conferred with ITT President Harold S. Geneen and Howard J. Aibel, its general counsel. As Walsh later testified: "Mr. Geneen was concerned that the Department's policy was really ignoring . . . the destructive economic effects of a rigid bar to conglomerate mergers even though they were of large companies. He felt . . . that these mergers, large and small, served an important purpose in avoiding stagnation in management, stagnation in industries and in giving companies like ITT, which has large foreign commitments and risks, a more stable and safe diversified base in this country."

Geneen testified that he "asked Judge Walsh . . . to see if he could persuade them, the Department of Justice, to consider a review of [its antitrust policies]. I do not consider that an interference. It was an open and honest request and judgment was to be made by them." In fact, Geneen deemed the matter so important that he wanted Walsh to make the presentation to the President, but Walsh dissuaded him. As it turned out, Geneen made the approach to the White House through others.

Attorney General Mitchell had disqualified himself in the ITT cases because his former firm, Mudge Rose, had handled some minor matters for ITT—$1,015 worth in 1969; $45,768 in 1970; and $44,047 in 1971. That left Kleindienst in charge of the case, presenting Walsh with a problem. Kleindienst could act on ITT, but only Mitchell could authorize the full-scale review Geneen wanted.

"We were confronted with a very serious obstacle by Mr. Mitchell's disqualification," Walsh said. "We went to Kleindienst with the hope that he could bring Mitchell back in and at least get his consent to a full-fledge presentation to him and the secretaries of Treasury and Commerce of Mr. Geneen's view of conglomerate mergers."

On April 16, Walsh called Kleindienst. With the meticulous logging necessary for billing, Davis Polk's records showed the conversation lasted two minutes. Walsh told him that he was sending down a memorandum requesting "Government-wide review of the Administration policy toward mergers and diversification." Sturve delivered the memo and a covering letter from Walsh that afternoon:

Dear Dick:, As I told you over the telephone, our firm has represented ITT, as outside counsel, ever since its incorporation over fifty years ago. A few weeks ago, Mr. Harold S. Geneen, Chairman and President of ITT, asked me to prepare a presentation to you as Acting Attorney General and, through you, to the National Administration on the question of whether diversification mergers should be barred and, more specifically, urging that the Department of Justice not advocate any position before the Supreme Court which would be tantamount to barring such mergers without a full study of the economic consequences of such a step.

To us this is not a question of the conduct of litigation in the narrow sense. *Looking back at the results of government antitrust cases in the Supreme Court, one must realize that if the government urges an expanded interpretation of the vague language of the Clayton Act, there is a high probability that it will succeed.* [My italics] Indeed, the Court has at times adopted a position more extreme than that urged by the Department. We therefore believe that the Department should not take such a step without all of the usual precautions that precede a recommendation for new legislation. . . .

It is our hope that after reading the enclosed memorandum, which is merely a preliminary presentation, you and Dick McLaren and the Solicitor General would be willing to delay the submission of the jurisdictional settlement in the Grinnell case long enough to permit us to make a more adequate presentation on this question. . . .

With kindest regards,

Sincerely yours,

s/ Ed

Lawrence E. Walsh

"There is a high probability that it will succeed." To some it seemed as if ITT was saying, You're going to win, so let's make a deal—and the government made a deal!

North Carolina Senator Sam Ervin, no novice at arguing before the Supreme Court, called it "a most interesting letter. . . . When I was practicing law, I did not make admissions of that character against my clients."

Walsh's first priority was to get the Grinnell case delayed, a touchy business since the normal ten-day deadline for requesting extensions of time had already elapsed.

McLaren was opposed. Solicitor General Erwin Griswold —in charge of Justice Department proceedings before the Supreme Court—was neutral. He noted that a last-minute request for an extension of time would be "quite unusual." Yet, he agreed to the delay because "the deputy attorney general wanted it." But Kleindienst had also professed neutrality. In fact, he claimed he hadn't even read Walsh's memo, merely turned it over to McLaren's office. Then who wanted the delay? Senator Edward Kennedy put the question to McLaren: "Who did care whether there was an extension . . . ?"

"I guess Judge Walsh cared," McLaren replied.

"And ITT cared?" Kennedy added.

The question of *why* remains open. The best answer seems to be that Kleindienst ordered the delay as a courtesy to Walsh.

"That is the relationship I had with Judge Walsh, the fact that he was a former deputy attorney general," he said. "He isn't an ordinary attorney, as far as I am concerned."

Three days later—on April 19—Kleindienst called this "extraordinary" attorney and told him the extension would be requested.

That ended Walsh's role in the case. While the Grinnell case remained pending, others representing ITT made contact with the Administration and worked out a satisfactory settlement.

Ironically, Walsh considers that he *lost* both the GM and ITT actions. With GM, he never blocked the grand-jury inquiry. With ITT, he never got the interdepartmental review he sought. "The value of the delay was really inconsequential," he insists. One wonders whether GM and ITT would agree.

The two cases illustrate the extraordinary power an extra-curricular lawyer like Walsh yields. From their service to city, state and federal officials, they incur obligations. Walsh naturally disagrees: "Most people who do public service do it because they get satisfaction from it. Any sense of building up good will is minimal." But human nature is human nature. A lawyer who has handled a touchy assignment for an office-holder is not likely to get slapped in the face when he comes asking favors for a client. And smart clients will seek out such lawyers. . . .

12

The Private Lawyer
as Public Servant

Brooklyn's Bedford-Stuyvesant section is only a short subway ride from the canyons of Wall Street, but it is another world. It is the nation's second-largest black ghetto—and, by every standard of social measurement, one of the worst. Crime, poverty, disease, infant mortality, illegitimate births, broken homes, unsafe and unsound buildings, un- and under-employment—on every one, Bedford-Stuyvesant ranks at or near the top of the list.

It has been more than thirty years since the subway replaced the El on Brooklyn's Fulton Street, but the change has not improved the thoroughfare as it did Manhattan's Sixth and Third avenues. In the long block east of Nostrand Avenue, many of the dingy buildings are abandoned, dozens of storefronts boarded up. No. 1368 is an anomaly—a solid structure with a colonial façade and modern gas lamps burning outside. Once it housed the Sheffield Farms dairy; now it is the headquarters of the Bedford-Stuyvesant Restoration, the antipoverty agency founded by Robert F. Kennedy. Inside it is as modern as the newest college student union.

In bright, fluorescent-lit, air-conditioned offices on the second floor is the Bedford-Stuyvesant Community Legal Services Corporation, funded by the federal government's Office of Economic Opportunity. It might be called a perfumed store front. For just a few minutes of listening to the problems that the agency handles is a grim reminder that modern walls of glass and brick cannot shut out the problems of the ghetto.

Christopher Norall is the newest addition to the office's legal staff, so new he doesn't even have a desk of his own. He works out of whatever office happens to be vacant. He is a serious-looking, balding young man of twenty-five with mod sideburns and a boyish bow-tie.

His first client of the day is a black man, deferential, dressed in denim, facing eviction. A new landlord bought his building and sued him for eight months back rent—$855. The man claims he paid. The landlord obtained a default judgment against him. The man claims he has never received the summons—"sewer service," in the jargon of the courthouse.

Norall outlines the steps he's going to take, the papers he'll prepare. "Then take it down to the judge and get him to sign it."

"I worked all night," the client complains. "I'm a bit tired. Will it take long?"

About a half-hour until the papers are prepared, Norall tells him, then the time it takes to deliver them to the court, the opposing counsel, the City Marshal. All are bunched in downtown Brooklyn. Nor are the papers a problem: Landlord-tenant cases are so routine that all the lawyer has to do is fill in the blanks on mimeographed forms.

The client heads for the lobby to wait until the papers are prepared. As soon as he's gone, Norall starts shuffling through the papers on his desk.

"These cases all tend to merge," he explains. "I can't distinguish in my head what happened to one from what happened to the other."

He finds the file he wants and picks up the phone. He has

difficulty dialing. "Push-button phones should be universal," he snaps. Finally the call goes through. No answer.

"We have a great problem getting hold of clients," he says. "Most of them don't have phones."

Another call. This time success. "Mrs.——, this is Chris Norall at Legal Services. Did you pay that money you owe? . . . You got a receipt? . . . Fine! Fine!"

Then he leads in another client—a fat black woman who also faces eviction. It seems she works as super in her building and shelled out $233 for emergency supplies over the winter. She's refused to pay the rent until the landlord—New York City— reimburses her.

She gives Norall her pedigree. She has a blind husband and three children, one of them in the hospital. She's a registered nurse and makes $175 a week.

Norall excuses himself and takes her papers to another office.

The client muses aloud: "I'm waiting for him to come and say, 'You're not going to get Legal Services.' This is the gripe of the middle-class worker. You're caught in the middle. I'm going to quit work and go on welfare."

Norall returns. "Do you really make $175 a week?"

She answers his question with another: "Do you want me to lie and say I make $110 a week?"

The lawyer explains that she's earning too much to qualify for Legal Services. She protests that she's not working at the moment. "I'm not going back to work until I get this whole business straightened out. I can't work all night and run around all day."

Norall sends her to the Brooklyn Bar Association. If two lawyers they recommend won't take her case—for a fee she can afford—then Legal Services will.

After she leaves, he explains: "I had a sense that one of the reasons she stopped working was that she could get a free lawyer. I don't believe in unemploying yourself into financial eligibility."

His next client is a husky black woman with two small, restless children. Throughout the interview, the girls are alternately climbing over their mother, crawling across the floor, prying into file drawers or wandering down the corridor.

The mother is listed on the court papers as " 'Jane' Morgan," but she has a definite Spanish patois. There's a barrier—if not of language, of life style. She has a habit of replying to the lawyer's questions with speeches on other topics, and the whole process has to start again from scratch. She has six children, no job, no husband. She's also been evicted. She hasn't paid rent for two months. The landlord claims six.

Why hasn't she paid? Norall asks. Eventually he gets his answer:

"Because things to be done. They didn't do none."

Has she gone to Welfare?

"They say I must try to find a place. I want to go to court to get more time. I have a place ready the first of June."

Where?

"It's on President Street."

Where on President Street?

"I don't know the address."

What's wrong with her present place?

Her answer is a litany of slum life: falling plaster, peeling paint, leaks, roaches, rats. "The man come around and use the rat poison. The rats just go in holes and die. And then they stink."

Norall calls the City Marshal, advising him that an order to show cause is on the way, staying the eviction. The woman will have to trek to the Bronx to deliver it.

Another wait while the papers are prepared. Norall lets loose a long sigh. "The most difficult interview I've ever had."

He pauses to take a call from a lawyer. Norall's client had bought a $300 set of books on credit. The man, Norall insists, is illiterate. His "wife" told him the paper he signed was for milk for her children. Then the "wife" died—and the children left, taking the books with them.

The opposing counsel apparently is insistent; after all, he's working for a percentage of the claim.

"He can't read," Norall argues. "He can barely talk." Norall cites a precedent—*Chicken* v. *Thoroughgood,* decided in the English courts in the 1600s!

No avail: The lawyer wants at least half payment; Norall won't settle for more than 10 per cent. The case is left open. The actual value of the books is never disclosed—or even discussed.

The next client is a black workman, asking Norall to interpret a clause in the Plasterers' Union constitution. Norall reads it. "It's not the clearest piece of English I ever read. . . . I'm not an expert on labor law," he adds. The client lets out a disappointed, "Oh." Unable to come up with an interpretation that will fit the client's particular problem, Norall finally sends the man to the National Labor Relations Board.

Then a well-dressed young black carrying a sheaf of religious tracts. He fell behind in his rent when his wife had a baby. When he got the money—$123.50—the landlord wouldn't accept it. An eviction is worth a 15 per cent rent increase.

Another wait for the client, another set of papers for the stenographer, another day without lunch for Christopher Norall. . . . And then, yet another client. . . .

The cases of the Bedford-Stuyvesant Legal Services Corporation are a far cry from the skyscrapers of Wall Street and Park Avenue and the operations of New York's Legal Establishment—except that Chris Norall is an associate at one of Wall Street's largest law firms.

He's not a part-time volunteer, nor is he on a leave of absence; he's drawing his full-time salary from Cleary, Gottlieb, Steen & Hamilton for working in the slums of Bedford-Stuyvesant. He symbolizes the latest turn of the blue-chip bar.

Like doctors—at least those the American Medical Association likes us to think of when we think of doctors—corporate lawyers and corporate law firms have long devoted a portion of their time to charity. Albeit, as *Fortune* observed, the typical lawyer "believes he has discharged his public obligations by contributing to the Legal Aid Society," "Even among the wealthiest Wall Street firms," the magazine continued, "only about 5 per cent of the lawyers' time is spent in any kind of public benefit work."

Virtually every large law firm has its pet charity, whose legal affairs are handled gratis or for a nominal fee. Usually, it's one brought in through the personal involvement of a partner (or a partner's wife), such as the link of the National Council of Churches through Charles Tuttle to Breed, Abbott & Morgan. Like the law firms that represent them, the charities themselves are a part of the Establishment.

But in recent years, under pressure from the new breed of associates, the firms' *pro bono publico* activities have been broadened to include services to organizations that not only don't represent the Establishment, but actively challenge it. Law firms as politically diverse as Paul Weiss and Mudge Rose send lawyers into the ghettoes to work in community law offices. In the argot of Wall Street and Park Avenue, all do-gooding activities are now lumped together under the title "Naderism." To some old-line lawyers, they represent a different sort of *nadir*. When asked about his firm's *pro bono* projects, one Wall Street lawyer sputtered, "A bunch of Reds!"

No firm has been more active in "Naderism" than Cleary Gottlieb. For more than three years, it has had an associate working full-time in a Legal Services office. In numbers, its *pro bono* manpower may not match that of other firms, which send as many as a dozen men to neighborhood law offices one day or one evening a week. But Cleary Gottlieb's volunteers spend three or four months at a stretch in the slums.

"We decided on this approach," a partner explains, "because there's no client responsibility the other way. If you've got lawyers coming in only one day a week, the client sees one lawyer one day, another the next. It's no good for the client, and it's not very helpful to the lawyer either."

All the Cleary Gottlieb associates who have worked in the Legal Services offices are volunteers. "There's no pressure in the sense of appeals to your desire to progress in the firm," Norall says. Just an appeal to conscience.

Norall is the seventh Cleary Gottlieb associate to work in a Legal Services office. Nothing in his background prepared him for the experience. Raised in England by American parents, he attended Cambridge, then returned stateside to the University of Pennsylvania Law School, where he was a law review editor. Before joining Cleary Gottlieb, he spent a year clerking for Federal Judge Edward Weinfeld. "And you might want to note this," he says, "my normal field is Eurodollar financing."

Once the lawyer volunteers, he meets with officials of Central CALS—Community Action for Legal Services—to determine which office he'll work in. So far, all the Cleary Gottlieb volunteers have chosen to go into the field where they deal with the unfamiliar nitty-gritty of landlord-tenant cases, matrimonial disputes and consumer complaints.* "All I know [of landlord-tenant law]," says Norall, "is what I learned from this little book on my desk." Surprisingly, none has chosen to work with Central CALS, where the lawyers probe the frontiers of poverty law, developing test cases and class actions—a field surely more in keeping with the volunteers' training and experience.

"I wondered about that," says a Cleary Gottlieb partner. "If they went into headquarters, they can be issue-oriented. But I guess they want to go out there and be with the people."

The volunteers represent only the tip of the iceberg. In cooperation with Willkie, Farr & Gallagher, Cleary Gottlieb also serves as counsel to a halfway house for ex-convicts in Bedford-Stuyvesant. But its chief *pro bono* contribution has been in developing minority capitalism.

"There are two reasons for this," a partner explains. "A, it's a good thing. B, it's something this firm can particularly help with."

Cleary Gottlieb has helped with the task of developing minority capitalism the same way many "green-goods" firms help the corporate giants—by serving as counsel to the investors. In this case, though, the investors are not banks and under-

---

* But not criminal cases. Except on murder indictments (where the state pays court-appointed private practitioners), indigent defendants in all New York City criminal cases are represented by the Legal Aid Society.

writers, but a host of public and privately funded alphabet agencies called MESBICs—Minority Enterprise Small Business Investment Companies.

Through Capital Formation, Inc., and its subsidiary, the Capital Formation Development Corporation, Cleary Gottlieb has advised going concerns on how to obtain Small Business Administration loans and job development grants, as well as helped set up Blue Ridge Farms, a processor of chopped chicken liver. Through Coalition Venture Corporation, a subsidiary of the Urban Coalition, it helped set up *Essense*, a magazine by and for black women, Cousin's Chicken Corporation, a soul food chain, and a microfiche concern. Through LESEDAC—Lower East Side Economic Development Association for Cooperatives—it has helped establish a co-op garment manufacturer and a co-op laundry.

Through an associate who had worked on an OEO project in the Far West, Cleary Gottlieb also acquired an unlikely *pro bono* corporate client—the *Navajo Times*, the newspaper of the Indian reservation in Arizona and New Mexico.

Both the Cleary Gottlieb partners and associates are proud of their role in the *pro bono* projects, but they are not overly optimistic about their effects.

"One thing that stands in the way of minority capitalism is the absence of a minority corporate bar," a partner explains. "There are more people in Harlem than in Lincoln, Nebraska. There are more lawyers in Harlem than in Lincoln, Nebraska. But the lawyer in Harlem has practically no real experience in representing a business. We thought we could—in a nonpatronizing way—train the indigenous bar. But when the minority businessmen come in, their lawyers are constantly Cravath, or Dewey Ballantine, or some guy named Goldberg who's cut himself in for eighteen per cent of the company as his legal fee."

He also wonders whether the lawyers aren't doing too good, too thorough a job for clients who don't need such elaborate legal services and who can't afford them once they learn to stand on their own middle-class feet. As an example, he cites the attempt to set up a black investment firm—a deal that finally fell through when one of the potential partners got a better offer from a white investment house. "They wound up with the greatest set of by-laws this office could produce," he explains. "They spent weeks down here going over every contingency that might arise. But what good was that to them? They spent all their time with the lawyers when they should have been hooked up with professional investment advisors."

But, so far, none of the Cleary Gottlieb partners—not publicly, at least—has questioned the basic premise of the firm's *pro bono* role: whether minority capitalism is really a good thing, whether black-owned "ma-and-pa" stores will be any better able to compete with the chains than white-owned ones, whether black businesses will prove any more beneficial to ghetto consumers than white ones.

As for the merits of the Legal Services there are even deeper doubts—especially among those who man the barricades.

"The trouble with the guys from the big firms is that they are gentlemen," said Miguel Hernandez, associate director of the Community Law Office in Harlem, a privately funded neighborhood law office, staffed largely by volunteers from major firms like Mudge Rose and Dewey Ballantine. "As gentlemen they are untrained in the ways of the ghetto. As a result, they often get hurt. And sometimes their client gets hurt with them."

Gerald McLaughlin, a Cleary Gottlieb associate who spent four months in a Legal Services office in Brooklyn, summed up his experiences there:

> The media may tout the legal services attorney as a tough, effective and glamorous store-front lawyer. But he is not always an asset to the poor for whom he works. In fact, some of his clients may be better off without him. . . .
> Many legal services attorneys are hampered by a lack of experience, particularly trial experience. Most are young and have worked in an office for less than two years. Few have been through a long trial, let alone a jury

trial and so try to avoid them like the plague. . . . Nuts-
and-bolts knowledge—such as how to bring particular
types of actions, gather facts, introduce evidence, prepare
witnesses, cross-examine and pick a jury—is the most critical need in legal services offices. . . .

The legal services attorney can actually render a dis-
service to clients. A poor person may be better off going
into court pro se or with an intelligent friend because he
is more likely to receive the judge's help and sympathy.
The rules of evidence may be relaxed, and pleading tech-
nicalities will probably be waived.

There's little doubt that working in the ghettoes is disillu-
sioning. The volunteer attorneys are overloaded with work;
their offices are often dingy and almost always understaffed
and underequipped, especially in comparison with the "law
factories" they've known on Wall Street or Park Avenue.

Some attorneys become disillusioned with their clients; they
find out the hard way that clients lie, that clients are unco-
operative, that clients often care less about their own cases
than does their attorney. But most become disillusioned with
the "system"—and radicalized in the process. Even Chris
Norall, who says, "I'm no more radicalized now than I was
before—and I wasn't particularly radicalized then," is forced
to admit, "Every now and then you get indignant."

The chief cause of disillusionment is the courts. Blue-chip
associates undergo a "culture shock" when they enter the
lower levels of the city's judicial system, especially in the out-
lying boroughs. Men who may have clerked for Supreme
Court justices suddenly find themselves arguing before political hacks whose knowledge of the law is minimal and whose
ethnic prejudices rival those of a Mississippi sheriff.

McLaughlin called the courts "instruments of obvious injus-
tice" and suggested that "Dante's inscription over the entrance
to Hades could appropriately be carved over the Family Court's
doors: 'Abandon all hope, ye who enter here.' "

Even Norall admits: "The courts by and large are not satisfactory. Most of the judges are sympathetic to the landlord.

There's one judge of whom it is said that he will always find for the landlord, except when the landlord is a Haitian. He just doesn't like Haitians."

Such is justice as the young lawyers find it. "It would be an understatement to say that I am pessimistic about the future of legal services as presently constituted," McLaughlin wrote. He went on:

> Even if every problem I have mentioned could be magically cured overnight—if the poor could receive decent legal services—the present defensive litigation orientation of legal services would still shortchange the poor. . . .
>
> One day when I was taking a mild ego trip after having prevented an eviction, I suddenly realized what I had really done. I had indeed helped my client to the extent of thwarting his eviction. But I had merely kept him in the same old rat- and roach-infested apartment. My time had been diverted from the real issue—forcing better housing for the poor.
>
> When all was said and done, was the poor person better off for having been exposed to "justice"? Was he better off for having been exposed to me? I wonder.

Musing openly about whether it wasn't time for the ghetto bar to become "legal guerillas," McLaughlin soon left both Legal Services and Cleary Gottlieb to teach at Fordham Law School. But Norall continues to find the work challenging. "There's not much law," he says. "But the human side is gripping. I'd like to do it again every year."

Meanwhile, in the mind of a young associate at Chadbourne festered deeper doubts about the efficacy of such *pro bono* projects. To twenty-eight-year-old Richard Kneipper, they seemed, first, a "misallocation of resources"—a waste of talent to let securities specialists and tax experts handle consumer complaints and landlord-tenant cases when their expertise could be mobilized for the public interest.

Second, the *pro bono* projects were haphazard. "The firms as firms have no commitment to public interest law," the thin, bespectacled Cornell law graduate says. "They're involved only because somebody there—usually one of the younger lawyers—is interested. And the firms only do it to the extent that it doesn't interfere with paying business. It's what I call 'the bottom-of-the-pile theory.' If a couple of cases for paying clients come along, the public interest stuff goes to the bottom of the pile. I'm not knocking it. Law firms have to operate that way. But there should be something else."

In 1971, Kneipper was invited by the Young Lawyers Committee of the Bar Association to conduct a seminar on public interest law. Rather than just talking about it, he suggested, why not do something about it? Why not put a positive proposal on the table?

"It was an idea that I'd been struggling with for a long time," he says. "I wanted to try to develop an innovative way of getting the firms as firms to do something about public interest law."

The "something else" he came up with was a plan for a public interest law firm, to be staffed and funded by the Wall Street and Park Avenue giants.

Kneipper got the go-ahead from the committee to work up the proposal. With the assistance of Nicholas Angell, the Chadbourne partner in charge of *pro bono* work, he drafted a twenty-five-page document that—appropriately for a securities specialist—reads like a stock prospectus. The format was deliberate. "We wanted to have all our homework done, all the questions answered, so people wouldn't sharpshoot us."

As Kneipper envisaged it, the firm—to be called Public Interest Legal Consultants, Inc.—would be a not-for-profit corporation, capitalized with $1,000 contributions from member firms. Each member firm would be expected to furnish, for one year with salary, an associate with at least three-years' experience.

With twenty firms participating, Kneipper projected a twenty-lawyer operation with an annual budget of $305,000, including the salaries of a permanent director ($40,000) and a non-legal staff of thirteen. The money would come from foundation financing, assessments of member firms and, in some cases, client fees.

The "prospectus" cited the advantages of such a public interest firm over present *pro bono* projects:

> The effectiveness of agencies and organizations providing full-time public interest legal services is limited by a serious over-all shortage of lawyers and financing. Although the effectiveness of public interest legal services is increased significantly by the part-time contribution of legal services by private law firms and lawyers, such legal services usually are contributed only to the extent that they do not materially interfere with the normal law practice of such firms and lawyers and frequently are not sustained.
>
> The [public interest law firm] will supplement, not duplicate, the efforts of most existing public interest agencies and organizations since it will not attempt to provide traditional "band-aid law" services for individuals with landlord-tenant, domestic relations, welfare and consumer problems, but instead will concentrate on providing legal consultation and representation to clients whose problems require specialized legal services and whose objectives involve a substantial public interest. Such concentration . . . will most effectively utilize for the public interest the substantial expertise of the Member Firms. . . .

Public Interest Legal Consultants, Inc., would represent only organizations and government agencies, not individuals. Among the projects it might handle would be organization of housing projects and other community facilities; civil rights actions; proposals for reform of public institutions such as prisons and the courts; and legislative drafting for local and state governments. But its field was restricted by a conflict-of-interest clause that barred it from bringing actions against clients of member firms.

The project was approved by the Young Lawyers Committee and by the Executive Committee of the Bar Association. Then the "prospectus" was sent to about sixty firms around town, directed in most cases to lawyers who were personal friends of Bernard Botein, the Bar Association's president.

"It was extremely well received," says Kneipper. "I was really quite surprised. The most-consistent flak came from the other public interest organizations—CALS, Legal Aid and the like. They weren't saying that what we proposed wasn't a good thing or that it didn't need to be done. They were just afraid that we were going to take some of the spotlight away from them and cut into their sources of support. That really surprised me."

About twenty firms expressed further interest in the project, and Kneipper organized what he calls "the traveling road show"—a group of young lawyers who went from firm to firm to sell the idea, answer any questions and dispel any objections. Finally, representatives of eleven firms were invited to a meeting at the Bar Association to whip the project into shape. Ten came. "They were all 'heavies,'" says Kneipper. "That really impressed me that they were serious about it."

They also had some serious objections to the details. The toughest problem was manpower. "Getting a third-year associate on loan for a year is like pulling eyeteeth," Kneipper says. "He's the most valuable guy in the office."

In general, the Brahmins of the Bar felt the project was "overly ambitious" and Kneipper was directed to scale it down in size and scope. And then Kneipper's pet project—"the most exciting thing I've done in four years of practicing law"—had to go to the bottom of his own pile, as the young lawyer got involved in a rush of stock registrations. But by mid-1972 revised proposals were circulated again among the firms.

When, if and in what form Public Interest Legal Consultants, Inc., will come about is not yet clear. But it could prove, as Kneipper says, "the first really big move on the part of firms toward public interest law."

13

The Greening of
the Bar Association

Just as the blue-chip firms were radicalized by the new mood
of "Naderism," so was the organization that represents the
Brahmins of the Bar, the Association of the Bar of the City of
New York.

Its building, at 42 West 44th Street, is a city landmark, mar-
ble and colonnaded, as solid as an old-fashioned bank. It seems
out of place amid the soaring skyscrapers of midtown Manhattan, their stainless steel and glass glinting in the sunlight. Instead, it squats in the shadows, a thing of the past, not a por-
tent of the future.

Like the building it occupies, the Bar Association seems
rooted in the past. It is commonly regarded as old-fashioned,
staid, respectable, and as Republican as the Union League
Club. Historically, it has not been receptive to young men or
to new ideas. Only one president in its 102-year-history took
office below age fifty; Charles Evans Hughes became a Su-

preme Court justice at forty-eight, but had to wait until he
turned sixty-five to head the Bar Association! It did not admit
women until 1937 and, in a city where 60 per cent of the
lawyers are Jewish, did not install a Jewish president until
1956. In theory, the Bar Association is a democracy; in practice, it has been run by a self-perpetuating oligarchy.

The Association of the Bar of the City of New York was
founded in 1870 as an instrument of uplift and reform in the
battle against Boss Tweed and Tammany Hall. From the start
it was an elite organization, almost as clannish as a country
club. Prospective members had to be proposed by present ones
and passed by a screening committee. In practice, few—if any
—were rejected (though Leo Gottlieb's application provoked
a furious fight in the 1920s; Emory Buckner had to "pack" the
meeting to get him admitted). And few outside the blue-chip
bar bothered to apply.* Max Steuer, the greatest trial lawyer
of his day, was never a member—nor is there any record that
he ever applied.

The association was prestigious, its presidents including
presidential candidates (John W. Davis), Supreme Court justices (Hughes) and Cabinet members (Elihu Root, Henry L.
Stimson and Herbert Brownell). But it represented only a minority of the Manhattan bar. As of May, 1969, its membership
was 9,294—perhaps 1,500 of them out-of-towners—about a
third of the 22,000 lawyers listed in Manhattan and the Bronx.

In contrast with the southern and small-town oriented
American Bar Association, it could be called liberal. But
among street-corner practitioners it was sneered at as "the blue-
chip association" which represented only the Wall Street and
Park Avenue firms. Sometimes the Establishment's sense of
noblesse oblige prompted it to take more liberal stands than

---

* This exclusivity led to the formation of the New York County Lawyers'
Association in 1908. The new organization had an unrestricted membership
drawn largely from individual practitioners and members of smaller firms. The
two groups have pursued parallel courses since. Both are confined to Manhattan. On occasion, the Bar Association has tried to exert its influence in other
boroughs, only to meet formidable opposition from the Bronx, Brooklyn and
Queens bar associations, which are practically adjuncts of the local Democratic
organizations.

other lawyers' groups. It successfully pushed a plan to have the Legal Aid Society represent indigent defendants throughout the city, and almost alone among the nation's bar associations, it supports "no-fault" auto insurance. But then blue-chip lawyers don't depend for their livelihood on criminal cases or personal-injury claims.

Some of the stuffiness was taken out of the association by Harrison Tweed, who became its president in 1945 and served an unprecedented three-year term. He opened the association's doors to alcohol and permitted it to present the annual "Twelfth Night" satirical shows. Tweed's appointment of Paul DeWitt as executive secretary, according to Edward Greenbaum, "changed the Association from being a respectable, gloomy mausoleum to a live-wire professional organization." "Harry Tweed brought an informality which was akin to liberalism," says one association insider. But the greening process had to wait until 1968, when the association installed a new president—Francis Taylor Pearsons Plimpton.

He has been described as "the quintessential WASP." An indentures specialist, senior partner of Debevoise, Plimpton, Lyons & Gates, he had served as Adlai Stevenson's second-in-command at the U.N. But he was better known as the father of George, founder of the *Paris Review*, all-purpose amateur athlete (*Paper Lion, Out of My League, The Bogey Man*) and occasional movie extra.

But father Francis, as Merrell Clark, Jr., noted, was something of a Renaissance man himself: "His abilities and interests run the full gamut. He is a tennis ace. He is a linguist, a poet, a wit and a classical scholar. His translations of Greek epitaphs once graced FPA's Conning Tower.

"He has held trusteeships in a stellar list of distinguished organizations from Athens College, Greece, Lingnan University in China, to overseer of Harvard University, and including the Metropolitan Museum of Art and the Philharmonic-Symphony Society of New York....

"He is an author, an outstanding lawyer, diplomat and a public servant. He does not shy from controversy. He once made a speech entitled 'In Praise of Polygamy,' and once, in a face-to-face audience, he tried to convert the Pope to Planned Parenthood."

At first glimpse Francis T. P. Plimpton did not differ from the typical Bar Association president. He surely looked the part—"the most distinguished-looking man in the country." And he fitted the role—WASP and white-shoe, from one of the bluest of blue-chip firms. He was sixty-eight when he took office.

Hardly a likely candidate to lead a revolution. Yet Plimpton's descent into the maelstrom of controversy started within a few weeks of taking office.

In 1968, after nearly a decade of delay, the legislature passed a bill creating 125 new judgeships in New York State. It was heralded as passed on a "no-deal" basis—which meant only that the local leaders in each district had to get together to divvy the spoils.

"The biggest judicial pie in almost half a century is about to be cut," *The New York Times* editorialized. "There are strong indications that the pie will mainly be one flavor—plum."

Nowhere was the plum pie juicier than in the First Judicial Department, which comprises Manhattan and the Bronx. Between new seats and vacancies, seventeen Supreme Court nominations were up for grabs. In mid-July word leaked out that the seventeen seats had been divided—six each to the Manhattan and Bronx Democrats, two each to the Manhattan and Bronx Republicans, one to the Liberal party.

Congressman James Scheuer called it "the biggest carving of 'swag' since the days of Boss Tweed. With multiparty endorsement, it is likely that all the public will be able to do is vote 'ja.'" He called for some sort of screening committee to ensure that only qualified candidates were nominated.

The cry was echoed by newspapers and good government groups. John J. McCloy, speaking as chairman of the Committee for Modern Courts, suggested the alternative of an independent slate if the political leaders didn't agree to screening. In a presidential election year, another costly campaign was the last thing the leaders wanted.

On July 23, Plimpton, acting in his capacity as Bar Association president, called the leaders to the association's headquarters and asked them to accept a screening panel headed by Herbert Brownell and Samuel Rosenman, both former Bar Association presidents.

"It seemed to me," he recalls, "that the way to get some decent judges was to go after the political leaders before they could do anything. My suggestion was to have a leading Republican and a leading Democrat, both of whom had high standards and political savvy. The leaders hemmed and hawed, and hawed and hemmed."

The leaders were naturally hesitant about any screening panel—especially one led by the blue-chip bar.

"We don't have any confidence in the Bar Association," said Frank Rossetti, the gravel-voiced assemblyman from Little Italy who presided over the shaky patchwork of the Manhattan Democratic party.

"Whom would you trust?" Plimpton asked.

"I'd trust a fellow like Judge Botein," Rossetti replied. "He gives nothing away, but he's on the level."

Bernard Botein has the look of an Old Testament prophet— dark, deep-set, intense eyes beneath black, bushy brows, a shock of white hair, imposing stature and a majestic manner. And he has an integrity to match the mien. He had spent nearly thirty years on the bench, having been named an interim Supreme Court justice by Herbert Lehman, promoted to the Appellate Division by Thomas E. Dewey and named presiding justice—"P.J." in lawyers' parlance—by Averell Harriman and reappointed by Nelson Rockefeller. He was the ranking state jurist in the city.

Although he had stature, Botein was hardly Establishment. Born in 1900 on the Lower East Side, he had worked his way through C.C.N.Y. and Brooklyn Law School. He brought to the bench a strong sense of social commitment and had long led the fight for court reform—so much so that at the 1967 Constitutional Convention the stand-pat politicians didn't dare put him on the judiciary committee. But he possessed what the political pros call "street smarts." As Plimpton puts it, "Bernie is much more knowledgeable about the City of New York than I am or ever will be."

At the time though, Botein was little more than a name to Plimpton. But "I went dashing out to call him up." It turned out that Botein was at his summer home on Long Island. "My wife and I went out to Westhampton," Plimpton continues, "and talked it over by the swimming pool. He hemmed and hawed, and hawed and hemmed."

"I was leery about it," Botein admits. "I wondered if it wasn't *infra dig* for a judge. Then I decided not to be so prissy."

Botein returned to the city, summoned the leaders to his chambers on 25th Street and secured what Plimpton had been unable to get—a firm commitment not to nominate anyone disapproved by the panel.

A nineteen-member panel was put together, representing all segments of the bar and including members of minority groups. "We have no monopoly on civic virtue," Plimpton explained. "The important thing is to see that we get good judges." The panel included three blacks, two Puerto Ricans and two women, but it had an even heavier representation of legal brahmins. In addition to Plimpton, there was Rosenman, Brownell, Louis Loeb and John McCloy.

Botein said proudly: "This is the first time in this state that the responsible leaders of the major parties have consented to be bound by the decisions of a citizens' committee, selected under nonpolitical auspices and representing a true crosssection of the community." If any of the leaders had reservations, none voiced them—then.

But some political practitioners had doubts. One Bronx reformer recalls his meeting with Plimpton: "You do not understand the meaning of judgeships to the leaders," he told the Bar Association president. "They are not going to abide by your screening procedures."

"I'm sure we men of reason can work it out," Plimpton replied.

"If I have ever seen a babe-in-the-woods, it was Mr. Plimpton," the reformer says. "He was a very delightful and bright elderly gentleman who didn't know what he was talking about. As I left, I had one clear impression—he had not understood a word I said. As we stood up to shake hands, I couldn't help but admire his suit. And the thought went through my mind—so help me!—'He's going to look awful funny without his pants.' "

Throughout August, while the nation reeled to the trauma of the presidential conventions, the panel plowed through the "laundry lists" of names submitted by the leaders—106 in all.

"We met every day, we talked to each one of them, we looked up records," Plimpton recalls. "We did a very good job. We turned down about a third of them."

In all, 37 of the 106 were rejected, including two of Bronx Democratic Leader Henry McDonough's favorites—District Attorney Dollinger, turned down both because of his age (sixty-five) and his handling of a controversial hit-and-run homicide involving a judge's son; and State Senator Ivan Warner, a black lawmaker who had sat in at a meeting where a legislative colleague asked for a $100,000 bribe to "fix" a narcotics case. Also rejected was Manuel Gomez, a Criminal Court judge, on grounds that he had "a horrible reputation for intemperateness."

As Labor Day neared, there were rumors that McDonough planned to ram through the nominations of some of those rejected by the panel. The Bronx leader denied it: "I have no intention of recommending anyone not approved by the screening committee." But he also insisted that he was not bound by the panel's recommendations, that they were "advisory" only.

By September 7, the day of the judicial conventions, McDonough was scoring the panel as "men who wear the halo of good government." It was a clear hint as to what was in the works. The Democrats duly nominated Dollinger, Warner and Gomez, while the GOP jointly slated Dollinger and Gomez. (Apparently Warner was too much even for them to swallow.)

The voters, in effect, were left without a choice; all three "unqualified" candidates were elected.

Some observers called the leaders' acceptance of the panel a cynical charade from the outset—a ploy to prevent formation of an independent judicial slate. Others argued that McDonough had bowed to pressures from below. But few denied that it was a crass double-cross.

Plimpton called it "a flat breach of faith." "I was abroad when it happened. I was so mad I almost turned around and came back." The panel, which was next to have passed on nominations for lower-court judges, closed up shop.

Despite the double-cross and defeat, Botein insists that "some good came of it." "I don't want to tell you the fellows that would have been nominated if we hadn't been there." He considers it a victory that only three "unqualified" candidates were elevated to the Supreme Court of New York State.

"Thus ended another noble experiment in attempting by *ad hoc* methods to improve on the selection of judges by political bosses," Plimpton said in his annual report. "Perhaps the failure of this attempt will in the long haul prove productive. . . ."

The next venture into judicial politicking was more successful.

On February 17, 1970, at the Bar Association's Centennial Convocation at Philharmonic Hall in Lincoln Center, wearing the crimson gown of a Harvard Law graduate, Plimpton rose to deliver the address expected of the Bar Association's president.

What he said was not expected, not the customary pablum of platitudes and praise. Instead, with Chief Justice Warren E. Burger seated on the dais beside him, he conjured up the vision of a Martian astronaut looking at America's judicial system "with a fresh and objective eye."

First there were some harsh words about local judges. Then he went on:

What would our Martian think of federal appointments? This association traditionally does not comment on nominations to the bench outside of our areas . . . but I cannot help expressing the wish that the President of the United States' second and third nominees to the Supreme Court of the United States could have approached, in stature, experience and integrity, his first nominee.

The first was Burger himself. The second was Clement F. Haynsworth, already rejected by the U.S. Senate. The third was G. Harrold Carswell. Although the nomination had stirred some senators to heated debate, confirmation seemed certain.

Although many harbored private doubts, until Plimpton spoke, no leader of the bar had come out publicly against Carswell. Plimpton's remarks obviously struck a responsive chord, for they drew loud and prolonged applause from the audience of fifteen hundred lawyers. "Unless you've lived in the New York City Bar Association," said Samuel Rosenman, "you don't know what an unusual thing that was to say, especially in the presence of the Chief Justice."

What prompted Plimpton to such an unprecedented action? "I just thought Carswell was no damn good."

A small step . . . but a giant stride in the greening process. More was to flow from it. A few days before, Irving Engel, an attorney active in civil rights, had called Plimpton and asked him to sign a statement opposing Carswell's confirmation. He also secured the support of Rosenman, Bruce Bromley and Bethuel Webster, another former Bar Association president.*

The statement, about three thousand words long, dealt mainly with Carswell's dubious role as an incorporator of a segregated golf club in Tallahassee, Florida. Its opening sentences were couched in unusually strong language:

The testimony indicates quite clearly that the nominee possesses a mental attitude which would deny to the

---

* The action put Bromley at odds with one of Cravath's most powerful partners, Albert R. Connelly, a member of the A.B.A.'s Committee on the Federal Judiciary which twice rated Carswell "qualified."

black citizens of the United States—and to their lawyers, black or white—the privileges and immunities which the Constitution guarantees. It has shown, also, that quite apart from any ideas of white supremacy and ugly racism, he does not have the legal or mental qualifications essential for service on the Supreme Court, or any high court in the land, including the one where he now sits.

The four lawyers originally planned to place the statement as a newspaper advertisement. But an aide to Indiana Democrat Birch Bayh, leader of the Senate opposition to Carswell, convinced them that it would be more effective circulated among their colleagues and released later.

Plimpton and Rosenman took charge of the operation. By March 12, they had secured the signatures of 133 other lawyers and 325 law professors at forty-two schools, including 19 deans. On that date, Plimpton and Rosenman, flanked by three law school deans—Derek Bok, of Harvard (now Harvard's president), Louis Pollack, of Yale, and Bernard Wolfman, of Pennsylvania—announced the results at Washington's National Press Club. There was a flurry of publicity and, within a few more days, another hundred lawyers added their signatures.*

"The outpouring of sentiment against Carswell from men in the highest positions of the legal world was astonishing," Bayh said. "And it was most effective."

Plimpton continued to work behind the scenes. When he

---

* Curiously, one who did not sign was Arthur Goldberg. During the gubernatorial campaign later that year, he accused Nelson Rockefeller of "silent acceptance" of Haynsworth and Carswell. Plimpton set the record straight, noting that Rosenman had solicited Goldberg's signature, only to be rebuffed. "He said that the place on the Court to which Carswell had been nominated was the place he had vacated and that as a consequence it would be inadvisable and counterproductive for him to make a public statement against the nominee. This seemed a curious excuse; one would think that the fact that it was his seat would have made him the more obligated to speak out. . . ." A month later Goldberg entered the gubernatorial lists. "Mr. Goldberg then seemed to forget his scruples, saw that it was popular in New York to oppose Carswell, realized there was a good possibility that Carswell would be defeated, and on March 23 publicly announced his opposition. . . . [But he] was unwilling to oppose it publicly at the time when public opposition really mattered."

learned that Senator J. William Fulbright was wavering, he recalled that George Ball was close to the Arkansas Democrat; he persuaded Ball to present the anti-Carswell case to him, and Fulbright eventually announced his opposition—an important southern convert to the cause. Plimpton also called Dean Acheson, a senior partner at the Washington firm of Covington & Burling, and persuaded him to put pressure on a colleague to release the so-called "Horsky memo"—a document drafted by a member of the A.B.A.'s judiciary committee which showed that Carswell had studied the golf club's incorporation papers the night before he told a Senate committee that he couldn't remember what was in them.

At Plimpton's prodding, the Bar Association itself got involved in the battle. The Executive Committee adopted a resolution urging the Senate to reject the nomination:

> Service on the United States Supreme Court requires that a Justice have exceptional qualifications of integrity, professional distinction, legal learning and proven sensitivity to human and civil rights. In our considered opinion, the public record demonstrates that Judge Carswell lacks these essential qualifications for a Justice of the highest court in the land.

In due course, Carswell's nomination was rejected by the Senate, 51-to-45. Some said the opposition of the organized bar was the decisive factor. "I think that really swung the votes against him," says Judge Bromley. "I really do."

Plimpton himself—with perhaps undue modesty—was not so sure. "Obviously," he noted in his final report as president, "members of our association, led by Judge Rosenman, were not solely or primarily responsible for the defeat of the nomination —full credit has to go to President Nixon for his letter telling the Senate that it is supposed to consent and not to advise, and to Senator Hruska for his stout insistence that there ought to be a mediocrity on the Supreme Court. But I think that it can be said that the insistence of members of the association that only excellence belongs on that court played an important part in the result."

Two years before Plimpton and the Bar Association had lost to the likes of Frank Rossetti and Henry McDonough and couldn't keep an Ivan Warner off the Supreme Court of the State of New York. Now they had triumphed over President Nixon and Attorney General Mitchell—two former members—and helped keep G. Harrold Carswell off the Supreme Court of the United States. Was it a case of the blue-chip bar's being prophets without honor in their own county?

"It's entirely different," Plimpton insists. "[On the local judgeships] Botein and I talked about the possibility of putting up an opposition slate. But it took time, money and a staff and we didn't have any of those things. With Carswell all we had to do was convince fifty-one senators that we were right."

Nor does Plimpton respond favorably to suggestions that he prodded the Bar Association to a more liberal stance—only that he reflected the changing political posture of the blue-chip bar. He notes that after the 1968 election, "I asked everybody [the association's Executive Committee] how they voted. It was something like twelve-to-seven for Humphrey, almost two-to-one. There you are. The general attitude of the Bar Association is pretty goddamned enlightened. They're a crowd of bright, intelligent, liberal, forward-looking people."

Perhaps so. But it took Plimpton to prod them to action. Botein, who succeeded Plimpton as president, says, "There's no doubt he nudged them into it. There is no doubt that Plimpton, with a lot of guts, started turning the corner on identification with burning issues which a lot of members thought were no business of the Bar Association. He really came to life."

Plimpton also notes that his stand on Carswell evoked scarcely a whisper of protest from the membership. His next venture into the political arena was not received so serenely.

"The presidential decision to invade Cambodia produced a galvanic shock in the New York legal community," Plimpton said in his 1970 report. It also produced a galvanic shock in the association.

The tensions started some months before when the first Moratorium to protest the Vietnam War was organized. Manfred Ohrenstein, a Democrat who represented Manhattan's West Side in the State Senate, sought a way to involve the legal community in the October 15 demonstrations.

"A few of us had this idea to have a lawyers' convocation," he recalls. Like Ohrenstein, the other organizers of the Lawyers Committee to End the Vietnam War were liberals, largely Jewish, definitely non-Establishment. Like Ohrenstein, most were not members of the Bar Association.

Then someone suggested the name of Orville H. Schell, Jr., senior partner at Hughes, Hubbard & Reed. "A very prestigious lawyer," in Ohrenstein's words. "He's just one of those guys who's a peace nut. You don't get a WASP Wall Street lawyer involved in these things every day."

Schell, who describes himself as "somewhat of a rebel all my life," had harbored growing doubts about American involvement in Vietnam since he'd visited Saigon on firm business in 1963. The doubts were fueled by his sons, Orville 3d, a Far Eastern scholar who heads the Bay Area Institute in Berkeley, and Jonathan, *The New Yorker* writer who wrote two of the most caustic critiques of American actions in the war, *The Military Half* and *Village of Ben Suc*. By mid-decade Schell was firmly against the war, taking part in one of the first peace marches in New York. At first he felt out of place amid the militant youths. But "as people threw stuff at us and screamed obscenities, I knew I was in the right pew."

So Schell joined Ohrenstein as co-chairman of the committee and they asked the Bar Association for use of its Meeting Hall for the October 15 convocation. That brought them up against Whitney North Seymour.

A colleague called Seymour "the quintessential bar association lawyer." He has served as president of both the American and New York Bar Associations. When he took the helm of the city Bar Association in 1950, he was forty-nine, the youngest man ever to hold the office. Although he was a senior partner of Simpson Thacher & Bartlett, he achieved the presidency not so much for his outside prestige as for his work within the association—"our first civil service president," says Paul De-Witt.

Even in 1969, nearly twenty years after his term as president, Seymour still felt a proprietary interest in the organization. He was chairman of the House Committee and his wife, Lola, was in charge of the headquarters' decorations and decor. He was also a Republican with close ties to the Nixon Administration; Whitney, Jr., is Nixon's appointee as U.S. Attorney. Seymour, Sr., turned down the request to use the Meeting Hall.

"His reply, as I recall," Ohrenstein says, "was that it might be confused as an activity of the association and the association didn't want to identify itself in that regard. So we dropped it. We held the meeting in a church."

Some weeks later, the committee again asked for use of the hall for a forum to discuss the legal aspects of the war. This time the request was made not to Seymour, but to Plimpton. The Bar Association's Executive Committee had already taken an informal vote to support Seymour's stand, but bucked the final decision to the president. "That was a hot potato in my lap," Plimpton says. "I said, 'let's do it.' "

"One of our lawyers approached him," Ohrenstein recalls, "and he said 'absolutely, yes,' and he didn't give a damn about what Seymour said, he was giving us permission. The only thing he asked was that we make a very definite announcement that this was not a Bar Association activity, which we agreed to do."

"The speeches were on a high professional level," Plimpton said, "and it was made clear . . . that the resultant resolutions were not official acts of the association."

The line could not be so finely drawn after President Nixon's announcement of April 30, 1970, that he was sending American forces into Cambodia. Some members of the Lawyers Committee urged mass action. They met at the conference room at Hughes, Hubbard & Reed's office on Wall Street.

One of them turned to Schell: "You're the only Wall Street

lawyer here. Is there any chance of persuading Wall Street lawyers to demonstrate against the war?"

"Not a Chinaman's chance," Schell replied. He suggested a more dignified protest, and the others decided to play the Schell game.

"The only way to move things is to make institutions within the system move," he explains. Schell recruited a large number of blue-chip lawyers to a May 19 convocation at the association and a lobbying effort in Washington the following day. "That gave it a stamp of respectability."

Again, the Lawyers Committee asked to use the Meeting Hall; again, Plimpton gave permission. This time, the convocation was announced in full-page newspaper ads:

> As members of the legal profession, we are alarmed by the action of the President in extending the war into Cambodia. We are deeply concerned that the divisions caused by this war endanger our fundamental institutions.
>
> On May 20, 1970, we will cease, to the extent consistent with our professional responsibilities, our usual business and devote our efforts exclusively toward ending with war in Indochina. We seek . . . immediate withdrawal from Cambodia, the earliest possible termination of our involvement in Indochina and a return to the rule of law at home and abroad.

Besides Ohrenstein and Schell, the sponsors included President Plimpton ("The invasion of Cambodia really upset me very much") and President-elect Botein; Morris Abram, Ramsey Clark, Adrian DeWind, Arthur Goldberg, Simon Rifkind and Theodore Sorensen, of Paul Weiss; Mayor Lindsay and Robert McKay, Dean of N.Y.U. Law School. The list of subscribers filled a half page with agate type.

In addition to announcing the lobbying effort, the ad announced the convocation at the Bar Association with speeches by former Chief Justice Earl Warren, Senator George McGovern, Lindsay, Plimpton and Botein. The association's name ran across the page in three-quarter-inch letters.

Two veteran members resigned from the association in protest. Plimpton later admitted, "The name *was* too prominent. . . . I am at fault for not having noticed and cut it down."

There was more adverse reaction among the bar. On May 19, Saxe, Bacon & Bolan—Roy Cohn's firm—sent an "open letter" to the antiwar protestors:

> Nobody from our firm will be on that train.
>
> By our absence from your convocation we hope to show our support for the President of the United States and our appreciation for the American fighting men abroad in their struggle in the cause of freedom. . . .
>
> We haven't formed a big-name committee or asked for signatures, but we believe that many lawyers still feel about America as we do, and won't be on that train with you either.

The opposition of Saxe, Bacon & Bolan could be dismissed as an outburst of the right, but three days later the Republican wing of the Legal Establishment (plus a few conservative Democrats) answered the Lawyers Committee to End the Vietnam War with a New York Committee to Support the President:

> We . . . support the President in his efforts to bring the war in Southeast Asia to a speedy conclusion. While we may disagree with specific actions, we collectively support the President, possessed as he is of all the facts, in those measures he believes necessary to protect the security of American troops in the field. . . .
>
> Our essential freedom is founded, particularly in critical times, on self-restraint and on trust in the wisdom of our Constitution.
>
> That is why we support the President.

The committee was the handiwork of Whitney North Seymour. Among the sponsors he corralled were Thomas E.

Dewey; Orison Marden, of White & Case; Edwin Weisl, Seymour's colleague at Simpson Thacher & Bartlett; Leo Gottlieb, of Cleary Gottlieb; George Leisure, Sr., of Donovan Leisure; John Wells, of Royall, Koegel & Wells; Maxwell Rabb, of Stroock, Stroock & Lavan; Murray Gurfein, soon to become a Nixon appointee to the federal bench; and Mayor Lindsay's old political ally, Robert Price, no longer practicing.

Meanwhile, about twelve hundred antiwar attorneys took a chartered train and descended on Washington—"well-barbered, well-tailored and well-prepared with legal arguments against the war." Plimpton, who had flown down, arrived at the Capitol steps to find the lawyers assembled for a press conference. "I arrived at the same time the bullhorn did," he says. "Jack Javits had captured the bullhorn and was telling how much he was in favor of everything he should be in favor of. Then Senator Goodell grabbed it and told how much in favor of the same things *he* was. I grabbed it and said, 'Hello, everybody. Let's go to work.' "

The lawyers fanned out across Washington to present their case to congressmen, senators and administration officials. Botein visited West Virginia Senator Jennings Randolph.

"We've encountered too many deaf ears and unseeing eyes," the jurist told him, "and from that has come frustration that has led to violence."

"You're opposed to violence?" Randolph asked.

"I am opposed to violence. I am a man of law."

Plimpton had been slated to see South Carolina's Ernest Hollings, but the senator was not available. So, as *The New York Times* noted, he "sent his greetings to the Senator, picked up his monogramed umbrella and went to a downtown church where about fifteen hundred Washington lawyers were meeting to plan an antiwar lobbying effort of their own." Actually, Plimpton noted later, the umbrella was a $5.98 special from Korvette's with a piece of adhesive tape wrapped around the handle on which he'd penned his initials, "F.T.P.P."

Later, he visited Solicitor General Erwin Griswold and Undersecretary of State Elliot Richardson, both of whom he knew from his activities at Harvard, then joined the delegation that called on Attorney General Mitchell.

"Mitchell wouldn't see us," Schell recalls. "Then Ramsey Clark said, 'Tell Mitchell we're going to hold a press conference at four o'clock.' I guess he imagined what the headlines would say—the chief law enforcement officer in the United States refusing to meet with his predecessor and two presidents of the Bar Association. So he saw us. Some of the younger members really let him have it."

Schell calls the effort "one of the best things for the bar that's ever happened. It bridged the generation gap." "The most exciting thing that's happened to the bar," Botein echoes.

But the question can be asked: Did the hegira have any effect?

Plimpton argued, yes: "In virtually every case, [the lawyers] were listened to carefully and earnestly . . . and the deep concern of the nonradical members of the New York bar—of what might loosely be called the New York Legal Establishment—definitely came across. And, after all, the Cooper–Church Amendment (cutting off funds for combat forces in Cambodia after June 30) *did* pass the Senate overwhelmingly, and the theretofore virulently hawkish Congressman Rooney (facing a primary battle) *did* announce repentant conversion, at the hands of his New York lawyer interviewers, into submissive dovishness, and introduced a Cooper–Church bill of his own into the House of Representatives!"

Others could argue, no. After all, the war still goes on.

The Washington trek did not end the association's involvement with Vietnam. On May 28, a special membership meeting was held to consider a resolution denouncing the invasion. Botein had assumed office as president three days before and presided over the stormy session—"a baptism of fire," Plimpton calls it; "Plimpton's legacy to me," says Botein.

"That was a shambles, that meeting," Plimpton says. "General Robert must have turned in his grave."

"The youngsters were out in full force," Botein says. "In the old days, associates were nice and meek and submissive. If the old guard wanted something passed, the word would just go through ten law offices and all the associates would turn out and vote for it."

But in 1970 the associates showed more independence—and militance. The original motion decrying the Cambodian invasion was amended and re-amended from the floor into something far stronger.

"It was the most heated meeting in history," Botein says. "I was scared stiff for the first half-hour. The quid-nuncs were challenging everything. I finally had to fall back on humor. I said, 'We'll get much further if I follow Wigmore's rules of evidence rather than *Robert's Rules of Order*.' "

After nearly four hours of debate, the vote was 197-to-64 to adopt the antiwar resolution:

> *Resolved*, that The Association of the Bar of the City of New York strongly opposes the continued American involvement in the war in Indo-China and strongly urges the immediate withdrawal of all American military forces therefrom.

The turnout was only a fraction of the association's nearly ten thousand members, but still far more than show up for most membership meetings.

Afterward, some attorneys charged privately that Botein's rulings had been biased and that he had "stacked" the debate by recognizing the least effective speakers for the opposition. But Seymour, who led the pro-Administration forces, has no quarrel with Botein, even though "he ruled against my point of view every time." But, "I don't think there was anything intentional about it."

Plimpton, who presented the case for the antiwar resolution, says, "I was strongly criticized by quite a few people. They were good-tempered about it, though. Nobody called me a son-of-a-bitch exactly."

In fact, the anti-antiwar forces were so weak that they did not debate the merits of the resolution, only the efficacy of the association's involvement.

"The thing that concerns me," Seymour says, "is stepping

out of the ordinary role of the lawyer. A lot of organizations can do that, but there's only one organization that can speak for the lawyer. The problem arises in all bar associations. On the whole, I think they do better to leave those questions alone and stick to those issues that they know best. Even there, the weight of the bar is not very great and the problem is not to lose what weight there is."

But Plimpton sees himself and the association in a far more activist role. "Should . . . each president inherit a muzzle with his nonexistent mantle?" he asks. "I think not, and I think that a president, being careful to emphasize that he is acting as an individual, should not hesitate to speak out forcefully on issues of legal significance as to which he has forceful convictions. If this association is to fulfill its function of leadership as to things legal in this city, state and country, its leaders must do their best to lead."

Botein obviously feels the same way: "I for one . . . believe that the bar must at long last exert its considerable influence to achieve certain reforms, which have been proven essential through informed research, logic and experience; but which have been blocked by selfish, short-sighted interests of political and other groups."

And so does Cyrus Vance, chairman of the association's "Second Century" Committee which is drawing up the blueprint for its future. "We're moving toward the direction of involvement in many issues which are not strictly legal," he says. "And I think that's a very good direction to move in."

In 1969, when Mayor Lindsay bucked the party machines of both the Republicans and Democrats to run for reelection on the Liberal line, a host of organizations sprang up to bolster his campaign. Among them was Lawyers for Lindsay, headed by Botein and staffed largely by associates from the large law firms. "They did all the work," Botein says. "One of the things they discovered was that they had great difficulty developing contacts from one firm to another."

Some of the associates decided to do something about this communications gap. Out of the temporary electoral alliance, a permanent organization was born to bridge the gulfs between the lower levels of the law factories—the New York Council of Law Associates.

With the backing of Plimpton and Botein, the new organization got Bar Association sponsorship—including free quarters in the 44th Street building—and foundation financing. Neil Johnston left Dewey Ballantine to become the council's full-time coordinator, with a grant as a fellow of the association. "The only establishment in history that subsidized its own destruction," says one Bar Association staffer. Within a few months the council had one thousand members.

The council published its own bulletin, held seminars and placed its members in *pro bono* projects. Within a year it decided to test its political mettle—as individuals, not officially as an organization—by running an insurgent slate for three of the four openings on the Bar Association's Executive Committee.

The idea had been tried the year before, when Stanley Arkin, head of the association's Criminal Court Committee, fielded a slate consisting of his law partner John Horan, Peter Fleming, of Curtis, Mallet-Prevost, Colt & Mosle and Leon Polsky, counsel to the State Narcotics Addiction Control Commission. They lost by a handful of votes.

In 1971, the Young Turks tried the same trick, this time with a slate of younger lawyers—Michael Varet, age twenty-nine, of Paul Weiss; Matthew Mallow, twenty-eight, of Marshall Bratter; and Sheila McLean, twenty-nine, who had gone from Milbank Tweed to the Ford Foundation.

"We asked for and received the mailing lists," Johnston says. "We sent out letters and did a lot of telephoning. There was a tremendous turnout of slightly post-pubescent faces at the stated meeting, and they won in a walk."

Other than the generation gap, there were no issues in the contest. Other than gaining a voice in its management, the Young Turks evinced no desire to take over the Bar Association and were content with presidents like Plimpton and Botein. In fact, having made their point, the new Executive Committee members joined with their elders the following year to push through a by-law change making future elections by mail ballot.

"It's the only bar association in the country that young lawyers really dig," Johnston says. "It comes out to be a really progressive place."

Though they could not comment officially—after all, it was their slate that went down to defeat—the elders seemed delighted at the development. "Out of this alliance," says Botein, "there'll be some fruitful cross-pollinization."

Vance predicts more changes: "Are the young and the minority groups properly represented? I think the answer is 'no' and we've got to change this."

Vance was the Establishment's choice to succeed Botein as president in 1972, but he turned down the offer—explaining that he was slated to become Secretary of State in the Muskie Administration! The Young Turks successfully pressed for the nomination of Orville Schell, a choice that left little doubt that the greening process would continue.

True, the Association of the Bar of the City of New York remains the Legal Establishment. It has not become Woodstock Nation, nor is it likely to. But it's a far cry from the clannish, clubbish organization the Whitney North Seymours and Herbert Brownells knew a decade ago.

As one lawyer puts it, "Why, even Bill Kunstler's a member!"*

---

* But not for long, perhaps. At last report, the Grievance Committee was considering disciplining the radical lawyer for discussing a pending case in a radio interview.

14

On Different Wavelengths

What of the future?

Prognosis is always difficult. But we may risk a few predictions: Some firms will decline and disappear; new ones will rise to take their place; but most will merely grow bigger, get richer—and become *less* powerful.

The reasons for growth and wealth are not difficult to discern. They are mainly extensions of present trends. The law is becoming more complex, the lawyer more specialized. Tasks that took one man a decade ago now need several, and in years to come undoubtedly will require even more.

As the pundits keep reminding us, ours is a government not of men, but of laws, more laws . . . and still more laws. Surely the United States is the most legalistic and litigious nation on earth. Republicans may promise to get government out of business and Democrats declaim about giving it back to the people, but regardless of who's in power, government regulation is bound to increase and with it more call for the attorney's talents.

Similarly, "Naderism" is on the ascendant and that, too, means more lawyers to defend the rights of erring corporations.

Finally, the seed only now is being sown, but there's increasing concern both within and without the profession for extending the availability of top-flight legal services to the middle class. Such a development may make it easier for the Archie Bunkers to divorce their "dingbats," but it will also make it easier for them to convert their gripes against General Motors into legal actions. Again, more work for the Brahmins of the Bar.

The concomitant of more work, of course, is more fees, more profits.

But the strange corollary is that growth and wealth undoubtedly will be accompanied by a decline in power. This also is an extension of the present trend. As Wall Street loses its strangle-hold on the American economy, so the Wall Street lawyer is losing his influence to those in the rising West and Southwest. As government continues to grow, so too will the role of the Washington "knifethrower."

Some of the New York brahmins may rage against the tide. Others may try to ride with it, opening new Washington offices or expanding present ones. But "green-goods" was, is and surely will remain the heart of the Legal Establishment. Top-notch Wall Street firms like Cravath and Sullivan & Cromwell have always eschewed political pull in favor of keeping a firm grip on the nation's bankroll.

Back in the 1930s, Liberty Leaguers like John W. Davis ranted against the reforms of the New Deal. But the powers at Sullivan & Cromwell were far-sighted enough to recognize that the securities regulations acts constituted a sort of permanent WPA leaf-raking project for the blue-chip bar. They joined eagerly in drafting the legislation and in carving a major role for their ilk. Similarly, while some crusty curmudgeons may curse Ralph Nader and his followers as "a bunch of Reds," those who know better relish the legal business created by their crusades.

So it bodes with the latest augury for change in the blue-chip bar—the new status of securities lawyers sought by the S.E.C. in the White & Case case and other actions. Some brahmins bemoan what might befall them should the commission carry the day. But the far-sighted see that such full and frank disclosure merely means more work for the lawyer . . . and still more profits.

The change—if it comes—will also make the "green-goods" lawyer less a lackey and more of an "expert," more detached, more independent, someone paid by the client but responsible to the general public. As a result, he could become even more valued for his advice and judgment by government, business and the bar itself. When he ventures an opinion, he will be saying, "Here's what I think . . . ," not the implied, "Here's what General Motors thinks. . . ."

Even now—in some areas—the Legal Establishment tends to pursue its own course regardless of what clients might think. Cravath, for example, is drafting a model water-pollution statute for New York State which is bound to contain provisions that will rile Bethlehem Steel, which has a large (and polluting) plant at Lackawanna on the Lake Erie shore.

Because of their background, their training, their immersion in the problems of society, there's little doubt that the Brahmins of the Bar are becoming considerably more liberal than the bankers, brokers and businessmen who head their corporate clientele. "We're on different wavelengths from many of our clients," says Cravath's Roswell Gilpatric.

But they both receive the same signals—the name of the game is making money. And that, we can be sure, the Brahmins of the Bar will continue to do.

Notes

The literature about New York's corporate bar is scanty. There are several privately printed histories, which are recommended reading only for insomniacs. As Dean Acheson observed: "An account of 'cases' undertaken turns into an unmitigated bore, as the recent epidemic of 'histories' of well-known law firms so amply proves." The list includes: Robert T. Swaine, *The Cravath Firm and Its Predecessors* (1946–48); Arthur H. Dean, *William Nelson Cromwell, An American Pioneer in Corporation, Competitive and International Law* (1957) [Sullivan & Cromwell]; *Seventy-five Years of Simpson Thacher & Bartlett* (1959); Otto E. Koegel, *Walter S. Carter, Collector of Young Masters or the Progenitor of Many Law Firms* (1963) [Hughes, Hubbard & Reed and Royall, Koegel & Wells]; Walter K. Earle, *Mr. Shearman and Mr. Sterling and How They Grew* (1964); Timothy N. Pfeiffer, *Law Practice in a Turbulent World* (1965) [Milbank, Tweed, Hadley & McCloy]; and Ralph Carson, *Davis, Polk, Wardwell, Sunderland & Kiendl: A Background with Figures* (1965).

Memoirs and biographies usually deal more with public service or dramatic trials than with the inner workings of the firms. For example, Corey Ford's *Donovan of OSS* (1970) has only one reference to Donovan, Leisure, Newton & Irvine. Milton Mayer's *Emory Buckner* (1968) provides a readable account of Root Clark's early years. Edward S. Greenbaum's *A Lawyer's Job* (1967) is also informative.

Mayer's *The Lawyers* (1967) includes a chapter on corporate practice. Beryl H. Levy's *Corporation Lawyer: Saint or Sinner?* (1961) is based largely on the firm histories. Erwin O. Smigel's sociological study *The Wall Street Lawyer* (1964, 1969) is filled with elaboration of the obvious and exegesis of the insignificant. For their ambiance, the novels and stories of Louis Auchincloss are highly recommended.

Magazine surveys include: Spencer Klaw, "The Wall Street Lawyers," *Fortune*, February, 1958; "Why Law Is a Growth Industry," *Business Week*, January 13, 1968; "The Law and the Profits on Wall Street," *Investor's Reader*, October 8, 1969; "The Gilt-Edged Profession," *Forbes*, September 15, 1971; and "Alexis de Tocqueville," "Money Talks," *Juris Doctor*, January, 1972.

In the notes that follow, I have not attempted to cite chapter and verse for every quotation or statistic, merely to give guideposts for future study. Needless to say, most of the information was obtained in oral interviews, much of it under the cloak of anonymity.

Many persons assisted in the research and writing, far too many to list here. If I'd been billed for all the time I spent in lawyers' offices, this book would have required foundation financing. Some persons provided information and documents. Others reviewed portions of the text and set me straight on matters of law or style, reminding me that there is no comma in *Simpson Thacher & Bartlett* and that *Stroock & Stroock & Lavan* takes two ampersands. The names of some are apparent from the text; those of others are not—because they wanted it that way.

I would especially like to thank Thomas Baer, John Lyon, Robert Poulson and my own attorney, Martin Garbus, for their help. Also a word of thanks to Nelson Seitel, associate publisher of the *New York Law Journal*, for opening the paper's files to me; to the officers and staff of the Association of the Bar of the City of New York for their assistance, including the invaluable use of the library; and finally to Congressman Edward I. Koch for his always speedy procurement of government documents.

1. *The Congress of Vienna Sits on the Fifty-seventh Floor*

White's comment is from "Human Dimensions of Wall Street Fiction," A.B.A. *Journal*, February, 1972, an interesting study of the lawyers in Louis Auchincloss' stories and novels.

Kelley's obituary is from *The New York Times*, February 18, 1972.

The chief source for Cravath is Swaine's history. The Moore case is detailed in Joseph Borkin, *The Corrupt Judge* (1962). The TFX controversy is summarized in Clark Mollenhoff, *The Pentagon* (1967, 1972). The fullest account of the "Jackie" letters is by Maxine Cheshire in the *Washington Post*, February 19, 1970, and subsequent days.

2. *Downtown, Midtown, All Around the World*

Fuller accounts of many of the firms may be found in the histories already cited. Cane's verse is quoted by Levy; I have been unable to trace the original source. Dulles' quotes are from the introduction to Dean.

The list of Royall Koegel clients was obtained from the weekly lobbying lists issued by the New York Secretary of State. For Rosenman's career, see his *Working with Roosevelt* (1952). Nizer discusses his cases in *My Life in Court* (1961) and *The Jury Returns* (1966). There is an interesting essay on Grant in David T. Bazelon's *Nothing But a Fine Tooth Comb* (1969). Morris Ernst's works, both philosophical and autobiographical, are too numerous to cite.

3. *The $100-an-hour Toll Collectors*

The cash statement is from R. Palmer Baker, Jr.'s unpublished memorandum, "Incorporation of the Firm" (1972). Hudson's study, *Outside Counsel: Inside Director*, was scheduled for publication in September, 1972; the figures were taken from a prepublication article on the study, "The High Cost of Corporate Law," *Business Week*, July 22, 1972. *TWA* v. *Hughes*, 312 F. Supp. 478 (1970); 449 F. 2d 51 (1971). The table on the firms' size was compiled largely from data in the *Fortune*, *Business Week* and *Juris Doctor* articles previously cited.

Background on the Twelfth Night shows was provided by Alan Littau.

Kheel's career is discussed in A. H. Raskin, "What Makes Teddy Kheel Run," *The New York Times Magazine*, December 5, 1965, and Fred Powledge, "How the Establishment Got Theirs: The Defeat of the Transportation Bond Issue," *New York*, January 3,

1972. Figures on his finances were obtained from reports filed with the S.E.C. and the Controller of the Currency.

4. Some Partners Are More Equal than Others

For background on Root Clark, see Mayer's *Emory Buckner*. No biography of Dewey has appeared, and the published accounts of his later years are scanty. The *Newsweek* quote is from the issue of May 16, 1955. Dewey's own comments are from *The New York Times*, January 4, 1955.

5. The Care and Feeding of Corporate Clients—I

The fullest account of the fallout of CBS and Colin is in *Variety*, February 25, 1970. See also *The Wall Street Journal*, February 13, 1970.

The chief sources for Milbank Tweed are Pfeiffer's history and Harrison Tweed's recollections in Columbia University's Oral History Project. The Tweed papers are badly transcribed (*e.g.*, "Brown, Carruthers, Harriman" for Brown Brothers Harriman); in some cases I have altered the wording to make the meaning clear. The Nader report is *Citibank* (1971); the final report has not yet been issued.

6. The Care and Feeding of Corporate Clients—II

Weisl's career is discussed in Arnold Beichman, "Pipeline to the President," "New York," *Herald Tribune*, January 17, 1965. Johnson's quote is from *The New York Times*, January 19, 1972.

Tweed's comments on the bonds between client and counsel are from *The Changing Practice of Law* (1955). Sullivan & Cromwell's role in the Dixon–Yates case is detailed in Chief Justice Warren's opinion in *U.S.* v. *Mississippi Valley Generating Co.*, 364 U.S. 520 (1961); Williams' role in the Penn-Central debacle from the S.E.C.'s *Staff Study of the Financial Collapse of the Penn-Central Company* (1972).

Sanford J. Ungar's *The Papers & The Papers* (1972) appeared after this chapter was written. The chief published sources are *Times Talk*, July–August, 1971, and *The New York Times*, June 15–July 1, 1971. The case is *U.S.* v. *New York Times, et al.*, 403 U.S. 713 (1971). Both the Pentagon Papers and the pleadings in the case have been published by the *Times*.

7. "As My Lawyer, Dick Nixon, Said the Other Day . . ."

Glimpses of the Nixon firm may be found in any of the presidential biographies or 1968 campaign accounts, especially Earl Mazo and Stephen Hess, *Nixon* (1968) and Jules Witcover, *The Resurrection of Richard Nixon* (1970). *Time, Inc.* v. *Hill*, 385 U.S. 374 (1967).

Paul Weiss is discussed in David Dorsen's "Paul, Weiss, Goldberg —What Kind of a Ticket is That?", *New York*, April 18, 1970. For the Crater case aftermath, see *The New York Times*, June 17, 1971. Goldberg's career is discussed in Victor Lasky's campaign tract, *Arthur J. Goldberg: The Old & the New* (1970). Costikyan's quote is from his *Behind Closed Doors* (1966). Goldberg's comments on leaving the firm are from *The New York Times*, June 17, 1971.

For Mudge Rose post-Nixon, see my "The Firm to See?", *New York*, April 26, 1971, from which parts of this chapter were adapted. Guthrie's role in the Penn-Central debacle is described in Joseph R. Daughen and Peter Binzen, *The Wreck of the Penn Central* (1972). For the Postal Service bond issue, see House Post Office and Civil Service Committee, *A Report on the Circumstances Surrounding the Proposed Sale of United States Postal Service Bonds* (1971); also *The New York Times*, July 30, 1971.

8. The Workers Are the Means of Production

Tweed recounted the Byrne anecdote many times, in many different words, probably embellishing it as the years passed. For the fullest flavor, I have combined the versions quoted by Mayer in *The Lawyers* and Smigel. Green's quotes are from his "The Young Lawyers, 1972: Goodbye to Pro Bono," *New York*, February 21, 1972.

Proskauer's quote is from his *A Segment of My Times* (1950). The ADL report was published in the *Yale Law Journal*, March, 1964; the quotations are from the abridgement issued by the ADL. For discrimination against women, see *The New York Times* and *New York Law Journal*, July 1, 1971. The report on Royall Koegel & Wells was issued by the Commission on Human Rights.

9. A Lot Goes on Behind Closed Doors

Jerome Carlin, *Lawyers' Ethics* (1966). The Grievance Committee's work is discussed in the centennial history of the Bar Association by George Martin, *Causes and Conflicts* (1970), and Murray Teigh Bloom, *The Trouble With Lawyers* (1969). Bonomi made available the annual reports of the committee. Erdman's quote is from James Mills, "I Have Nothing To Do With Justice," *Life*, March 12, 1971; Plimpton's from the supplement to the Bar Association *Record*, March, 1970.

U.S. v. *Greater Blouse Assn.*, 228 F. Supp. 484 (1964); all quotations are from the court record.

In the matter of Javits, 35 AD2d (1971). Bonomi made available the hearing record. For background on the Javits family, see Milton Viorst, "Can this Jew be President?", *Esquire*, April, 1966.

10.   *The Green-goods Counsel as the Big Board's Cop*

Escott v. *Bar-Chris Construction Corp.*, 283 F. Supp. 643 (1968).
Feit v. *Leasco Data Processing Equipment Corp.*, 332 F. Supp. 544 (1971).

The S.E.C. provided a copy of its complaint in the National Student Marketing case; it has since been printed by Bowne of New York City, Inc. For the case's repercussions, see *The Wall Street Journal*, February 15, 1972, and *New York Law Journal*, March 10, 1972, and June 6, 1972. For its background, see Andrew Tobias' amusing *The Funny Money Game* (1971).

The Vesco case is summarized in *The Wall Street Journal*, November 28, 1972.

11.   *The Public Servant as Private Lawyer*

McCloy's quotes are from "The Extracurricular Lawyer," *Washington and Lee Law Review*, Fall, 1958. Kraft's quotes are from his *Profiles in Power* (1966). Donovan gave his account of the Abel case in *Strangers on a Bridge* (1964). The *Hecate County* case is *Doubleday* v. *N.Y.*, 335 U.S. 848 (1948). *Attica, The Official Report of the New York State Commission on Attica* (1972).

Burns' battle against pollution is discussed in the *New York Daily News*, January 7, 1971; for his ouster, see *The New York Times*, January 10, 1971, and subsequent days. Walsh's role in the ITT case is abundantly documented in the Senate Judiciary Committee hearings on Kleindienst's nomination for attorney general and the committee's majority, minority and individual reports (1972).

12.   *The Private Lawyer as Public Servant*

Hernandez' quotes are from "Wall Street Law Goes into the Ghetto," *Signature*, February, 1970, which discusses the Community Law Office. McLaughlin's quotes are from his article "A Storefront Lawyer and 'Wild West' Justice" which appeared in *Juris Doctor*, February, 1971, and the *New York Law Journal*, March 8, 1971.

Kneiper provided a copy of his "A Proposal for the Organization of Public Interest Legal Consultants, Inc., A New York Not-for-Profit Corporation" (1971).

13.   *The Greening of the Bar Association*

For background on the Bar Association, see Martin's history. Plimpton was profiled by Geoffrey Hellman in "Periodpiece Fellow," *The New Yorker*, December 4, 1971. Resolutions and reports are from the Bar Association's *Yearbook* for 1969, 1970 and 1971 and the supplement to its *Record* for March, 1970.

For the Botein committee's work, see *The New York Times*, July 18, 1968, and subsequent dates.

The Carswell fight is chronicled in Richard Harris' *Decision* (1971). For the text of the Rosenman statement, see the *New York Law Journal*, February 25, 1970. Plimpton's comments on Goldberg appeared in a letter to *The New York Times*, October 12, 1970.

The antiwar ad appeared in the *New York Law Journal*, May 14, 1970, and *The New York Times*, May 17, 1970. The Saxe, Bacon & Bolan letter appeared in the *New York Law Journal*, May 19, 1970. Seymour's statement appeared in the *New York Law Journal*, May 22, 1970. For accounts of the Washington lobbying effort, see *The New York Times* and *Washington Post*, May 21, 1970.

Index